ADDITIONAL PRAISE FOR
HER HONOR

As someone who's often critical about the progress of women in the legal profession, I found this book to be a much needed antidote to my cynicism. It's an illuminating, honest look at how female judges overcame substantial obstacles with grit and grace—and triumphed.

— Vivia Chen, Opinion Columnist, "Unfiltered,"
BLOOMBERG Law

This remarkable volume of 25 essays practically oozes with perseverance and pride—with a dizzying array of our most accomplished women jurists recounting the stories of both familiar and less-well-known lawyers who were each, in their own rights, trailblazers. The stories are remarkable as much for what they have in common as for how they differ, and they provide page after page of inspiration not just to the next generation of aspiring trailblazers, but to those looking for reminders of how injustices in the legal system—and in the legal practice—are not necessarily a permanent feature. Indeed, the identities and resumes of the authors of these essays only proves the point.

— Stephen Vladeck, Charles Alan Wright Chair in Federal Courts
at the University of Texas School of Law; Author,
The Shadow Docket

Her Honor is a breathtaking collection of the stories of pioneering women judges who made the nation's courts look more like the nation they serve. Their stories are at once humbling for the obstacles they fought and inspiring for their determination and dedication to the rule of law.

— Prof. Steve Wermiel, American University Washington College of
Law, Co-Author, *Justice Brennan: Liberal Champion*

Her Honor is a magnificent anthology of the professional and personal reflections of some of the country's leading women jurists. The chapters in this volume bring to life the challenges, the pain, the joys, and the resiliency of female judges representing three generations of judicial icons. These stories will surely inspire not only the next cohort of women lawyers and judges, but anyone interested in promoting gender equality in the American legal profession and the United States more broadly.

— Ajay K. Mehrotra, Research Professor, American Bar
Foundation; William G. and Virginia K. Karnes
Research Professor, Northwestern University
Pritzker School of Law

Foreword by Dahlia Lithwick

HER
HONOR

Stories of Challenge
and Triumph from
Women Judges

Lauren Stiller Rikleen
Editor

AMERICANBARASSOCIATION

Judicial Division

Cover design by Monica Alejo

Printed in the United States of America.

27 26 25 24 23   5 4

Library of Congress Cataloging-in-Publication Data

Names: Rikleen, Lauren Stiller, editor. | American Bar Association.
   Judicial Division, sponsoring body.
Title: Her honor : stories of challenge and triumph from women judges /
   Lauren Stiller Rikleen.
Description: Chicago, Illinois : American Bar Association, [2022] |
   Includes index. | Summary: "This book contains personal stories by and
   about some of the most revered and influential judges in the United
   States. They also provide a unique and deeply instructive glimpse into
   our justice system. In the following pages you will come across a
   remarkable array of female jurists: trailblazers, legal entrepreneurs,
   political strategists and mentors. This is a book about imagination, and
   what it took and still takes for women, and by extension other
   minorities invisible to the constitution and the law, to imagine
   themselves into a structure that didn't include them"-- Provided by publisher.
Identifiers: LCCN 2022043483 (print) | LCCN 2022043484 (ebook) |
   ISBN 9781639052400 (paperback) | ISBN 9781639052417 (epub)
Subjects: LCSH: Women judges--United States--Biography.
Classification: LCC KF372 .S76 2022 (print) | LCC KF372 (ebook) | DDC
   347.73/14092--dc23/eng/20221201
LC record available at https://lccn.loc.gov/2022043483
LC ebook record available at https://lccn.loc.gov/2022043484

www.shopABA.org

To Sander, with constant gratitude; to our children, for their unconditional love of us, just as we have always given them; and to their wonderful spouses and growing family who give special meaning to the importance of legacy—a word at the heart of every chapter in this book.

Contents

Foreword

Dahlia Lithwick, Senior Legal Correspondent Slate,
Author, Lady Justice *(Penguin Press, 2022)*

I have spent many years pondering the question of whether women judges and justices are "different" than their male counterparts. Do they think differently? Write in a singular fashion? Do they tend to arrive at substantially distinctive outcomes? It's a question that ultimately divided Justice Sandra Day O'Connor and Justice Sonia Sotomayor. The former always insisted that "a wise old man and a wise old woman will reach the same conclusion in deciding cases." The latter argued that, at least with respect to certain matters, a wise Latina might sometimes arrive at better ones.

The question of how women judges tend to judge has—in recent decades—been measured and assessed and tested in the academy and debated in the media. But until I sat down to read *Her Honor: Stories of Challenge and Triumph from Women Judges*, I hadn't quite arrived at a satisfactory answer.

In the following pages you will come across a remarkable array of female jurists: trailblazers, legal entrepreneurs, political strategists, and mentors. Many were and are also wives, mothers, and caregivers, balancing the needs and individual traumas of complicated families and the pushes and tugs of the seductive dance we once called "having it all." They are different in every particular, yet what unites them in the aggregate is profound: This is a book about imagination, and what it took and still takes for women, and by extension other minorities invisible to the constitution and the law, to imagine themselves into a structure that didn't include them.

In these pages you will encounter—at the most basic level—young girls who at first couldn't even envision themselves applying to college suddenly matriculating with honors from law school. You will hear from and about women who were persistently advised by academic advisors, spouses, spiritual leaders, and their mothers that women stay home. More urgently, you will find yourself among young women entering the field of law in which workplaces were incompatible with their reality, and the laws and statutes with which they were engaged often failed to see anything but women who stay home.

I use the word "imagination" because there is virtually no way for women to engage with the law unless it begins with a capacious moral imagination—an ability to simultaneously acknowledge what is and also what could be. At its best, as Justice Ruth Bader Ginsburg explains in these pages, law is a profession "that enabled one to aid and repair tears in the community."

As I type this, American women have just been told by mostly male jurists at the highest court of the land that they have no rights, no interests, no privacy or dignity that was not explicitly "deeply rooted in this Nation's history and tradition." As Yale Law School professor Reva Siegel has noted, the majority opinion in *Dobbs v. Jackson* rests upon "laws enacted during a period when women were wholly disfranchised. And they signed on to an opinion in which a body of decisions and laws written by White men was presented as representing America's history and traditions, without a single woman's voice represented."

It is easy to do law without imagination—one simply looks backward and stands perfectly still. But if you were, by design, carved out of writing laws, interpreting laws, applying the law, or changing the law, your work must inevitably sound in the key of what might be, as opposed to the insistent one-note thump of what has always been.

I also use the word "imagination," because the work of these jurists involved adapting, analogizing, empathizing, and expanding, both a legal and cultural regime that needed to be bent toward justice. In so many of these profiles you will come across visionary jurists who came to both understand and insist that the jurisprudence of "hearth and home" is as urgent as the law of contract, property, and tort; and who established commissions, task forces, scholarships, and educational opportunities to level the playing field—not simply as between men and women, but as between what the law treated as serious and dismissed as trivial, or "Mickey Mouse," concerns. Whether they were hearing cases about indigent defendants, abortion rights, violence against women, all-male golf clubs, or sex discrimination in the military, the body of work stands for the fundamentally imaginative project of more equality, more dignity, more opportunity for all.

Many if not most of the jurists in this collection grew up amid poverty and hardship. One might venture, as does Marci Hamilton, reflecting on Sandra Day O'Connor, that they would have become pathbreakers in any field, even if they had not clawed their way to the highest echelons of the legal profession. But each describes being drawn to the law as a force for producing change and progress.

With varying degrees of patient civility and concessions to "lady-like" behavior, in the face of sexism, racism, and antisemitism in their workplaces and confirmation hearings, they persisted, or as the Hon. Bernice B. Donald puts it, after each fall, they always "get up." And over their careers in law firms, in courtrooms, and on the bench, these attorneys all found in the practice and application of law, a way to change the world, from the inside out, in deceptively radical ways.

But perhaps the most powerful imaginative project evident in these pages is that of mentorship and friendship, jurists who elect to serve as "path markers" as RBG would put it, for the road still ahead. So many of these judges describe an obligation to pay it forward, to help others, to reach out to young people to help *them* imagine a place in the machinery of law and governance and power.

In short, these judges were never dreaming merely for themselves, but for future generations, and in so doing they aren't just legal luminaries in their own right, but also act to shine a light into the future. The lives chronicled and celebrated in these pages illuminate a time, in the not-too-distant past, in which remarkable women persisted in the face of formal discrimination and overt bias.

Yet nobody believes that their fights are behind us. Their warmth, generosity, compassion, and advice should serve to remind us that even when the path is dark and lonely, legal heroes walk among us, and we are never, ever alone.

About the Editor

Lauren Stiller Rikleen, president of the Rikleen Institute for Strategic Leadership, is a nationally known speaker, trainer, author, and consultant focused on building a diverse, respectful, and inclusive workplace culture. She is also a board member and interim executive director of Lawyers Defending American Democracy, an organization devoted to the protection of democracy and the rule of law.

Lauren is a former law firm equity partner and founder of the firm's environmental law practice. For 20 years, she was recognized in Best Lawyers in America; she was also recognized in Chambers USA America's Leading Business Lawyers and in Massachusetts Super Lawyers.

Lauren's extensive background of community and professional leadership includes serving as a former president of the Boston Bar Association and a former trustee of Clark University. Within the American Bar Association, she co-chairs the ABA Women's Caucus and is a member of the Standing Committee on Publishing Oversight. Among her many past ABA leadership roles, Lauren is a former member of the Board of Governors, the Commission on Women in the Profession, and the ABA Journal Board of Editors. She is also a former chair of the Section of Civil Rights & Social Justice.

Lauren is the recipient of numerous awards, including the prestigious American Bar Association's Margaret Brent Women Lawyers of Achievement Award presented by the Commission on Women in the Profession, the Lelia J. Robinson Award from the Women's Bar Association of Massachusetts, and the Boston College Alumni Award for Excellence in Law. She was also named by Public Media's Next Avenue as one of the 50 Most Influential People in Aging.

The author of more than 200 articles, including topical commentary and op-ed pieces, Lauren has written for or been interviewed by such publications and media outlets as: Fortune.com; the *Harvard Business Review;* BBC; Public Media's Next Avenue; *The Washington Post; The Boston Globe; The New York Times;* MSNBC; National Public Radio; *The American Lawyer; The National Law Journal;* and Law 360.

Lauren's previous books are:

The Shield of Silence: How Power Perpetuates a Culture of Harassment and Bullying in the Workplace

You Raised Us – Now Work with Us: Millennials, Career Success, and Building Strong Workplace Teams

Ladder Down: Success Strategies for Lawyers from Women Who Will Be Hiring, Reviewing, and Promoting You

Ending the Gauntlet: Removing Barriers to Women's Success in the Law

Introduction

Lauren Stiller Rikleen, Editor

This book, *Her Honor: Stories of Challenge and Triumph from Women Judges,* contains personal stories by and about some of the most revered and influential judges in the United States. They also provide a unique and deeply instructive glimpse into our justice system.

Here we strive to present the human face of the judiciary—judges who steadfastly maintain compassion for the litigants before them, a humble appreciation for the power they wield, a desire to serve with distinction, and a commitment to the rule of law that is foundational to every American's faith in the judicial branch of government.

They also understand that judicial decisions are but one avenue within the court system for tackling tough problems. Accordingly, they have found a myriad of ways to create and participate on commissions and task forces to analyze endemic societal problems and promote positive change, through the law and administratively.

In other words, they see the good that our justice system can accomplish and they have a reverence for serving within it.

At a time when surveys reveal declining trust in the judiciary, this book offers reasons to be confident about our court system. The judges featured here have each been honored with the prestigious Margaret Brent Women Lawyers of Achievement Award from the American Bar Association's Commission on Women in the Profession.[1] They are not, however, an anomaly; rather, they are

---

[1.] The American Bar Association's Margaret Brent Women Lawyers of Achievement Award, created in 1991, recognizes and celebrates the accomplishments of women lawyers who have excelled in their field and have paved a path for other women lawyers to succeed. Honorees are selected by the ABA Commission on Women in the Profession.

exemplars of judges around the country who, each day, bring to their work a deep commitment to the justice system.

Their stories show that judges can have a desire to ensure an accessible and fair system of justice without a political agenda. Their written decisions reflect a deep compassion for humanity along with an abiding respect for the law. They respect precedent but will act with courage if the law offers a way forward.

All of the judges have lived lives of deep influence. The stories they share in this book will extend that influence further and, we hope, inspire future generations of lawyers and judges.

THE FORESIGHT OF CHIEF JUDGE JUDITH KAYE

When the American Bar Association's Judicial Division first asked me to compile and edit a book featuring the wisdom of judges honored with the Margaret Brent Women Lawyers of Achievement Award, my first thought was of a particular Brent recipient, Judith Kaye, the former Chief Judge of the New York Court of Appeals, a position that includes serving as the Chief of the state's court system. In many ways, Judge Kaye (who died in 2016) exemplified the extraordinary qualities of the distinguished judges whose voices are heard in this book.

I first came across Chief Judge Kaye's work when I was researching my first book, *Ending the Gauntlet—Removing Barriers to Women's Success in the Law*. My research brought me to a 1988 article she had written for the *Fordham Law Review* about women in large law firms.[2] Her article identified the challenges that women were facing as they entered the legal profession in increasingly larger numbers after decades of full exclusion.

Her premise was prescient: the long-held belief that women would advance in greater numbers once the pipeline was filled was (and is) a myth. That is, a mere increase in the number of women graduating from law school would not itself eliminate their barriers

---

[2] Judith S. Kaye, *Women Lawyers in Big Firms: A Study in Progress Toward Gender Equality,* 57 FORDHAM L. REV. 111 (1988), *available at* https://ir.lawnet.fordham.edu /flr/vol57/iss1/3.

to advancement. Inequities will invariably continue until organizational leaders understand and remove the institutional and cultural barriers to women and all other excluded groups. And she explicitly recognized the importance of women succeeding in large firms, precisely because these institutions have an outsize influence on our profession and society as a whole.

Yet even with her realistic assessment of the status of women in the profession, Judge Kaye exuded optimism and a sense of hope—qualities that were clearly a part of her writing, her speeches, and her life's work.

At some point around the time *Ending the Gauntlet* was released, Judge Kaye reached out to me with kind words that I have always treasured. Subsequently, our paths crossed through the American Bar Association and our mutual interest in the Commission on Youth at Risk, she as a member of its Advisory Committee and me as a liaison from the ABA Board of Governors. Being in her presence was always an opportunity to be inspired and to learn.

In preparation for this book, I read *Judith S. Kaye, In Her Own Words*,[3] a book that is part memoir and part a selection of her opinions and articles. Her book was grounded in the abiding respect for both federal and state constitutions and the rule of law that she employed in serving as the leader of the New York State court system.

The book also revealed the Chief Judge's clear-eyed vision of what a just society should look like. Most significantly, her words were always forward looking and, read in the light of today's challenges, offer instruction for where we need to be. For example, in a lecture about former New York Chief Judge and later Supreme Court Justice Benjamin Cardozo, Chief Judge Kaye reached back to the Talmud in describing the qualifications that each judge should bring to the awesome responsibilities of that role. She stated:

[J]udges must show patience, humility and respect, hear both sides, be impartial, proceed with care and deliberation, considering again and again before announcing a decision,

---

[3.] JUDITH S. KAYE, IN HER OWN WORDS (Henry M. Greenberg, Luisa M. Kaye, Marilyn Marcus, & Albert M. Rosenblatt eds., State University of New York Press 2019).

yet not unduly delay justice. A judge must conduct himself so that justice is not only done *but also seen to be done, and is so understood by the participants*. [Emphasis added.]

As I read those words in the context of her speech about a revered Supreme Court jurist, I wondered how she would have viewed the institution's current unprecedented use of a "Shadow Docket" that provides no opportunity for care and deliberation, no sunlight into the process of judging, and no ability for the participants to understand the result.

Her book also includes portions of the commencement address she gave to the 1991 graduates of New York University Law School, where Chief Judge Kaye spoke eloquently about some of the topics that constitute the theme of this book:

> As I myself can attest . . . jobs for women lawyers . . . were hard to find: quotas were commonplace; compensation lower; partnerships all but impossible. Women were excluded from bar associations, lawyers' luncheon and athletic clubs, and even firm outings. Humiliation and degradation at the hands of judges, fellow lawyers, and support personnel were the order of the day. The law tolerated this behavior long into the twentieth century, and . . . so did many of us. Getting in was what mattered.
>
> But while the stereotypes and inequities are by no means yet eradicated, efforts that began more than a century ago at last have borne fruit. . . . And the law and the courts have had a substantial role in facilitating that change.[4]

The qualities that Chief Judge Kaye described in her lecture about Justice Cardozo are the same ones that she brought to her hundreds of articles, speeches, and court decisions, and the many commissions, task forces, committees, and other governing bodies on which she served—many of which she also created. It is the significance of her impact and the strength of her legacy that Chief Judge Kaye shares with the others featured in this book.

[4.] KAYE, supra note 3, at 361.

THE ENDURING RELEVANCE OF THEIR STORIES

For each of the judges featured in this book, research can provide information about their career milestones, correlating dates with jobs, marriages, promotions, and other measurable facts in their lives. But timelines do not reveal the moral fiber that underlies their success, and they omit the messiness of life: the challenges of relationships, the politics of work, the burdens and joys of raising a family and caring for relatives, and the difficulty of working through career and life choices (or the lack of choice altogether, as many women have faced at different stages of their careers).

Timelines, however, do not reveal what it took to achieve each life stage, nor the grace, courage, and resolve required to overcome the obstacles and make a positive difference in the world. The stories in this book move beyond timelines, providing an understanding of each judge's devotion to the justice system, the rule of law, and the law's power to make a difference in people's lives, even as they have sought to use that privilege wisely.

They also understand that when women work together, their impact can be profound, even as some shared stories of hurt and disappointment when opposition from other women thwarted their efforts. But still they persisted, moving past roadblocks to build coalitions wherever they could to accomplish their goals. They are inspirational figures who made our justice system better by their service, and all of us better by their presence.

THEIR LEGACY IS NOW OUR RESPONSIBILITY

In addition to describing the personal qualities that underlie the successful careers of the judges featured here, their stories offer important lessons to combat the subtle and less overt discriminations and unexamined biases that exist today, and that pose barriers that are as insidious as the ones that result from outright discrimination.

The task of overcoming these barriers can be more difficult when a response feels impossible and is, instead, replaced by a silence born of fear. But as some of the judges' stories make clear, it was their silence they regretted the most.

I hope that readers of this book will see approachable role models who achieved the pinnacle of their profession with the dignity, grace, and resilience that helped them overcome the many challenges they encountered along the way. The organizing and coalition building they employed remains essential today.

Much more work is required to achieve the full equality they envisioned for this country. We cannot rest on their laurels.

METHODOLOGY

Significant efforts were made to reach every living recipient of the Margaret Brent Women Lawyers of Achievement Award. Some were unable to participate for a variety of reasons; a few others could not be reached. In some instances, we reached out to colleagues of judges who are no longer with us or who otherwise would be unable to participate, to ensure that the voices of some of these remarkable women could still be heard from those who knew them well.

The letter inviting the judges to participate included guidelines for their potential submission. The result is seen in the following chapters that form a compendium of stories from current and former judges from courts throughout the country.

Each judge responded movingly to these guidelines, openly and reflectively sharing nuanced stories about stereotyping they faced, barriers they encountered, difficulties they had to overcome, criticism they endured, work-life challenges, pay and promotion inequality, asserting their power, overcoming fears, responding to critics, and support from other women. In addition to these individual contributions, we have a collection of articles in honor of several other towering Brent Award recipients whose work on the bench made a tremendous difference for civil rights, civil liberties, and women's advancement, including Justice Sandra Day O'Connor and Justice Ruth Bader Ginsburg.

Considerable thought went into the order of these chapters. While the original inclination was to arrange them thematically, it soon became clear that there were many overlapping themes. It also became clear that, whatever the age of the writer, each submission had deep relevance to today's challenges. Accordingly, each chapter is ordered chronologically by the birth year of the judges, bookended by contributions about Justice Sandra Day O'Connor and Justice Ruth Bader Ginsburg.

This framing reveals that every contributor, from the oldest to the youngest, has faced the sting of biases that range from the overt to the unconscious. This order also reminds us that even as gains are made, biases are deep and systemic, requiring the vigilance of every generation to continue the difficult work of achieving full equity for all.

The Independence, Strength, and Professionalism of Justice Sandra Day O'Connor

1

Marci A. Hamilton

*P*rofessor Marci Hamilton's reflections on her experience clerking for Justice Sandra Day O'Connor provide a vital lesson about the importance—and fragility—of the Supreme Court. Professor Hamilton includes anecdotes that demonstrate the deep roots of the Federalist Society's efforts to influence the Court, just as she demonstrates Justice O'Connor's steely resolve and deep devotion to the Constitution's meaning in a modern world.

The description of Justice O'Connor's approach to her work and the way in which she comported herself on the nation's highest Court serves as a crucial reminder that the strength and integrity of the judiciary depend on judges who refuse adherence to political agendas and the influence of outside organizations.

Lauren Stiller Rikleen, Editor

1

I had the deep honor of clerking for Justice Sandra Day O'Connor, or "SO'C," as her clerks call her, during the Supreme Court's 1989 term. By example and explanation, she instilled in me the values of independence, strength, and professionalism.

I. INDEPENDENCE

Justice O'Connor was her own person. She was born in El Paso, Texas, in 1930 and raised on her family's Lazy-B ranch in Duncan, Arizona, where she loved the outdoor life of the ranch. Her high intelligence was clear: she learned to read by age four. With school options near the ranch not ideal, and to ensure she received a high-quality education, she returned to El Paso to live with her grandmother.

SO'C graduated high school two years early and, against the odds—because few women were admitted—she was enrolled at Stanford University to major in Economics when she was just sixteen years old. In 1950, SO'C entered Stanford Law School, where she was one of five women in the class and an editor on the *Stanford Law Review*. It's also where she met John Jay O'Connor III, her beloved husband. Future Chief Justice William Rehnquist was the class valedictorian, and although Stanford did not officially rank their students, many say SO'C was third, leading many a fellow classmate to claim in jest to have been second!

Despite her intelligence and academic achievements, she could not find a paying job as an attorney after graduation. Why? Because she was a woman. So, she forged her own path.

SO'C turned down the paid legal secretary job offered by the law firm of Gibson Dunn; instead, she took an unpaid position with the San Mateo County, California, County Attorney's office. It did not take long for her to be promoted to Deputy County Attorney. In 1954, she and her husband headed to Germany, where he would serve in the U.S. Army Judge Advocate General's Corps and she would serve as a civil attorney for the U.S Army Quartermaster Corps. Three years later, they settled in Arizona, and she entered private practice, where she remained for eight years. That was followed by four years as an Assistant Attorney General.

She then served for five years in the Arizona Senate, which culminated in her being the first female Majority Leader at any statehouse in the country. Her legislative service distinguished her from the other Justices once she joined the U.S. Supreme Court, because she had "boots on the ground" insight into how the law is made and what lawmakers need from the Court to guide them. SO'C was always a pragmatist, as you can see from her very first decision in the law to reject a secretarial position in favor of becoming an unpaid county attorney. With her legislative knowledge combined with her pragmatism and common sense—reinforced by her upbringing on a Western ranch—she brought a fresh and important viewpoint to the Justices' Conference Table.

In 1975, she was elected to the Maricopa County Superior Court and, four years later, appointed to the Arizona Court of Appeals in Phoenix. Not a bad record for someone who couldn't get hired out of law school! As you can tell, SO'C never looked back; she just kept forging ahead as her tenacity combined with her high intelligence made her a leader wherever she landed.

After two years as an appellate judge, in July 1981, she received the historic phone call from President Ronald Reagan informing her that he intended to nominate her as the first woman on the U.S. Supreme Court. During his campaign, Reagan had pledged to put a woman on the Supreme Court for the purpose of shoring up the women's vote. It worked. He made the promise, he won, and then he fulfilled it when Justice Potter Stewart resigned. SO'C was perfect for the position: smart, experienced, congenial, and athletic, with a resume bristling with high achievement. She was both approachable and admirable and was confirmed unanimously by the U.S. Senate.

SO'C's upbringing on an active ranch, where she rode with the ranch hands daily, served her well as she entered the Court's fraternity. I have never known anyone better than SO'C in sending subtle messages to make major points. If Reagan hadn't selected her for the Court, she would have been a standout diplomat and even Secretary of State; honestly, she would have been a formidable President, but I digress.

It was important to her to signal to her male colleagues at the Court that she would be equal and independent. The Supreme Court building has a basketball court above the courtroom, which many call the "highest court in the land," where the guys in the building, including the justices, would play basketball. Early in her tenure, she made it clear that this was her space, too, when she established her weekday morning exercise classes for the women in the building. I was the "exercise clerk" during my year, and it was a blessing to have one hour each weekday to clear my brain before heading back to another long day in chambers, researching and writing without having to be concerned about in-chambers face time.

From the day SO'C arrived at the Court to the day she retired, she took very seriously her obligations to Lady Justice and the Court. At the same time, she made time and space to fulfill the demands placed on her because she was the first woman on the Court. No other Justice received remotely as many invitations to speak and be honored. She gave freely of her time to the public, which sought her out incessantly.

The public also wrote thousands of letters to her on many topics. During the late eighties, when *Roe v. Wade* was aggressively under attack, she received bags of mail from both sides. Of course, they were irrelevant to her own decision making, but they were a visual reminder to all on the Court of her role as the one female Justice deciding women's rights at the time.

There was an era when the Supreme Court issued approximately 160 decisions each year, because most of its jurisdiction was mandatory. That is a heavy load for nine Justices and led to Congress during the 1970s and 80s amending many federal statutes to permit discretionary jurisdiction for the Court. By 1989, when I started clerking, the number of cases taken for full consideration had slipped to 130. More recently, the Court selects approximately seventy-five cases each year. With this shift to discretionary certiorari for the vast majority of cases, the Justices cut their docket in half, making each case more consequential.

It also tempted some Justices to treat their jurisdiction as larger than the case before them. For example, Justice Antonin Scalia had a tendency to treat each case as an opportunity to decide an issue for decades. It was as though he was Zeus, throwing down legal rules from the heavens—which meant he was scaling the heights from common law to a modified version of civil law. SO'C wasn't interested.

In contrast, her feet were firmly planted on the ground. She considered each case on its own facts, understood the challenges faced by local and state governments, and held true to the Constitution's "case and controversy" requirement that limits the federal judiciary's jurisdiction to cases with live controversies brought by those who have active standing. Each case for her was to be decided narrowly with respect to the facts in front of them so as to let the law develop organically and to ensure fairness to the parties before them.

II. STRENGTH

Many think of Justice O'Connor as the "swing vote" of her era. It has been common in some quarters to assume that meant she couldn't make up her own mind, as though in each case she was eyeing who to follow. Was she the swing vote because she needed guidance from the other Justices to make a decision? Hardly.

SO'C had a backbone of steel. No man (or clerk) was going to dictate case outcomes to her. She was in the middle because that's where her views lay. Note that she did not change her views as the Court moved farther to the right. She did find it astonishing that she would become a "liberal" Justice, but of course the Court was shifting to the right, and the right was increasingly dogmatic in a way she would never find comfortable.

SO'C was a Goldwater Republican, who supported the civil rights of women and others, including a right to abortion. As the Republican party shifted, the openness to individual rights shifted to rights-reducing dogma derived in part from religion. That was never going to sit right with SO'C.

This new wave crashed into the Court with Federalist Society law clerks forming a secret "cabal" to advance their agenda. During the 1989 term, the cabal was in full operation. These were deeply conservative male clerks, who were united in a Federalist Society vision of the Constitution and determined to set the Court's agenda behind the scenes. They would meet in private to coordinate their strategy for both the shadow docket and the merits cases. Of course, their highest priority was to overrule *Roe.*

Justice O'Connor assigned to me the abortion docket that year. There had been an opening to reconsider it in *Webster v. Reproductive Health Services* during the previous term, but SO'C refused. Scalia couldn't contain himself, declaring in his concurrence that her approach to the case *"cannot be taken seriously."* Unfortunately for him, she was dead serious and never did waver from her refusal to overrule *Roe.*

During our term, the Court had granted several abortion cases where the petitioners were arguing to overturn *Roe,* which meant I was approached by many a cabal member in the halls. I honestly couldn't decide whether they were suffering from youth or hubris, thinking SO'C was going to change her mind. The cabal once again failed to move the needle. They would casually chat me up to see what SO'C was thinking and suggest arguments to try with her. I marveled at their assumption that I was on their side, or that SO'C ever would be.

There was this underlying assumption that she wasn't that bright compared to the smart conservative Justices and that she could be bullied into changing her view of women's rights. They were dreaming if they thought that Scalia's jab at SO'C might have persuaded her to follow his demand. Let me repeat: she had a backbone of steel. There was no persuading her to do what she had already decided she would not do.

After I wrote copiously long bench memos on each case, around Thanksgiving, all of the direct *Roe* challenges were settled or withdrawn. The word must have gotten out that SO'C was not going to be the fifth vote to overrule *Roe.* Setting aside the many hours I had spent on what had become a dead letter, I was at least thoroughly prepared for the next abortion case: *Hodgson v. Minnesota.* Once again, she voted according to her own lights.

The *Hodgson* case involved a Minnesota law that required pregnant minors to notify both parents forty-eight hours before they could obtain an abortion. While SO'C was determined to preserve *Roe*, she had voted to uphold many a restriction over the years. In this case involving the safety of a girl who found herself pregnant and sought an abortion, SO'C drew the line at the two-parent requirement standing by itself. The District Court had made copious fact-findings that requiring a girl to notify both parents, particularly in dysfunctional families, could be dangerous for the girl. The law had another element, however, that would permit a girl who feared telling both parents before the abortion to obtain permission through a judicial bypass system.

SO'C was determined not to expose the girls to even more trauma than they had already suffered and voted to uphold the two-parent notification requirement only if it was paired with the judicial bypass. She was being strong for the vulnerable in an arena where she was being pressured by the conservative Justices, and I so admired her for that.

III. PROFESSIONALISM AND LIVING YOUR LIFE

Justice O'Connor insisted on a high level of professionalism in her chambers, which was an integral element of her worldview where one watches one's words and never burns a bridge.

I experienced her insistence on civility firsthand. She assigned to clerks the job of drafting opinions, and then she reviewed them closely. I had drafted something at one point, and I included some strong language describing another Justice's opinion, which I thought was just right. One day, seated at my desk, I heard her call out, "Marci!" across the chambers, which was not a good sign. Knowing I must have done something problematic, I hurried to her office. She pointed to my words and her red lines through them, saying something like, "We don't talk like this." When I started to defend those clever words, let's just say she cut me off. She was so right.

Now I understand more deeply what she was teaching us: don't waste time on squabbles or creating personal discord; it will just create an annoyance in the future when you are working hard to make progress on another issue. The ranch and her private and public practice of law had taught her to avoid wasting time on such. She was not saying that you shouldn't criticize those who deserve it, though. SO'C's later opinions were fiery, and she more than once told me that she admired my rather direct public advocacy. It was not that she was teaching me to be a "lady," but rather how to pave the way to success most expeditiously.

Her insistence on civility was an element of her entire life actually. SO'C's clerkship wasn't like the other clerkships. The chambers were decorated to reflect her Southwestern roots. She made lunch for us when we came in on Saturdays to discuss the cases to be argued the next week. We carved pumpkins for Halloween, went to see the cherry blossoms regardless of the workload, and ended the year on a clerk retreat with her. She asked us how our spouses were and made sure we were doing something other than sitting at our desks all day, every day.

SO'C called our kids her "grandclerks," and even had T-shirts made with a grandclerk Supreme Court seal. I treasure the pictures of my kids in those T-shirts.

She clearly loved her husband and her sons, who she spoke to regularly while in chambers. It was the 1980s and women were still finding their rhythm with work and family, but she had chosen love and work. That meant she wasn't "just" a mother and a Justice. She also had a social life! The message was don't make your successful career and happy home life an "either-or" proposition. Do all that makes you happy. I am eternally grateful to her for that.

More often than not, SO'C headed out in the evenings with John to attend an event, dance, or concert. Even with all the pressures on her, she was going to have fun while doing it. Then there were her sports—she was a terrific tennis player and played regularly with Rehnquist, and she also skied. How can you not be impressed by a woman who decides in her middle years to take up golf, plays alone for months and even years, and then emerges as an accomplished golfer?

When she retired for the sake of her husband, who was ill, she wasn't done with the law. She had come to see judicial elections as an opportunity for corruption that was destroying the professionalism and trustworthiness of the judiciary, and actively fought to end judicial elections in numerous states, while she also continued to push for the rule of law in Eastern Europe.

One of her most important and enduring contributions post-retirement is iCivics,[1] the website for civics education, which draws in children with online games and engaging lesson plans. I will never forget the day she proudly demonstrated a template to me. In true SO'C style, she wasn't interested in something boring. It had to be active, it had to be intelligent, and it had to succeed. Just like her.

[1.] See https://www.icivics.org.

BIO

Marci A. Hamilton

Marci A. Hamilton is the founder and CEO of CHILD USA, www.childusa.org, a 501(c)(3) nonprofit think tank fighting for the civil rights of children. Its mission is to employ in-depth legal analysis and cutting-edge social science research to protect children, prevent future abuse and neglect, and bring justice to survivors. She is also a Professor of Practice in Political Science at the University of Pennsylvania. Before moving to Penn, Professor Hamilton held the Paul R. Verkuil Chair in Public Law at Benjamin N. Cardozo School of Law, Yeshiva University.

Professor Hamilton is the leading expert on clergy sex abuse and child sex abuse statutes of limitation (SOL). She has been invited to testify and advise legislators in every state where significant SOL reform has occurred. She is the author of *Justice Denied: What America Must Do to Protect Its Children* (Cambridge University Press 2008), which advocates for the elimination of child sex abuse statutes of limitations. She has filed countless pro bono amicus briefs for the protection of children at the U.S. Supreme Court and the state supreme courts. She is the coauthor of *Children and the Law* (Carolina Academic Press 2017).

Professor Hamilton is also a leading and influential critic of extreme religious liberty and the author of *God vs. the Gavel: The Perils of Extreme Religious Liberty* (Cambridge University Press 2015), which was nominated for a Pulitzer Prize. Hamilton successfully challenged the constitutionality of the Religious Freedom Restoration Act (RFRA) at the Supreme Court in *Boerne v. Flores* (1997) and defeated the RFRA claim brought by the Archdiocese of Milwaukee against hundreds of child sex abuse survivors in *Committee of Unsecured Creditors v. Listecki* (7th Cir. 2015). She has represented numerous cities, neighborhoods, and individuals dealing with church-state issues as well as claims under the Religious Land Use and Institutionalized Persons Act (RLUIPA).

Professor Hamilton was honored by Governor Tom Wolf with the 2019 Distinguished Daughters of Pennsylvania Award and is the recipient of the 2018

Louis H. Pollak Award for Public Service by the University of Pennsylvania Law School; the 2015 Annual Religious Liberty Award, American Humanist Association; the 2014 Freethought Heroine Award; the 2016 Voice Today, Voice of Gratitude Award; the National Crime Victim Bar Association's Frank Carrington Champion of Civil Justice Award, 2012; the E. Nathaniel Gates Award for outstanding public advocacy and scholarship, 2008; and selected as a Pennsylvania Woman of the Year Award, 2012, among other awards and honors. She is also frequently quoted in the national media on child sex abuse, statute of limitations issues, and constitutional, RFRA, RLUIPA, and First Amendment issues.

Professor Hamilton clerked for U.S. Supreme Court Justice Sandra Day O'Connor and Judge Edward R. Becker of the U.S. Court of Appeals for the Third Circuit. Professor Hamilton is a graduate of Vanderbilt University, BA, *summa cum laude*; Pennsylvania State University, MA (English, fiction writing, *High Honors*); MA (Philosophy); and the University of Pennsylvania School of Law, JD, *magna cum laude*, where she served as Editor-in-Chief of the *University of Pennsylvania Law Review*. She is a member of Phi Beta Kappa and Order of the Coif.

BIO

The Life and Highly Interesting Times of Betty Roberts: The First Woman to Serve on Oregon's Appellate Courts

2

Attorney General Ellen Rosenblum
and S. Diane Rynerson

M*any years ago, I read—and was deeply influenced by—the memoir of Justice Betty Roberts,* With Grit and by Grace. *I was struck by the many parallels between her role as a lawyer and pioneer of women's rights, and the relevance of her experiences to women lawyers today.*

I wrote at the time that women would benefit from studying the extraordinary efforts of and brilliant strategies employed by this lawyer, activist, legislator, and first woman judge to sit on the Oregon Court of Appeals and, subsequently, the Oregon Supreme Court. Justice Roberts' book laid out a blueprint for how she built coalitions to eliminate many of the overt sources of discrimination that women faced at that time. That many other barriers still persist suggests it is a blueprint worth reviving.

Attorney General Ellen Rosenblum and Diane Rynerson both knew Justice Roberts well, and beautifully capture for us her dedicated efforts and accomplishments, as well as offer insight into her personal challenges, demonstrating the inevitable complexities of life. They clearly capture Justice Roberts' tireless energy for making the world a better place, and how her success in doing so made a difference.

Lauren Stiller Rikleen, Editor

Betty Lucille Cantrell was born on February 5, 1923, in Arkansas City, Kansas, but moved at an early age to northern Texas to be closer to extended family. When she was six, her father became desperately ill from drinking tainted bootleg alcohol and had to leave home for treatment. As a result, the family's comfortable existence changed dramatically.

External events proved equally disturbing. In her autobiography, *With Grit and by Grace: Breaking Trails in Law and Politics—A Memoir* (2008: Oregon State University Press), Betty described how as a child she witnessed smoke and flames coming from the local courthouse. Betty watched her mother wringing her hands and repeating over and over, "That poor man, that poor man." She later learned what had upset her mother: The fire had been set by an angry mob that wanted access to a Black man who was on trial for rape. The man was lynched and his body dragged by a car through the Black part of town. It was experiences like this that made Betty want to make public institutions more accountable and equitable.

There were times when the family went hungry. Receiving food from the Salvation Army helped. When her father returned from the sanitarium during the summer after Betty was in third grade, it was clear that he could not walk without assistance and would never work again. Although her parents could not vote because they couldn't afford to pay the poll tax, they were heartened by the election of President Franklin Delano Roosevelt and soon benefited from the opening of a local commissary under the new Federal Surplus Relief Corporation, where they could acquire foodstuffs which couldn't otherwise be sold.

After Betty's high school graduation at age 16, she had a series of unfulfilling jobs but an active social life. Beginning in the fall of 1941, she was able to take classes in the morning at Texas Wesleyan in Fort Worth while supporting herself by working long hours at a department store. In January 1942, while home in Wichita Falls during a semester break, she met Bill Rice, someone her mother approved of and determined would be a good provider. Betty and Bill were married on September 25, 1942.

After the war, Betty, Bill, and their daughter, Dian, moved to Oregon, where Bill resumed his work as a banker. The work required them to move to a series of small towns. Betty was restless but threw herself into the role of banker's wife and mother of four young children. It was while living in LaGrande, a short distance from a state college, that she decided to continue her formal education. She reached the decision in part because she worried about what would happen if, like her mother, she should have to become the sole support for her family.

Without discussing her decision with her husband, whose work caused him to travel extensively each week, she enrolled in Eastern Oregon College of Education. A year later, Bill was transferred to Gresham, near Portland, and Betty was able to continue her studies at the newly formed Portland State College, from which she graduated in 1958 with a degree in education.

When Betty found a position as a high school teacher and dean of girls, Bill made it clear that he didn't want her to work. Betty did not want to give up her new career and the chance to continue her education. Against the advice of many, including her pastor, who told her, "If you were my wife, you would not have gone to college and you would not be teaching," she sought the help of one of the few women lawyers in Portland and filed for divorce.

Betty continued teaching high school while she worked toward a master's degree in political science and became interested in politics. She was appointed Democratic precinct chairwoman. Her involvement with schools as an educator and a parent led her to run for an open seat on the local school board despite being advised that, as a recently divorced woman, her chances for election were not good. Betty typed up a fact sheet with her qualifications and, with the help of fellow teachers, distributed copies to voters. Her two male opponents didn't appear to campaign, and Betty won the election.

In November 1960, Betty married Frank Roberts, a speech professor at Portland State College and chair of the Multnomah County Democratic Party. By 1962, both Betty and Frank were running for political office. She ran as a candidate for the Oregon State House of Representatives, and he ran for Oregon State Senate. They both lost their elections. In her memoir, Betty wrote, "The lesson I learned in that campaign was how tough it is to lose." Betty didn't let that loss end her political career.

The year 1962 marked another turning point. Having received her master's degree from the University of Oregon, Betty wanted to work toward a doctorate at the University, focusing on behavioral politics, specifically on public opinion and polling. The chair of the department told her that, as she was 39 at the time, he couldn't allow her to pursue a PhD. He explained that she would be 45 by the time she completed the program and would only have 20 years in which to repay the taxpayers of Oregon for their investment in her education. As she wrote in her memoir, "It was well known that there had never been a woman professor or PhD candidate in his department. I knew my age was not the real reason."

Although Betty had not previously contemplated a legal career, having the door shut so completely on pursuing a PhD made her consider alternatives. She applied to a night law school in Portland, where she was readily accepted. She began law school at age 39—with three children still at home, a daughter at Stanford, a full-time teaching job, and responsibilities as a school board member. Her decision in 1964 to campaign for a seat in the Oregon House of Representatives meant her life became even more hectic. She won the election and joined the six other women in the House.

During her first term in the House, she was assigned to the Education Committee. She sponsored unsuccessful bills to reinstate state spending on kindergarten and on the relatively new idea of victim compensation. In her memoir, she had positive reflections on that first term: "I had made my mark as a freshman legislator who was a 'quick study,' as one newspaper reported, and ended the session recognized as a lawmaker who was willing to work hard and take tough stands."

In 1966, Betty and one other woman graduated from the Northwestern College of Law of Lewis & Clark College. Passing the Oregon bar exam was the next hurdle to be faced. She felt well prepared, but the distractions of professional and family life proved to be too much, and she failed by one point. Although her score was within the margin for appeal, she decided to study harder and try again. The following year she took a bar review course and was coached for six weeks by Jena Schlegel, who at the time was counsel to the House Judiciary Committee and had received the top score on the 1958 Oregon bar exam. Betty was the only female among the 208 applicants sitting for the Oregon bar in 1967 and, just as with her campaign for a House seat, on the second try she was successful.

Frank Roberts had been elected to the Oregon House of Representatives for the term beginning in 1966, but their marriage was coming to an end, and their divorce became final in March 1966. She decided to continue to be known as Betty Roberts, as in her words, "the voters had, in effect, named me." That decision created difficulties with the Registrar of Elections, the Oregon State Bar, and Oregon's newspaper of record, but Betty ultimately prevailed.

Betty easily won reelection to a second term in the Oregon House. She served on the Education Committee, the State and Federal Affairs Committee, and the Planning and Development Committee, where she chaired a subcommittee that brought forth successful legislation to create a Sea Grant College at Oregon State, making Oregon the host of one of the four initial federally recognized Sea Grant Colleges.

Two years later, Betty ran a successful campaign for the Oregon Senate, where no woman had served in the previous session. In the 1969 session, Betty worked to decriminalize abortion and introduced a bill to end employment discrimination based on sex and race. In subsequent sessions, as the number of women legislators increased, she worked to end sex discrimination in public accommodations, regulate deceptive trade practices, and pass the Equal Rights Amendment. In terms of her legislative work, she is perhaps best known for spearheading Oregon's Bottle Bill: the nation's first effort to encourage recycling through a deposit on soft drink containers.

In the 1977 legislative session, she was the sole sponsor of a successful bill that required a judge to grant joint custody of the children if requested by both parties. As a lawyer, she had experienced the need to "judge shop" in cases like these, even when the parties agreed that joint custody would work best for their children.

Another significant success in the 1977 session was the expansion of the rape shield law to make the victim's reputation for chastity inadmissible for any purpose. By 1977, with Betty still serving in the state senate and as a leader of the Women's Caucus, Oregon ranked ninth in the nation in terms of the percentage of women in the state legislature (13.3 percent).

Throughout the ten-year period Betty was serving in the Legislature (1967 to 1977), she taught business law and political science at Mt. Hood Community College. In the fall of 1977, Betty's career took an unexpected turn when she was appointed by Governor Straub to a newly created panel of the Oregon Court of Appeals, making her the first woman to serve on an Oregon appellate court.

At the time of her appointment, there were five women trial judges in Oregon. The chief judge was not welcoming, and her early days on the court were marked with tension, slights, and snide remarks from some of her colleagues on the bench as well as court staff. Over the next few years, Betty persisted, not being confrontational or combative but also refusing to be silenced. Betty wrote in her memoirs that by 1980, "While the workload of the court was still a killer, the emotional strain had diminished significantly, making it easier for me to turn all my mental energy to my work."

On September 22, 1981, the day after Sandra Day O'Connor was confirmed by the U.S. Senate as the first female U.S. Supreme

Court Justice, Betty filed for a seat on the Oregon Supreme Court. Due to ill health, Justice Thomas Tongue, one of Betty's law school professors, had determined he could not complete his term.

Although Betty thought it was unlikely that Republican Governor Victor Atiyeh, who had been her colleague in the legislature, would appoint her, she thought it important to let him know that she wanted the position and was confident that she could win a race just a few months later against someone he might appoint. (In Oregon, all state judges must run for election after their appointment.) A number of Republicans encouraged him to take the practical and historic step of appointing her to the vacancy, and on December 17, 1981, Governor Atiyeh announced that Betty Roberts would be Oregon's first female Supreme Court Justice.

So, on February 8, 1982, at age 59, Betty was sworn in as an Associate Justice on the Oregon Supreme Court. The transition to the Supreme Court had none of the discomfort she'd experienced in her first years on the Court of Appeals, and she quickly settled into her new role.

The case for which Betty is best known, *Hewitt v. SAIF*, 653 P.2d 970 (1982), came in her first year on the court. The claimant, an unmarried man, had cohabited with an unmarried woman for several years prior to the woman's death in an industrial accident. The couple had a child together, and they had jointly executed a declaration of paternity, naming the claimant as the father. A state statute clearly permitted that Workers' Compensation benefits could be granted for the surviving unmarried woman and children of an injured male worker "the same as if the man and woman had been legally married." The Oregon Court of Appeals reversed the Workers' Compensation Board's dismissal of the claim and ordered that compensation should be granted as if the statute were written in gender-neutral terms.

Writing for the court, Betty analyzed the statute in light of the Oregon Constitution, Art. 1, Sec. 20, which states that "No law shall be passed granting to any citizen or class of citizens privileges or immunities, which, upon the same terms, shall not equally belong to all citizens." She wrote that "Oregon has no equal rights provision related specifically to gender, yet we do not feel constrained to limit our application of Article 1, Section 20 on this basis." At a time when national ratification of the Equal Rights Amendment had failed, the holding in *Hewitt v. SAIF* was hailed by many as effectively giving Oregon its own Equal Rights Amendment.

Two other cases from the following year show the importance of having a woman on Oregon's highest court.

In *State v. Middleton*, 294 Or 427 (1983), Justice Roberts joined the majority opinion that permitted expert testimony about the behavior of a child abused by a family member. Her concurring opinion was significant, as it highlighted the growing body of study explaining the behaviors of victims of intra-family abuse—including battered woman syndrome—and endorsing such expert testimony.

Then, in *Nearing v. Weaver*, 295 Or 702 (1983), Justice Roberts joined the majority in recognizing a civil action on behalf of a woman and her children who suffered injuries from an abusive spouse when police failed to enforce a judicial restraining order. Betty first urged the court to take review from the lower court decisions denying relief, and then worked successfully to persuade colleagues to support recovery for the plaintiffs.

In 1986, at age 63, Betty resigned from the court. Although she was conflicted about leaving the high court after only four years, she wanted to spend more time with her ailing third husband, Keith Skelton, whom she absolutely adored and who had retired from the legislature, as well as to free herself from the tedious commute between Salem and her home in Portland.

In the years that followed, Betty kept to a busy schedule, lecturing, writing, and helping to pioneer acceptance of alternate dispute resolution. She did not like being described as a "retired judge," and took an active role in political and civic life, serving as a visiting professor in state and local government at Oregon State University and mentoring countless young men and women.

In March 2004, well before the federal courts legalized same-sex marriage, she made history by conducting the first same-sex marriage ceremonies in Oregon during a brief period that year when Multnomah County (Portland) issued marriage licenses to gay and lesbian couples.

Betty received numerous honors, most notably the American Bar Association's Commission on Women in the Profession's Margaret Brent Women Lawyers of Achievement Award in 2006. In Oregon Betty received the first award named after her from then-recently formed Oregon Women Lawyers. Since then, the coveted award has been bestowed upon an individual who lives up to Betty's example.

Even after she was diagnosed with pulmonary fibrosis, she continued to mediate cases, mentor women lawyers and judges, and maintain an extensive correspondence. She died on June 25, 2011, at the age of 88, surrounded by her four children.

Does it make a difference having a woman on the court? Here are Betty's thoughts on that topic as expressed in her memoir:

> My friends asked me regularly whether a woman on the court made any difference in how the law is interpreted and in the outcome of cases. I had to answer candidly that I didn't think my presence on the court had made much of a difference yet, but that when more women became judges that would make a difference. It's inevitable, I thought, that when we have judges who are biologically different from men, who have different cultural training and uniquely different life experiences, they will see the law from a different set of values.

Did it make a difference having Betty Roberts on the court? The answer must be a resounding YES. Everything about Betty—from her lived experience to her deep and practical approach to solving problems to her skill as both a listener and a speaker—made her a memorable jurist *and* made Oregon's appellate courts the better for her presence. Betty Roberts's legacy remains an inspiration to all of us who work to make our justice system more accessible and equitable for all.

I.   PERSONAL REFLECTIONS FROM ATTORNEY GENERAL ELLEN ROSENBLUM

Betty Roberts was pathbreaking as an appellate judge in Oregon. Her extraordinary life experiences, her many years as a teacher, her deep understanding of how a legislature works, and her powerful personality all contributed to her success on the bench. These qualities also made all the more meaningful her mentorship of countless Oregon women lawyers aspiring to judgeships. Betty's life experiences tell of a world few of us can imagine these days, and far fewer of us have had to endure.

I was fortunate to meet then-Senator Roberts in 1975, when I was a third-year law student at the University of Oregon, assigned to her for my legislation clinic. In truth, she was too busy to spend much time with me, but I got to watch her in action presiding over the Senate Business and Consumer Affairs Committee; her strength and decisiveness offered lessons I'll never forget.

Much later, in the late 1980s, I would become reacquainted with Justice Roberts, who took it upon herself to mentor a lucky group of us women lawyers who began to see the judiciary as within our grasp. After most of our group was appointed by various governors—and then elected (as required by Oregon law)—we came to think of ourselves as "Betty's Bench"—even posing at one point for a "court" pictorial in our judicial robes that made it appear all the justices on the Oregon Supreme Court were women!

Incredibly enough, today that very court is led by a woman Chief Justice and four other women Justices, making it only two shy of being an all-female court. Without Betty's influence, this may not have happened at all—and certainly not this soon.

I—and my women-in-law colleagues who knew and were mentored by Betty—still feel the love and strength of this remarkable woman, who continued to support and care about us to her dying day. She is missed, but her legacy is carried on as we pursue our legal careers that have been so greatly influenced by her.

BIO

Attorney General Ellen Rosenblum

A former federal prosecutor and state trial and appellate court judge, Ellen Rosenblum was elected the first woman to serve as Oregon Attorney General in November 2012. Attorney General Rosenblum has been reelected twice and is currently serving her third four-year term. Her priorities include consumer protection and civil rights, with a focus on addressing hate crimes and bias incidents.

As "the People's Attorney," Rosenblum is a fierce advocate for Oregon's children, seniors, students, crime victims and survivors, and BIPOC communities—including immigrants and refugees. She has led successful statewide policy reform task forces on topics including Police Profiling, Public Records, and Hate Crimes, and is currently leading initiatives on Consumer Internet Privacy, Labor Trafficking, and Police Standards for Training and Discipline.

Attorney General Rosenblum is active in local and national organizations of lawyers, judges, and attorneys general. She is the Vice President of the National Association of Attorneys General and a past Chair of the Conference of Western Attorneys General. She has served as Secretary of the American Bar Association (ABA) and as Chair of the ABA Section of State & Local Government Law. She has been the recipient of numerous honors and awards, including, most recently, the ABA Commission on Margaret Brent Women Lawyers of Achievement Award.

Rosenblum is a proud "Double Duck" graduate of the University of Oregon College of Arts and Sciences (BS) and Law School (JD).

BIO

S. Diane Rynerson

S. Diane Rynerson has been active with women's bar associations since 1989, in roles ranging from committee volunteer to staff member. She served as the first executive director of Oregon Women Lawyers, and was the long-time executive director of the National Conference of Women's Bar Associations.

Diane received her undergraduate degree from Portland State University's Honors College and her law degree from Santa Clara University. She is admitted to practice in California and Oregon but is retired from the practice of law.

Diane shared a deep interest in the history of women lawyers and their life stories with Betty Roberts, whom she was honored to know as a friend and mentor.

The Honorable Joan Dempsey Klein: A Relentless Quest for Gender Equality

Drucilla Stender Ramey

3

When learning about the early pioneers who broke through the centuries-long prohibition against women serving as judges, there is a tendency to idealize their life and assume that what they accomplished was so super-human, it can be seen only as admirable, not aspirational. But as their stories come to life, we learn that their achievements were built on challenges that fueled their drive to make life better for others.

Justice Joan Dempsey Klein was an iconic figure in the California bar and judiciary. Her friends and colleagues remember her with reverence and deep gratitude. Drucilla Ramey, a trailblazer in her own right, reflects on Justice Klein's life, legacy, and continued relevance.

Lauren Stiller Rikleen, Editor

California Senior Presiding Justice Joan Dempsey Klein, who died on Christmas Eve 2020 at the age of 96, was a trailblazing judicial pioneer and iconic feminist powerhouse who epitomized the qualities celebrated by the Margaret Brent Award. Over the course of her fifty-two-year judicial career, Justice Klein authored more than 500 opinions, including landmark decisions in areas including products liability, equal access to the courts, and sex discrimination. But it was in her relentless quest for gender equality in the legal profession and the courts that she played her most pivotal role, helping to irrevocably change the face of the profession and the judiciary.

Smart, tough, tenacious, disarmingly frank, and often funny, Justice Klein was a force of nature who always saw the best in people but did not suffer fools gladly. Perhaps best known for cofounding and leading powerful statewide, national, and international professional organizations dedicated to the advancement of women lawyers and judges, she pioneered the formation of groups including

California Women Lawyers (CWL), the nation's first, and still largest, statewide women lawyers' organization, as well as the National Association of Women Judges (NAWJ), and the International Association of Women Judges (IAWJ).

As movingly highlighted in two compelling oral histories—the California Appellate Court Legacy Project and the ABA's "Women Trailblazers in the Law Project"—Justice Klein, born just four years after women got the vote, was most assuredly not to the manor born.

A proud fifth-generation Californian, Justice Klein's forebears included Maria Refugio de Bernal, a daughter of a nineteenth-century Mexican land grantee, and her Austrian-born husband John Kettinger, California's first Caucasian judge and founder of Pleasanton California. The Justice's immediate family, however, followed a swift downhill trajectory, owing to her father's problems with alcohol, gambling, and gainful employment, with the family making successive moves south until finally landing in a small rural town just north of the Mexican border.

Though the Justice's mother was an educated woman of great beauty and talent, she nevertheless tied herself to the fortunes of her improvident husband, subordinating her own autonomy and dreams to a lifetime of subservience. Justice Klein's own dream thus became "having a life unlike that of my mother, who had no independence about anything, and to put as much distance as I possibly could between her lifestyle and my own."

Justice Klein attributed her lifelong determination to pave the way for and mentor the women coming up behind her to the complete absence of any positive role models in her childhood. "If I can be some kind of role model, a catalyst for somebody whose face has seen hurdles along the way," she said, "I say, 'Go for it,' because I didn't have role models at all, none . . . I had no money, had nothing but negative impetus from those around me." The seeds of her ambition for higher education instead were first planted by way of a random bus ride conversation with a teenage friend who insisted, "You will never get anywhere in life unless you go to college."

Justice Klein's newfound urgent quest for higher education led her to enter and work her way through San Diego State, supporting herself via a hodgepodge of jobs, including riveting bomb bay doors on military aircraft and teaching swimming at the Y. Upon graduation, her swimming prowess fortuitously landed her a spot on a nine-month European synchronized swimming tour with the famed Buster Crabbe Aqua Parade. As she later summed up that extraordinary experience, "It was a ball."

Upon returning to California, Justice Klein was able to parlay a one-year fellowship to the University of California, Los Angeles (UCLA)—where she was encouraged to pursue a degree in physical education—into admission to the third entering class of the new UCLA School of Law. While finding it a consummately inhospitable environment for women, she married "one of the good guys" and gave birth to her first child while still in law school.

Ultimately crediting her law school education as "giving me a life," she later paid it forward with an endowed scholarship fund in support of "students with financial need and outstanding academic credential who show a strong commitment to advocating for gender equality or to promoting the advancement of women in the law and society."

As an immediate graduate, Justice Klein and her friend and fellow UCLA Law graduate Dorothy Nelson (and later Ninth Circuit Judge and first Dean of an ABA-accredited law school) recognized there were, as Justice Klein put it, "no opportunities for women anywhere. No law firms were hiring women." Partly owing, however, to the fact that her then-husband had landed a job at the California Attorney General's Los Angeles office, Justice Klein was able to secure employment there as a Deputy A.G. She worked right up to the day she delivered her second child and returned to work three weeks later.

As she came to fully comprehend the wholesale exclusion of women from most law jobs and the lack of any accommodation by employers for pregnancy, childbirth, or child-rearing, Justice Klein experienced an epiphany that was to thereafter guide her life. "There was a point in my life," she said, "when I recognized discrimination against women for what it was . . . and made a commitment to myself that I would devote a certain portion of every day to try to eliminate discrimination against women."

Consciously taking a page from the civil rights movement, Justice Klein further recognized that group action by women, speaking truth to power with a unified voice, was the *sine qua non* for meaningful change.

Governor Pat Brown's 1963 appointment of Justice Klein to the Los Angeles Municipal Court ("that's where the women were") was the first appointment of a UCLA Law graduate to the bench. Ultimately rising to serve as the Court's Presiding Judge, she thereafter was elected to a seat on the L.A. Superior Court in 1975.

It was perhaps the complete absence of mentors or moral and professional support systems for women judges in those early years that caused Justice Klein to lead in the creation, first, of CWL in 1974, then of the NAWJ in 1979, and, finally, of the IAWJ in 1991. (As a fledgling lawyer in San Francisco, I, for example, first came within Justice Klein's considerable sphere of influence in 1974, in what might fairly be described as a two-day slumber party she hosted at her Los Angeles home for the Provisional Board of Governors of California Women Lawyers, out of which emerged CWL's by-laws and a lifelong friendship.) In her international travels, the Justice similarly campaigned for equality and adherence to the rule of law in justice systems across the world.

In 1978 Justice Klein was appointed by Governor Jerry Brown to serve as the first woman Presiding Justice of a Division of the California Court of Appeal (Division Three of the Second District Court of Appeal), a position she held with distinction until her retirement in 2014. The appointment leapfrogged her over long-tenured male colleagues, making for "a few hard years" working to bring around some of her initially disgruntled fellow justices. While her superior rank entitled her to the best chambers, for example, "I sure didn't claim the corner office."

Characteristically, Justice Klein's insistence on collegiality and mutual respect among the judges and staff, as well as on objectivity, impartiality, and fair treatment of women, people of color, and other marginalized groups before the Court, ultimately set the tone for the Division's success over the ensuing decades. As she summed up her judicial philosophy, "It's very simple. It's fairness. Fair and reasonable." Former State Senator Sheila Kuehl put it another way. "She was an inspiration and a perfect example of the intersection of justice and common sense."

Among Justice Klein's most significant opinions on the Court was the landmark 1980 products liability holding in *Sindell v. Abbott Laboratories*, addressing manufacturers' liability for cancer and sterility caused in daughters of women who took DES (diethylstilbestrol) while pregnant. Because DES was a fungible product produced by numerous manufacturers, the damages from which were known only decades later, it was effectively impossible for most plaintiffs to identify the specific company whose product had caused their injuries. Justice Klein's opinion (later expanded upon by the California Supreme Court to establish the theory of market-share liability), created a rebuttable presumption in favor of a plaintiff who could prove actual damages, shifting the burden to the defendant manufacturers of a substantial market share of DES in the relevant timeframe to prove that the injury was not caused by their own respective DES.

A huge fan of the necessity for, and power of, affinity bar associations for women and other marginalized groups in the profession and the judiciary, Justice Klein also famously devoted herself to leveraging her powerful position to support the founding of women's bar associations across the country. These efforts included Southern California, Arizona (at the behest of her friend Sandra Day O'Connor), Virginia, and Tennessee.

Justice Klein was also instrumental in launching landmark studies of gender differentials in the courts and broader justice system, subsequently pushing for systemic reforms in response to that research. These efforts included assisting in the launch of foundational gender justice studies in courts across the country, including in New Jersey and California, which in turn revealed glaring gender disparities not only in the actual treatment and experiences of men and women in the courts, but also in the perceptions held by each group as to the existence, nature, extent, and impact of such discrepancies.

In her own backyard at the Court of Appeal, Justice Klein implemented reforms ranging from generous maternity leave policies to efforts to affect more diversity among law clerks. She pushed for public education and advocacy for survivors of domestic violence, and for rigorous diversity training in judicial education, including on issues of human trafficking, domestic violence, and disparate conditions for women and girls in juvenile facilities, jails, and prisons.

Justice Klein also vigorously rose to the defense of her friend and colleague, California's embattled Chief Justice, Rose Bird, who ultimately was voted out of office in 1986, together with two other liberal justices who had the bad luck to come up for confirmation in the same year as the Chief Justice—Mexican American icon Cruz Reynoso and past labor professor and arbitrator Joseph Grodin.

A former public defender and the state's first woman to hold a cabinet position, Chief Justice Bird had been a surprise appointment to California's highest judicial post in 1977 by then-Governor Jerry Brown, catapulting her over several senior male Justices serving on what was widely viewed as the most progressive state supreme court in the nation. As the Court's first woman and only the second woman to sit on any state's top court, Chief Justice Bird was soon publicly excoriated by conservatives for failing to vote in support of death sentences in capital cases, though death penalty reversals perforce required the votes of at least three additional Justices.

Although Chief Justice Bird was subjected to repeated and unprecedented efforts to unseat her that were purportedly death penalty-based, she had in fact early become a lightning rod as the female leader of what had long been a liberal majority on the Court. Influential sectors of big business, banking, and agribusiness deplored the Court's decisions, ranging from broadening the rights of consumers and injured plaintiffs, to upholding environmental protections and strengthening the rights of workers, including the outlawing of growers' rules requiring farmworkers' use of the physically devastating short-handled hoe.

As observed by then-*New York Times* reporter and columnist Tom Wicker, "Thus the death penalty is only the trumped-up excuse for the anti-Bird campaign—the actual purpose of it clearly is to put a conservative majority on the California Supreme Court." And so they did, despite the efforts of Justice Klein and a broad coalition who worked indefatigably in defense of the Justices and, more fundamentally, judicial independence.

In 1981, Justice Klein provided testimony on behalf of the NAWJ before the Senate Judiciary Committee in strong support of the nomination of Sandra Day O'Connor to the United States Supreme Court. Justice Klein—herself on the short list—declared, "As women jurists, we are keenly aware of the spotlight focused on our every act and the scrutiny to which we are continually subjected," emphasizing that Justice O'Connor would rise above such scrutiny to thrive as a member of the Court. In what today seems an impossible dream, the full Senate vote was 99–0.

Upon assuming the position of Senior Presiding Justice of the California Court of Appeal, Justice Klein also served with distinction on the three-member Commission on Judicial Appointments, which, among its other responsibilities, is charged with confirmation of all California Supreme Court nominees. That Commission, for the first time in history, was shortly to become composed of three extraordinary women: California Chief Justice Tani Cantil-Sakauye, then-California Attorney General Kamala Harris, and California's Senior Presiding Court of Appeal Justice Joan Dempsey Klein.

Over the course of her remarkable career, Justice Klein was the recipient of a great many awards, including, in addition to the American Bar Association's Margaret Brent Women Lawyers of Achievement Award, the *Los Angeles Times* Woman of the Year Award and the California State Bar's highest honor, the Bernard Witkin Medal. A number of awards today are named in her honor, recognizing the overarching achievements of feminist lawyers and judges who have followed in her footsteps.

Devoted to her second husband, Conrad Klein, and consummately proud of their large blended family, Justice Klein often spoke of the centrality in her life of their five children and eight grandchildren. She reveled as well as in the achievements of the wide-flung network of women, BIPOC, and LGBTQI+ judges and attorneys whose careers she had nurtured throughout her long and storied career.

Justice Klein herself saw it all this way: "I was originally anxious and tentative, and now am secure and confident, a whole different person . . . I just had a sense that I was going in a direction, and I wasn't about to take a couple of detours along the way which I saw as interfering with my movement forward." In speaking of her steady transformation into the powerhouse she became, she said, "I think my impact has been my personality, just who I am." As she related in her ABA interview with former U.S. Attorney Andrea Ordin, "I like people. I do well with people, I have a sense of humor, I respond to them and we're just fine."

BIO

Drucilla Stender Ramey

Dean Emerita Drucilla Stender Ramey is a national leader and speaker on equality of access and opportunity in the legal profession, the justice system, and the broader society.

Attorney Ramey was formerly an attorney with the Mexican American Legal Defense and Educational Fund, specializing in employment class actions and tri-ethnic school desegregation cases, including the generations-long Uvalde, Texas, litigation. She went on to lead the Bar Association of San Francisco (BASF) as its long-time Executive Director and General Counsel, helping to establish the BASF as a leader in nationally replicated programs of provision of pro bono legal services and racial, gender, disability, and LGBTQI+ diversity initiatives, including the BASF's Goals and Timetables for Minority Retention and the San Francisco Unified School District Law Academy and School-to-College Program.

Attorney Ramey then served as Executive Director of the National Association of Women Judges, where it was her privilege to work with women judicial pioneers across the country, including its peerless cofounder, Senior California Court of Appeal Presiding Justice Joan Dempsey Klein.

As Dean of Golden Gate University School of Law, Attorney Ramey helped to broadly expand the School's clinics and other public interest programs, and founded the Chief Justice Ronald George Lectureship Series. The first woman Chair of the Board of the American Civil Liberties Union of Northern California, Ramey chaired the San Francisco Commission on the Status of Women and, later, of Equal Rights Advocates; was a cofounder of California Women Lawyers and the California Minority Counsel Program; and currently serves on the Board of Public Advocates.

Having served on numerous ABA diversity-related entities, she currently is Special Counsel to the Section on Civil Rights and Social Justice Council and serves as a member of the Standing Committee on Pro Bono and Public Service. A graduate of Harvard University and Yale Law School, her honors and awards include the ABA Margaret Brent Women Lawyers of Achievement Award, the American Jewish Committee's Learned Hand Award, the National Bar Association's Wiley Branton Award, and the National LGBTQ+ Bar Association's Allies for Justice Award.

Rosalie Erwin Wahl: Tested by Tragedy, Fueled by Idealism, Accomplished Beyond Measure

4

Harriet Lansing

The stars must have been aligned in August of 1924, when Rosalie Erwin (Wahl) was born, a mere nine days after Joan Dempsey (Klein), as the power of their contributions to the legal profession and the judiciary were luminous. Harriet Lansing, a retired judge of the Minnesota Court of Appeals, brings the power and force of Justice Rosalie Wahl to life. She also shares fascinating details that reveal the additional roles that judges fill to improve the law and the court system through important task force and commission work.

It is important to understand the roadblocks and difficulties endured to reach that "first woman" status in the state court system, particularly at the highest levels. And here, too, we see that the drive to make a difference can be grounded in the toughest of challenges and life experiences.

Lauren Stiller Rikleen, Editor

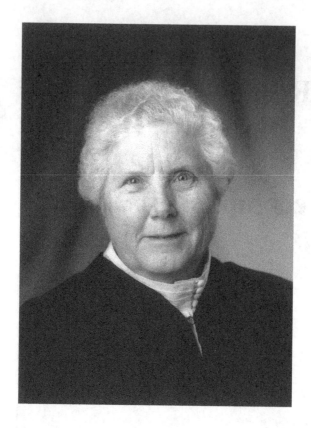

Rosalie Erwin Wahl served as an Associate Justice on the Minnesota Supreme Court from 1977 to 1994. As the first woman Justice on that court (preceded by seventy-one men), her appointment was a monumental event for Minnesota women.

The selection process was an open and very public procedure with an initial slate of eighteen that narrowed to six. These developments were taking place in the summer of 1977 when states were holding federally funded women's conferences preparatory to a National Women's Conference in Texas that November. Minnesota's state-level conference was held in the Fieldhouse at St. Cloud State University with an estimated attendance of more than 4,000 people.

The governor made his decision to appoint Rosalie only hours before the opening of the Conference and communicated it to the convenor, Secretary of State Joan Growe, to announce. As journalist Lori Sturdevant recounts, "No one present that night is likely to forget the jubilation of that moment. The auditorium erupted in pure joy.

Laughter, tears, hugs, cheers, and applause rocked the room." And when the arena finally fell quiet enough for her to speak, Rosalie's carefully chosen words left so indelible an impression that they were published in their entirety in the next morning's *Minneapolis Star*.

Leading up to that appointment, Rosalie had already been recognized as a force in Minnesota's mid-twentieth-century women's movement. She had also established herself in the vanguard of the rapidly expanding clinical legal education front that was developing nationally and in Minnesota law schools. And in the five years between graduating from law school and beginning her clinical teaching career at the University of Minnesota and William Mitchell law schools, she distinguished herself as a dedicated and able appellate attorney. Employed in the state public defender's office representing defendants charged with criminal offenses, she argued 109 cases before the State Supreme Court.

As journalist Sturdevant observed, "Affirmations outweighed criticism" that summer and fall as the investiture approached, but there was enough of each to make Rosalie—and the governor—aware of many watchful eyes. Rosalie was warmly and genuinely welcomed by the Chief Justice and the members of the supreme court. But other judges and lawyers, some of whom had sought their own appointment to the position, did not respond positively to a woman joining the male-occupied highest state court, particularly a woman who had been a nontraditional student, entering law school at the age of thirty-eight.

Her past participation in the activities of the women's movement and her history in criminal defense as a representative of indigent defendants caused concern among prosecutors and hardliners. But those who had known Rosalie for a long time, were familiar with her work, and knew the challenges she had encountered and overcome in her life, were deeply confident that she had the strength, courage, resolve, and quality of mind to more than match any obstacles in this new challenge.

Rosalie's encounters with hard and painful circumstances arose early in her life. Born in hard economic times in Kansas, Rosalie was only three years old when her mother died. Her father had to move frequently to find work, and Rosalie stayed with her maternal grandparents on their Chautauqua County farm. Four years later, her grandfather and younger brother were killed at a railroad crossing in conditions of poor visibility when a late train neglected to sound its whistle as it came over a rise.

Seven-year-old Rosalie, who had hopped off the horse-drawn wagon to open the crossing gate, witnessed the tragedy. There was no personal injury recovery—no settlement of any kind. The local lawyer conditioned representation on a retainer of $100. Rosalie said it might just as well have been a million. It was an unimaginable sum in those hardscrabble times of Depression-era poverty. Their farming implements were sold at auction, and Rosalie and her grandmother moved to the old stone house on their few remaining acres.

These were hard times, with Kansas at the center of the American Dust Bowl crisis. Rosalie attended the one-room country school at Birch Creek and, with the help of her Aunt Sara, moved into town when it was time to attend high school.

Rosalie started college at Kansas University (KU) in the fall of 1942 in the shadow of the Second World War. In 1943, her fiancé, who had enlisted in the Air Force, died tragically in a military training accident. Rosalie sought solace in her return to the old stone house, where she again lived with her grandmother and took charge of Birch Creek's one-room country school that she herself had attended.

In the summer of 1944, she decided to go back to KU, but changed her academic focus from journalism to sociology, hoping to prepare for a life that was more directed toward "mak[ing] the world a better place." To that end she became involved in the Young Women's Christian Association (YWCA) and its civil rights work on the KU campus. Shortly after her return to the campus, she actively took part in cofounding Henley House, one of the first interracial student-housing programs. It was during her residency at Henley House and through their initiatives that she learned about the Quakers' Religious Society of Friends. By 1946 she had become a member and remained a member throughout her life.

Rosalie obtained her bachelor's degree in sociology in 1946. That same year she married Roswell Wahl, a student she first met in her initial year at KU. Ross had left the University to enter military service, experiencing a brutal deployment on the European Front that yielded a Bronze Star and traumatic memories of the harrowing Battle of the Bulge and a grisly winter in the Ardennes Forest. He returned to the KU campus in 1945 to continue work on an engineering degree and premed studies. During this time, the Wahls formed strong friendships with Quaker social activists who were drawn together by mutual interests in pacifism and cooperative living.

Through the American Friends Service Committee, the Wahls and their friends made connections with a new cooperative living project that had been formed north of the Twin Cities in Circle Pines, Minnesota. In 1949, the Wahls moved to Circle Pines to join this shared ownership village that aimed "to unite the habitation benefits of a functional and contemporary community with the economic advantages of a consumer's cooperative."

After early successes, the intentional community and its core members encountered challenges, and the cooperative spirit that had inspired its creation began to erode. Just four years after its founding as a cooperative, Circle Pines was incorporated as a conventional village. Parts of the core community relocated to rural Lake Elmo, southeast of Circle Pines. By 1960, the intentional community had dissolved. Nonetheless, many of the close relationships continued throughout Rosalie's life by virtue of the proximity of their houses in Lake Elmo and a Twin Cities Friends Meeting group that they had mutually formed.

Rosalie began her public life by extending the reach of the county library system. Her love of books and her desire to make them more available to the children in rural Lake Elmo gave rise to a community venture that secured a bookmobile route that would include a weekly stop at the end of Rosalie's Lake Elmo driveway. This limited achievement encouraged the group to aim for a true county library system with structural branch libraries.

Despite enthusiastic support and a carefully planned presentation, their formal proposal was rejected. At the end of their presentation to the county board, the library proponents were ushered out of the room and not permitted to remain for the vote. Rosalie's disappointment in the way in which the county board meeting was conducted influenced her to think about how governmental decisions were made. She later recounted that getting shut out of those decision-making rooms encouraged her to enter into politics and ultimately consider becoming a judge. As journalist Sturdevant said in her superb biography of Rosalie, "[w]hen she set a goal with the aim of benefiting others, she pursued it with intensity."

In those early days of the 1960s, Rosalie began to think deeply about how she would be able to get by with their day-to-day expenses and still save money to help her children attend college. Ross's bouts of discouragement and depression, related to his traumatic war-time experiences, added to the strife of the difficult circumstances. In 1962, when the Wahls and their four children were living on their Lake Elmo farm, Rosalie made the decision to begin law school at William Mitchell. Only one other woman was among the members of that entering class. The Wahl's fifth child was born while she was in her second year, but the personal strife deepened, and Rosalie and Ross were divorced in 1972.

These personal tragedies tested and toughened Rosalie, but they did not erode her compassion, compromise her energy, or defeat her idealism. In the Foreword to Rosalie's biography, Senator Amy Klobuchar recognized a key force that Rosalie had used to describe what had impelled her momentum: "She was tired of sitting outside doors waiting for the men inside to make the decisions." Senator Klobuchar chronicled what that momentum had actualized:

> After defeating three men in her reelection to the state's highest court, she heard countless cases, argued persuasively in judicial conference, and tackled gender discrimination and racial bias in our judicial system—and she did all of this with uncommon humility and an unerring commitment to justice.

And, Senator Klobuchar added, Rosalie had marched down this remarkable path, always with an "uncanny combination of grit and grace."

Rosalie needed every ounce of that grit and grace as she prepared to stand for election in the fall of 1978, only one year, one month, and four days after joining the court. The 1978 contested election was universally observed to be one of the roughest high-court elections in Minnesota history. It came as no surprise.

In his decision to appoint a woman, the governor knew that there would likely be strong opposition in his candidate's first election. Rosalie's nontraditional background and her experience coming from a criminal defense rather than a prosecutorial or civil law career made opposition even more likely. Several lawyers and sitting judges had indicated early on an interest in running—both because of their belief in the superiority of their own qualifications and because they believed it would be easy to defeat a woman for this position. The governor had told members of women's organizations that they would need to be prepared and committed to the campaign.

And they were. By 1978, Minnesota feminists had organized contact lists that numbered in the thousands. Both the Democratic-Farmer-Labor Party (DFL) and the Republican Party had Feminist Caucuses and the Minnesota Women's Political Caucus had effective rosters that had come from the organizing for the Minnesota Women's Meeting in June 1977. Rosalie's friends, lawyer colleagues, legislators, and former students stepped up. They organized fundraisers, debates, speaking engagements, and, in the final stages of the campaign, chartered an airplane to fly her to appearances all around the state.

Rosalie's three opponents were formidable. The first to announce was a former state Attorney General who had told the governor that if he appointed a woman, he would run against her. The other two opponents were both state district court judges with long and well-regarded records of judicial service. Each had significant political experience before being appointed to the bench, and they were serious campaigners. The former state Attorney General came through the primary with Rosalie in September and was, therefore, the opposing candidate in the general election. His attacks were the most visceral and distorted, and they continued and escalated throughout the fall.

Rosalie was a robust campaigner and kept up a hectic pace. She would leave her office at the court in late afternoon and climb into a waiting car to travel to destinations outside the Twin Cities. The Secretary of State who had announced Rosalie's appointment, and who was herself involved in a state-wide campaign, said, "Nobody worked harder than Rosalie." She was at weekend events across the state on a regular basis.

In the state bar association's judicial candidate survey, Rosalie was deemed the better-qualified candidate by 76 percent of respondents. And on November 6, she came out of the election with a much greater victory than her most avid supporters had dared to predict—a solid win with 57 percent of the vote. As journalist Sturdevant, who was also her biographer, summarized,

> That solid victory assured that, though she would stand for
> election again in 1984 and 1990, she would not again face
> serious electoral opposition. . . . But its import was much

larger. Wahl's success gave future governors a green light to appoint women to the state's judicial benches.

Rosalie, showing her usual humility, credited the Minnesota women's movement for her success, saying that she would not have been appointed to the court or elected in that jarringly rough election if it had not been for the women's movement. Biographer Sturdevant aptly expressed the opinion universally held that although the women's movement made her public service possible, it was Rosalie who made it exceptional.

The criteria for exceptional service are readily established by a review of Rosalie's 549 judicial opinions. William Mitchell Professor Ann Juergens describes them as written with "elegant clarity and deep sensitivity to the minds and souls of the people seeking justice." They illuminate a judicial philosophy strongly grounded in due process, equal access, equal justice, and fundamental fairness.

Professor Jane Larson of Northwestern University Law School traced these constitutional doctrines in Justice Wahl's opinions and summarized five key elements of her jurisprudence: (1) requiring laws to represent legitimate governmental purposes in both intention and execution; (2) interpreting statutory language to ensure that laws have the intended impact on society; (3) using appellate review to encourage trial courts to accept and implement legislative policy choices; (4) narrowing the space preempted by federal law to give Minnesota room to apply its own policy considerations; and (5) defending the right of Minnesota courts to establish and enforce independent state constitutional standards.

These elements are visible in all of Rosalie's opinions, both in her majority opinions and her dissents. But the analytical language stands out most clearly in her opinions in criminal cases, cases involving gender and racial discrimination, cases related to spousal maintenance and displaced homemakers, cases applying child custody standards, and in cases relating to mental illness in the criminal justice system.

As the only justice on the court with criminal defense experience, she brought an invaluable perspective to the court's consideration of criminal cases. She fully apprehended the stark violation of equal protection and due process in unjustified sentencing disparities. In *State v. Russell*, 477 N.W.2d 886 (Minn. 1993), writing for the majority, she brought home her realist version of rational basis review, ruling that the statute's distinction between crack and powder cocaine is arbitrary, unreasonable, and irrelevant to the purpose of penalizing drug dealers and consequently violates the equal protection clause of the Minnesota Constitution. Characteristically, Rosalie was ahead of her time in perceiving the issue.

In an opinion with similar foresight and far-reaching implications, *State v. Scales*, 518 N.W.2d 587 (Minn. 1994), she recognized the critical importance of a recording requirement to discourage unfair and psychologically coercive police questioning at all stages of detention. Rosalie's opinion, relying on the court's supervisory power, ushered in a sea change to professional law enforcement that has swept the entire country in these last decades.

In *Sigurdson v. Isanti County*, 386 N.W.2d 715 (Minn. 1986), writing for the majority in an employment discrimination case, Rosalie remanded to the trial court when the judge had dismissed the sex discrimination claim on the merits, despite an advisory jury's finding based on uncontroverted evidence that sex discrimination had occurred. The opinion gently set forth the analytical framework that the trial court should use and the necessity of setting forth the court's factfinding clearly so an appellate court could conduct effective and meaningful review.

On remand and more careful consideration, the trial court changed its position. In this way, Rosalie led the court in fashioning an effective methodology for areas where some trial court judges in the state were ambivalent or even hostile to policy mandates from the legislature that contradicted their traditional family values or sought to restrict the traditionally broad discretion granted judges in family law cases. The court also used this demand for particularized findings in cases involving child custody when it was apparent that the trial courts were having difficulty applying the required "best interests of the child" standard.

Rosalie's efforts to achieve fair results and properly ascertain and effectuate legislative purpose sometimes required a dissent or a series of dissents. An important issue that required repeated dissents was the availability of permanent rather than rehabilitative maintenance for long-term homemaker spouses. Her persistence was ultimately rewarded. Following her sharp dissent in *Abuzzahab v. Abuzzahab*, 359 N.W.2d 12 (Minn. 1984) (joined by Justice Mary Jeanne Coyne, the only other female justice on the court), the legislature amended the law to emphasize that temporary awards should not be favored over permanent awards in traditional long-term marriages or other circumstances where earning capacity was affected. In *Gales v. Gales*, 553 N.W.2d 416 (Minn. 1986), a case decided after Rosalie had left the court, the court acknowledged that the "legislature has established with unmistakable clarity" a presumption in favor of permanent maintenance in cases involving traditional marriages or where earning capacity has been affected.

In cases involving the mentally disabled in the criminal justice system, Rosalie worked valiantly on developing careful jury instructions on what constitutes diminished capacity to form criminal intent. She also guided the court through a course of developing thoughtful commitment procedures and, consistent with the constitution and state statutes, identifying a wider range of alternatives to commitment.

In her early years on the court, she was the most frequent dissenter, but as time passed, her insights, her powers of persuasion, and her strong analytical and writing skills brought more justices around to her way of thinking, and she was more often writing the majority opinion. Part of Rosalie's power of persuasion was anchored in a deeply rooted philosophy that I think of as her "jurisprudence of inclusivity." By that I do not mean only her life-long perseverance in eliminating barriers created by sexism, racism, or social and economic disparities, but the significant capacity that Rosalie had to understand what Professor Juergens referred to as the wholeness of a legal solution.

Rosalie knew that an enduring legal solution must incorporate a comprehension of the full emotional, social, and economic context of a legal problem.

This was, of course, evidenced by wanting everyone at the table or to be represented when decisions affecting them were being made. And it was evidenced in her commitment to legal education that took into account the value of experience and the importance of the moral and ethical component of our careers as lawyers and judges.

She knew that lawyering skills and sound judicial decision making could not be compartmentalized to a category of narrowly bordered mental reasoning or rational thinking but had to incorporate the whole content of consciousness and that it was important to be aware of these influences. She understood that experience and emotion played a significant part in every stage of the rule of law—shaping laws, applying laws, interpreting laws, and determining the priority of doctrines in analyzing legal questions.

In her book and articles on gender and justice, Professor Sally J. Kenney of Tulane University similarly recognized Rosalie's emotional intelligence as well as her rational intelligence as a component of wisdom and good judgment. Rosalie's former clerk, Jane Larson, said that she had learned the law through focusing on legal doctrine, like musical scales—mastering the necessary components on which all else is based. But from Rosalie, she learned it is the social, political, and philosophical content that brings meaning to doctrine and makes music out of the law.

Minnesota's former Chief Justice Eric Magnuson referred to that global quality at Rosalie's memorial service when he said, "I have known many jurists who have worn the robes of authority at both the trial and appellate levels, but none who have worn them with greater humanity than Rosalie." Rosalie's humanity and the context in which she analyzed and reviewed the law was a full 360-degree projection.

These cords of philosophy are visible throughout the fabric of Rosalie's opinions, but her legacy is greater than the sum of her opinions. The responsibilities that Rosalie took on when she joined the court extended beyond the pages of the *North Western Reporter.* Rosalie was instrumental in forging significant changes in legal standards related to the intersection of law and mental health, system-wide changes in gender fairness, and groundbreaking work on systemic problems of racial bias.

And Rosalie did not stop at the courtroom doors. In her work on clinical education through the American Bar Association's MacCrate Report and the Final Report of the Wahl Commission, she went to the very heart of the law—the way in which lawyers are trained and educated.

I.   STUDY COMMISSION ON THE MENTALLY DISABLED AND THE COURTS

Within days of her appointment to the State Supreme Court, the Chief Justice prevailed upon Rosalie to serve as the court's liaison to a new Study Commission on the Mentally Disabled and the Courts. The Chief Justice knew of Rosalie's interest and concern for the problems of mentally disabled persons. Her new colleagues on the court similarly understood that Rosalie had valuable insight obtained through her painful years observing and helping to work through the struggles that two of her sons and her former husband confronted with mental health and chemical dependency issues.

During the intense days leading up to the election in the fall of 1978, Rosalie's opponent had attempted to obtain and use her sons' medical information as ammunition against Rosalie's qualifications to serve on the court. Commendably, the news media was not persuaded of its relevance. Rosalie remained stalwart and undeterred throughout the tense and deeply unsettling episode. She did not distance herself from the difficult issues on which the Commission was working or from the people who needed her help and support. Although her days were full to overflowing, she would not turn away from work that was so near to the center of her heart. The Commission's work was anticipated to last for eighteen months, and it occupied a strong share of her time and attention throughout the tumultuous election year of 1978.

"There are imperfections in our system," she said, "none of them more troublesome than those in the area where psychiatry meets the law." Rosalie worked within the judiciary to bring a heightened sensitivity and understanding of mental illness. She worked to establish recognized standards of diminished capacity to form criminal intent and against the misuse of mental health categories and institutions to confine the criminal and antisocial. And she worked both on the court and in the community to develop a wider range of less restrictive alternatives to commitment.

II. TASK FORCE FOR GENDER FAIRNESS IN THE COURTS

One of her most comprehensive and far-reaching commissions while on the court was her work chairing the Minnesota Supreme Court Task Force for Gender Fairness in the Courts. Created in 1987, the Task Force was established by the supreme court to investigate the nature and extent of gender bias in the state's judicial system and to formulate specific recommendations for reforms.

Although the Task Force was created by a unanimous order of the court, it was Rosalie who worked from the very beginning to initiate the idea, to demonstrate to her colleagues the need for the internal and external analysis, and to do the long and hard work of seeing it through and creating the commissions to oversee the implementation of the recommendations.

I served as Vice Chair of the Task Force and became keenly aware of the innate judicial resistance to undertaking this type of evaluation. Rosalie understood that courts were insular institutions. She also understood that, in some ways, that insularity served the purposes of justice and the rule of law because constitutional precepts impose a duty that can require courts to stand against the majority.

But because of that very insularity, judges do not always have the opportunity to test their own perceptions, intuitions, and default premises. And Rosalie knew from her years representing indigent defendants in the trial courts and arguing more than 100 cases before the supreme court that as judges, even though we are well meaning, we are sometimes blind to our limitations and biases.

The thirty-member Task Force held hearings, gathered evidence, and, in June of 1989, produced an extensive report with ninety recommendations for reform on issues of family law, domestic violence, criminal and civil justice, and the courtroom environment. The report, which included actual examples and very specific accounts of courtroom and systemic gender bias, created what Federal Judge Mike Davis called "a judicial firestorm," and led to prompt and wide-ranging changes in statutes, judicial education, and court procedures.

The national leader and inspiration for the gender and race bias task forces around the country, Dr. Norma Wikler of the University of California, said,

> Within this national judicial reform movement, no one is more respected or loved than Justice Wahl. Rosalie can articulate better than anyone else what the struggle for gender and racial fairness is about—the horrendous costs for the victims of bias and the obligation of the judicial system to rectify it.

III. RACIAL BIAS TASK FORCE

The Racial Bias Task Force, appointed in 1990 with thirty-two members, delivered its report in 1993. The Task Force held ten public hearings, all of which Rosalie chaired, and fifteen focus groups.

The proceedings were complicated and the hearings were emotionally charged.

Rosalie's deep commitment to due process and fair treatment fueled her work on this Task Force, just as that commitment had motivated her on the Gender Fairness Task Force. The reports of racially biased treatment took Rosalie back to her time at the University of Kansas in 1944 and 1945 when she successfully cofounded the integrated Henley House and staged sit-ins in the University's restaurants that refused to serve food to African Americans.

Judge Michael Davis, who chaired the Criminal Process Committee of the Racial Bias Task Force, said the hearings were exhausting, but Rosalie was never exhausted. She was an essential component of the trust on both sides of the racial divide. Rosalie had become the face of equal justice under the law in Minnesota.

The many recommendations that grew out of the hearings and reports became the workplan for the Implementation Committee that was chaired by Justice Alan Page. Despite the difficulties of the process and the painful testimony at the hearings, Rosalie continually exhorted the audiences not to give one inch to despair.

As she said in the preface to the Task Force Report:

> This cannot be just another study. People trusted us enough to come and make their feelings known. We who are the stewards of the justice system cannot fail the people that it belongs to. . . . This we vow: that we will not cease our efforts until this court system, of which we are so proudly a part, treats every person equally before the law—and with dignity and respect regardless of such irrelevancies as race or gender or class.

IV. CHAIRING THE ACCREDITATION COMMITTEE OF THE AMERICAN BAR ASSOCIATION SECTION OF LEGAL EDUCATION AND ADMISSIONS TO THE BAR

In addition to her other leadership responsibilities on the supreme court, Rosalie agreed to take on the job of liaison to the Board of Bar Examiners. The Chief Justice knew that she was interested in "the whole process of who gets into the bar and how diverse is your bar and what are your processes and are they fair." Rosalie's background as a former clinical professor and her desire to have more women involved in leadership led to an invitation to become a member of the American Bar Association Section of Legal Education and Admissions to the Bar and also to the Section's Accreditation Committee. The next year, Rosalie became chair of the Accreditation Committee, the first woman to hold that position.

As chair of the Accreditation Committee, Rosalie began working together with the ABA's consultant on Legal Education, James White, to develop plans for a conference on clinical education to be held that fall. She opened the conference with these words:

> The issue then is not whether the law schools should go on teaching legal analysis, or conducting skills training but which legal analysis and skills the law schools should teach and how much of each. Have we really tried in [our] individual law school's self studies to determine what skills, what attitudes, what character traits, what quality of mind are required of lawyers?

The conference lasted for four days and focused on the importance of working together to ensure adequate or mandatory skills training, and to integrate into the skills training matters of the heart alongside matters of the intellect in law school and practice.

The success of the conference led to further discussions between Rosalie and the ABA's Jim White, and then to a proposal to create the Task Force on Law Schools and the Profession that would build on previous studies of the ABA related to professional skills. Rosalie and Jim persuaded the highly respected and former ABA president Robert MacCrate to chair the Task Force. As Rosalie explained, "The stage is set for fundamental changes in law school instruction. All that is missing is clear guidance and motivation. This project can provide it."

According to the consultants, "Rosalie picked every member of the Task Force, with an eye for heft and balance and recruited them." The twenty-six members and consultants labored for three years, and in 1992 published a lengthy report entitled Legal Education and Professional Development—An Educational Continuum (also known as the MacCrate Task Force Report).

As Ann Juergens summarized in her excellent account of Rosalie's vision for legal education with clinics at the heart,

> Wahl's gift to legal education was the MacCrate Task Force and her conviction that every lawyer should have instruction in professional skills, that lawyers do not exercise their skills in a moral or social or economic vacuum, and that every lawyer must "learn to learn from experience."

V. THE WAHL COMMISSION TO REVIEW THE SUBSTANCE AND PROCESS OF THE AMERICAN BAR ASSOCIATION'S ACCREDITATION OF AMERICAN LAW SCHOOLS

The MacCrate Report's seminal recommendation that law schools be obligated to prepare students for the practice of law and to participate effectively in the legal profession and not merely to prepare them to pass the bar, was adopted into the ABA standards in 1993. According to the consultants, the MacCrate Report's recommendation was met with recalcitrance by the Section of Legal Education and Admissions to the Bar. And, as Professor Juergens recounted, "It was then that Wahl rolled up her sleeves again and accepted the charge of the Commission to Review the Substance and Process of the ABA's Accreditation of American Law Schools."

After a year's study, the Wahl Commission called for amendments to the ABA Standards that would implement the spirit of the MacCrate Report's recommendations. Those amendments included (1) that all law graduates should understand that "law is a public profession requiring the performance of *pro bono publico* legal services"; (2) the program of education must offer all students instruction in professional skills in the same way as other "core" subjects such as at least one rigorous writing experience; (3) when law schools conduct their self-studies for accreditation they should be required to show how the school is seeking to prepare students to participate effectively in the legal profession; and (4) the ABA Standard requiring that all law schools offer students instruction in professional skills should be set forth in a formal interpretation of the Standard.

Within a year from when these recommendations were submitted, all of them were enacted into the ABA Standards by the ABA's House of Delegates. As Rosalie concluded:

[The ABA] standards . . . if not the battleground, at least have been the field of action on which the Section and the ABA House of Delegates are hammering out recognition by the profession . . . that clinical legal education, with its emphasis on lawyering skills and values, with all its pedagogical and philosophical ramifications, is an essential, integral, legitimate part of legal education.

VI. AN IMPACT BEYOND MEASURE

In a speech at Hamline School of Law shortly after her appointment to the court, Rosalie described her commitment to never cease to work for the goals that were based on values sprouted by the hearth—the sense of justice and fair play, the sense that every individual in the human family is a unique and precious being, and the sense of compassion in those times when justice ends or fails.

Throughout her judicial service she faithfully kept that promise. And she coupled that commitment with two other fundamental beliefs—that women had experiences that could bring intellectual and emotional values to our legal framework and that the underlying unity that lawyers must seek is that of heart with intellect.

In her years of work, Rosalie kept heart and hearth at the center. The dedication of her court papers is first to her children, whose love, she said, "surrounds and upholds me, as does my love for them." They in turn recognized that she left a piece of herself in the hearts of each of them. They treasured her loving and compassionate nature, her feistiness, her steely resolve, and the joyful spirit with which she approached life—positive, optimistic, and hopeful of a better world, and in the words of her daughter Sara Wahl, "always, always with a song in her heart."

As William Mitchell's Dean, Eric Janus, emphasized, "the genius of Rosalie Wahl is that she did not simply have the idea, she didn't just hope to change legal education and improve the practice of justice and fairness in our society—she had the practical wisdom, in her gentle but cleared-eyed way, to see that it happened." It was not an accident that Rosalie's service on the court was the prelude for Minnesota becoming the first state to have a majority of women on its Supreme Court. As her daughter Sara said, "She encouraged women to spread their wings and pursue their dreams."

Her seventeen years of high-visibility judicial service was heralded by the *Minneapolis Tribune* as the "human bridge between Minnesota's highest court and the people it served." In their words, "Few state Supreme Court justices have made a larger impact for good or commanded more respect."

BIO

Judge Harriet Lansing

Harriet Lansing is a retired judge of the Minnesota Court of Appeals. She was appointed to the court when it was established in 1983 and served for twenty-eight years before her retirement in 2011. Prior to serving on the Court of Appeals, she was a trial court judge in Ramsey County, served as the St. Paul City Attorney, and practiced civil, criminal, and administrative law in the firm of Lansing, Oakes, and Caperton.

Judge Lansing has been involved in legal and judicial education, serving as a faculty member of New York University Law School's Appellate Institute for Judicial Education for almost a decade, has served on the adjunct faculty of William Mitchell College of Law and Hamline School of Law, and chaired the University of Minnesota Law School's Board of Visitors.

Since her retirement from the court, she has continued her legal work, focusing on issues relating to state law and international law. From 2013 to 2015 she was the President of the National Conference of Commissioners on Uniform State Laws. In 2015 she became a fellow of the European Law Institute and was the keynote speaker for the Institute's Annual Conference and General Assembly in Vienna, Austria. In 2018 she also delivered the keynote speech for the Institute at its meeting in Riga, Latvia. From 2015 to 2018 she served as a member of the United States delegation to the United Nations Commission on International Trade Law on Enforcement of International Commercial Settlement Agreements.

Judge Lansing received her BA from Macalester College and her JD from the University of Minnesota Law School. Among other recognitions and awards, she has received a Distinguished Alumni Award from Macalester, a Minnesota State Bar Association Award for Judicial Excellence, and a Minnesota State Bar Association Award of Excellence for Improvement of the System of Civil Litigation. For her work in international law, she was honored by the International Women's Forum in 2015 with the Woman Who Makes a Difference Award. She is a life fellow of the American Bar Foundation and a member of the American Law Institute.

Patricia McGowan Wald: Role Model for Doing the Right Thing

5

Marcia D. Greenberger and Sarah E. Wald

W*hen two trailblazers talk about someone who has been a major influence in their lives, the result is a deeply moving description of why legacies matter. Marcia Greenberger, herself an iconic figure in the fight for women's rights, and Sarah Wald, a highly accomplished lawyer who was fortunate enough to grow up as the daughter of Patricia Wald, paint a fascinating picture of Judge Wald—a mother of five whose barrier-breaking career was profoundly rooted in her life experiences.*

As with so many of the other richly detailed stories in this book, we are permitted to see the real person that exists behind the titles and the accomplishments. We are given an understanding of a jurist who built upon her experiences to serve the justice system with compassion, integrity, innovation, and an unfailing understanding of humanity.

Lauren Stiller Rikleen, Editor

She was the smartest and most ethical person I have ever known. But she was, well, my mom. It was only as I got older that I would continually hear from people—both women and men—passionate about how much she motivated and inspired them. (Sarah Wald)

Pat Wald was my role model and inspiration, as I was just starting law practice . . . She told me about openings at the Center for Law and Social Policy, including one to start a Women's Rights Project. The Project grew, we created the National Women's Law Center, and because of Pat Wald, I ended up with a 45-year women's rights career while my husband and I raised two children. (Marcia Greenberger)

To look at the simple facts, few would have predicted that little Pat McGowan would have grown up to be a pioneer in the law. But her keen intelligence, her intense drive, and her unwavering ethical compass steered her from the earliest age, through challenges and life changes, to become one of the most influential, accomplished, and inspiring women judges in the country.

Born into a working-class Irish family in Torrington, Connecticut, Pat's early years were shaped by her family and her very modest roots. An only child, her father abandoned the family when she was two years old. She and her mother moved back into her grandparents' home, which they shared with several adult aunts and uncles.

They had very few resources; she remembered borrowing puzzles from the library so the family would have an activity to do. Most of her family worked their entire lives in the factories owned by the

Torrington Company, which produced steel instruments and ball bearings. (Later, when Pat was a mother herself, roller skates were a frequent gift to her children from the Torrington relatives.)

When Pat was four years old, her mother, Margaret, lied about her age so she could be enrolled in kindergarten. This would allow Margaret to go back to work. Margaret, who did not have extensive formal education herself, recognized Pat's talents. When high school started, the school system sorted students into "tracks," and Pat, coming from her modest background, was initially slotted for the vocational, "secretarial" track. Margaret marched into the office of the school principal and successfully insisted that Pat deserved to be placed in the "pre-college" track. She was, and graduated valedictorian of her high school class.

The first person in her family to go to college, Pat won a scholarship to what was then Connecticut College for Women (now Connecticut College) in New London. Success was not preordained. Pat was almost three years younger than most of her classmates (from entering school early and then "skipping" two grades based on her academic performance). She was not from a privileged background, as were many of the other students, and she lived in a separate "scholarship" dorm. But her work ethic, and the fact that she was always interesting to be around, resulted in her friendships with classmates, her mentoring by faculty (particularly her government professor, who thought she'd make a good lawyer), and in her selection to Phi Beta Kappa.

Pat did not know any lawyers growing up, though she later said she was inspired by the activists who supported labor actions at the factory in Torrington, where she worked during summers. Pat went on to join a small cadre of women (11 women in a class of 160) at Yale Law School. At that time, Harvard and a number of other law schools did not admit women.

Her experience at Yale was generally a happy one; she and her roommate and lifelong best friend, Jodie Zeldes Bernstein (who went on to a distinguished legal career herself in private practice and the federal government), lived together in the "women's dorm," which was situated a mile away from the convenient campus-adjacent law school dorms that housed the men, so their women classmates would not "distract them."

Pat said that she did not feel marginalized by her male class-mates, who pretty quickly figured out that having her around for their academic activities would be a boon. She described the men, many of whom were returning to school after their service in WWII and thus were older and had families, as viewing her "like a little sister," coaching and supporting her. She and Jodie were elected to the *Law Journal*, the only women to be asked to join. She excelled in her classes.

In her third year, she started dating a classmate, Bob Wald. The story is that when Bob first asked her out, she told him she would do so only if he raised his grades (her children later fully believed she would have that reaction!). They married in 1952, and Bob was always her biggest professional booster and fan.

The career path for women attorneys was not a straight one at that time. Law firms came on campus to interview students at Yale; none would interview a woman. Jodie and Pat decided to undertake their own job search, and in the spring of their third year, they took the commuter train to New York and went door to door at major law firms in which they had a contact, with their resumes, their law review credentials, and their stellar work examples. Jodie ended up being hired at Shearman & Sterling; Pat ended up going on to a judicial clerkship instead of a firm.

It is remarkable that Pat and Jodie did not view the differential treatment of women law students as something to be bitter about; they seemed to accept it as just another challenge in the world of legal learning and practice.[1] Pat made lasting friendships and professional relationships and retained an affection and appreciation for Yale Law her whole life.

After graduation, Pat clerked for Judge Jerome Frank on the U.S. Court of Appeals for the Second Circuit. She was based in New Haven and traveled to New York monthly for the oral arguments. She was connected with Judge Frank by two of her professors, Boris Bitker and Fred Rodell, who told the Judge that she was the smartest

---

[1.] Jodi Enda, *Three Audacious Women before Audacious Was In*, WASH. POST, Mar. 6, 2015, *available at* http://www.washingtonpost.com/lifestyle/magazine/three-audacious -women-before-audacious-was-in/2015/02/26/9dd26308-9c1f-11e4-bcfb-059ec7a93ddc _story.html.

student they had. Again, her hard work and support from mentors who recognized her talent helped propel her forward.

The early years of her legal practice were marked by life choices and changes. After she and Bob married, and moved to Washington, DC, Pat was hired as the only woman at Arnold, Fortas and Porter (now Arnold & Porter Kaye Scholer). She continued there until she was expecting her first child (including hiding her pregnancy from the firm until that was impossible), at which point she stopped her work with the firm to stay home to care for her children.

This period of not working outside the home was typical for women at that time. The fact that Pat had five children in seven years influenced her choice to be at home, both personally and practically (there were very few organized childcare options, and it was "expected" that women professionals would give up their careers in order to be full-time mothers). She remembered this period fondly in many ways, despite not practicing: "I was lucky, however, in important ways: my husband was by then practicing law in a DC law firm and we traveled socially in legal circles. As a result, I had access to legal periodicals and trade-talk so that I never felt professionally isolated."[2]

But despite her nonstop mothering of five young children, it was clear to both her and her family that she needed to use her talents in the law. Ironically, being out of the formal workforce for close to ten years did not disadvantage Pat disproportionately. Because women lawyers had a harder time being hired anywhere for any job, her absence from holding a traditional legal position did not necessarily make it substantially harder to get a job—it was already so hard for women that this was just another factor.

She edged her way back into the workforce when, in 1963, she was hired to work part time on a project involving bail reform, with a former law school classmate at the Department of Justice where (again) her extraordinary talents were recognized. In the few years following that, she was hired to work on reports and books for several government commissions, and went on to serve on the DC Crime Commission and other projects related to criminal justice reform and poverty law. (Her appointment was reported in the "Style" section of

---

[2.] Hon. Patricia M. Wald, *Six Not-So-Easy Pieces: One Woman's Journey to the Bench and Beyond*, 36 U. Toledo L. Rev. 979, 982 (2005).

the Washington paper under the headline "Mother of Five Named to Crime Commission.")

This period started a fruitful and impactful period of Pat's practicing public interest law. She worked in the late 1960s for the newly formed Neighborhood Legal Services, representing low-income clients on a range of cases. She left to join the emerging public interest law movement in 1970 and worked for the Mental Health Law Project, as a litigator on major law reform cases involving juvenile justice and rights of institutionalized psychiatric patients.

Pat was first woman lawyer I ever met who was married with children, and with a public interest career to boot. I turned to her for advice on handling legal matters, and on how she managed work and five kids. (**M.G.**)

Juggling a busy legal practice with raising five children was not straightforward. There were not many models in the profession for how to accomplish that balance. She tried to end her workday early to be home for dinner. She worked in the evenings in her small den while the kids did homework and watched TV. She ran from her office to grade school classrooms to deliver birthday cupcakes. She and the family relied heavily on Bob's parenting (and driving) skills—Pat never got her driver's license—to ferry kids around on errands, evenings and weekends. In typical Pat style, though, she just "powered through."

We were the original latchkey kids. My brother Doug got to be an expert in breaking into the house when none of us remembered our keys. Once mom just sent a key home to us from her office in a DC yellow cab. (**S.W.**)

Nominated by President Carter in 1977 to be Assistant Attorney General for Legislative Affairs in the Department of Justice (DOJ), her well-received work on criminal justice reform, public interest law, and legal services provided relevant policy and practical experience on top of her superb credentials. For once, being a woman was not a barrier she had to overcome in the first instance.

President Carter was explicit in his support for women holding senior positions in his administration, as well as for women serving as judges on the federal courts. She and Barbara Babcock were the first women Assistant Attorneys General to lead their divisions at the DOJ. (When asked by a reporter how it felt to be named to a senior government role "because you are a woman," Barbara Babcock responded, "A lot better than NOT being named because I am a woman.")[3]

While at the Justice Department, Pat worked on an array of matters, including the ratification of the Equal Rights Amendment and the expansion of the number of federal judgeships below the Supreme Court level. Having very little direct experience working with Congress, Pat again dove into learning her new role and spent extensive effort building relationships with Congress and congressional staff. A substantial increase of women on the federal bench resulted from the expanded number of judgeships and, in 1979, Pat became the first woman nominated and confirmed to the U.S. Court of Appeals for the D.C. Circuit.

Her confirmation process was an early omen of some of the bruising political battles over judicial appointments that are so unfortunately common today. She had strong support from important senators such as Ted Kennedy, Birch Bayh, and Barry Goldwater. But right-wing groups were unhappy that President Carter was given the opportunity to appoint so many new judges, and decided symbolically to target a few. Pat was one of these, and a campaign of prepackaged editorials (one called her "a wild and wooly" woman) were sent to newspapers across the country. She faced some opponents who argued that she was "anti-family," based on articles she had written regarding children's rights. No doubt it helped that some Senators had gotten to know her during her work at the Justice Department, as did having her husband Bob and five children at her side during the confirmation hearing. She was confirmed with nineteen votes opposing her on the Senate floor, but with bipartisan support.

[3.] Transcript of Interview with Barbara A. Babcock (Feb. 22, 2006), *available at* https://purl.stanford.edu/nq979sp5101.

There was a surreal moment during her confirmation hearings when Reverend Bob Jones (of Bob Jones University), stood up with a Bible in his hand and said Mom was "an instrument of the devil." Senator Bayh, who was chairing the hearing, stopped and asked Bob Jones if he had ever met the nominee. Jones stammered "no," and Senator Bayh said, "Why don't you go over and shake her hand. She's a very nice person." It totally stopped his attack. (S.W.)

Pat served twenty years on the D.C. Circuit, five of which she was Chief Judge (the first woman Chief Judge of the D.C. Circuit). During her tenure, she wrote over 800 opinions. One of her colleagues on the court, Judge David Tatel, has described her as a "widely admired intellectual leader of the federal judiciary" and as "having a pro-found impact on the law." She was also known for her ability to bring colleagues together through diplomacy and to navigate challenging political waters.

On the D.C. Circuit, she was involved in many important cases, including the first Microsoft antitrust appeal (*United States v. Microsoft Corp.*, 147 F.3rd 935 (D.C. Cir. 1998)), the conviction of Iran-Contra mastermind Oliver North (*United States v. North*, 910 F.2d 843 (D.C. Cir. 1981)), and crucial administrative law cases such as *Sierra Club v. Costle* (657 F.2d 298 (D.C. Cir. 1981)).

One of her opinions of which she was most proud was actually a dissent, taking a position that ultimately became the law of the land. It dealt with the now-discredited federal government "don't ask, don't tell" policy, under which those serving in the armed forces could not reveal their sexual orientation if they were not heterosexual. If they did "tell," they faced discharge. Pat, in her ringing dissent, ana-lyzed why the policy "runs deeply against our constitutional grain."[4] Ultimately, the government dropped the policy, a development she fortunately lived to see.

Pat left her mark even beyond her legal opinions. Half of her law clerks were women, a remarkable record. During her years on the bench, many federal judges still tended to select men as their law clerks, even if few explicitly maintained the position she had to con-front when finishing Yale Law School, when most judges refused to

---

[4.] Steffan v. Perry, 41 F.3d 677 (D.C. Cir. 1994).

consider women clerks at all. Her law clerks, both male and female, have been highly sought after and are in academia and throughout the legal profession, where they are well positioned to mentor women themselves.

As Chief Judge, she also supported the work of the D.C. Circuit Task Force on Gender, Race and Ethnic Bias, put in place to review D.C. Circuit policies and practices. Not all similar task forces at work in other circuits received such support. Creation of these task forces was controversial in a number of circuits, including D.C. The Board of the Federal Judicial Center offered to help the circuits with research, but passed a resolution in 1993 to note that "The Board takes no position with respect to the desirability of the appointment of gender bias task forces in the various circuits."[5]

As one judge noted:

> Forming a task force and gaining acceptance for it to study and report on gender fairness in the courts are not simple undertakings. Some believe gender bias does not exist in the courts to any significant extent and that any study is unnecessary. Others believe that earlier studies from federal or state courts provide all the information needed, and that resources should be directed toward implementing educational programs and other changes to eliminate bias, rather than studying it.[6]

Supporting the D.C. Circuit Task Force on Gender, Race and Ethnic Bias was a major commitment from her. These Task Forces were a priority of civil rights and women's rights organizations concerned that any biased practices in the courts be removed to promote equal justice. (**M.G.**)

Further during her tenure, the first woman, and then a second, was selected to be the Circuit Executive, the top management position for the Circuit; women advanced to other senior-level administrative

---

[5] MOLLY TREADWAY JOHNSON, FEDERAL JUDICIAL CENTER, STUDYING THE ROLE OF GENDER IN THE FEDERAL COURTS: A RESEARCH GUIDE, ii (1995), *available at* https://www.ojp.gov/pdffiles1/Digitization/155454NCJRS.pdf (iii, xiii).

[6] *Id.* at xiii.

positions for the first time as well. Important changes followed for the court workforce. New policies were adopted, for example, to make it easier for employees of the Circuit to deal with family and other responsibilities.

Pat was incredibly supportive of women in the profession, but she would at times bristle at being categorized primarily by her gender. If you asked her, she would have said that her sympathies lay with the "underdog"; and that women were often treated as inferiors, but other categories of people were also. She acknowledged that:

> [B]eing a woman and being treated by society as a woman can be a vital element of a judge's experience . . . I can think of a few cases where being a woman entered into my conscience, but I can think of just as many where having worked in a factory, having been a Legal Services lawyer and having been a government official who dealt with Congress affected my perspective just as much.[7]

In 1999, she was appointed a judge on the International Criminal Tribunal for the former Yugoslavia (ICTY), the international war crimes tribunal (the first international criminal court established since Nuremberg) set up by the United Nations in The Hague to address atrocities during the Balkan wars in the early 90s. She resigned from the D.C. Circuit to take on this new challenge and moved to the Hague, where she was the only woman judge in a sea of male judges and prosecutors. She had never lived abroad before; her husband Bob visited frequently but stayed in their DC home.

The ICTY, which was in place from 1993 to 2017, was established to provide mechanisms to hold accountable war crimes and war criminals from the Balkan conflict. Among its accomplishments was the conviction and sentencing of high-level officials who ordered and countenanced genocide, and wider recognition of both the frequency and the severity of violence against women as war crimes. One of the cases Pat sat on was the heartbreaking case of General Radislav Krstić, convicted of genocide in the Srebrenica massacres of as many as 8,000 Muslim men and boys in one week in 1995.

[7.] Wald, *Six Not-So-Easy Pieces*, supra note 2 at 989.

The proceedings and materials were conducted in French, a language she did not speak, and the norms and procedures were not as developed as the courts in which she was experienced. As could have been predicted, she just put her head down and held firm to her ethical standards. She said decisions and orders could take a long time because of the careful translations; she would not sign or agree to anything that she did not fully understand.

At the ICTY, Pat brought her commitment to fairness to the proceedings, and worked to improve the tribunal's procedures, transparency, and protection of and respect for witnesses, particularly women and children victims.

She did not see herself as a "representative" of women; nonetheless, her perspective and strong sense of fairness were instrumental in ensuring that the stories and interests and dignity of women were given weight in the tribunal. The tribunal has been noted for, as she described, its:

> . . . path-breaking decisions regarding the status of rapes, sexual violence, and sexual enslavement as crimes of war and crimes against humanity when committed in the context of a widespread campaign against civilians. An estimated 20,000 rapes were committed in wartime Bosnia as part of a campaign of terrorism against civilians or inside the prison camps. For the first time in history an entire war crimes prosecution at the ICTY was devoted to crimes against women.[8]

When her two-year appointment term at the ICTY ended, Pat returned to Washington. She was active in legal reform organizations such as the American Law Institute and the American Constitution Society and was named to the U.S. Privacy and Civil Liberties Oversight Board (PCLOB), a bipartisan independent commission charged with monitoring the intelligence community's actions on terrorism. The Board released a controversial report in 2014, in which the PCLOB found programs of the National Security Agency for warrantless bulk surveillance of telephone records in Section 215 of the

---

[8.] Hon. Patricia M. Wald, *Punishment of War Crimes by International Tribunals*, 69 Soc. Res. 1119 (2002).

Patriot Act were both without legal basis and ineffective in terms of uncovering evidence of terrorist activity.

Pat's strong view of what was "right" was in evidence here. As she noted once, "Looking back, I do not regret the times I stuck my neck out or departed from the prevailing view. My regrets are confined to the times I didn't."[9]

In 2013, Pat was awarded the Presidential Medal of Freedom by President Barack Obama, the highest civilian award in the United States. President Obama, when awarding her the Medal of Freedom, said she was "one of the most respected federal judges of her generation."

It was such an amazing moment to be there in the East Wing with her as she was being honored by President Obama and sharing that day with other honorees, including Ben Bradlee, Bill Clinton, and Loretta Lynn. My sisters and I had taken her shopping beforehand for the occasion. I remember sitting and watching her on the stage, in her new teal velvet blazer, laughing with fellow recipients Gloria Steinem and Oprah Winfrey. We were so proud of her and it was so well deserved. (**S.W.**)

It is impossible to summarize a life in neat themes—life is too unpredictable, messy, and surprising to fall into clean categories. Still, there are repeated threads that run throughout Pat Wald's life. She was incredibly smart and also worked incredibly hard—a combination that was recognized by the nuns in her grade school, by teachers in college and law school, by Attorneys General, and by Presidents.

She did not engage in lots of self-promotion; she relied on the notion (whether justifiably or not, in all cases) that integrity, commitment, and contributions were what made a person "successful." She was both fortunate and open enough to get support from those around her—men as well as women—from her law journal colleagues, to the judge who recommended her for her first job, to her devoted and superhuman husband and co-parent of five, Bob.

She was adamant about "doing the right thing"; her moral compass was unwavering, even when that meant that she was in

---

[9.] Hon. Patricia M. Wald, *Unfinished Business: Reflections from an Alumna*, YALE L. REP., Winter 2015, at 42, *available at* https://ylr.law.yale.edu/pdfs/v62-1/W15-features -pat-wald.pdf.

the minority on a decision or in a group or on a commission. She had high and demanding standards for herself, but also for everyone else—her kids, her colleagues, her country; and she was determined to push all of them to be their ethical best.

She was a loyal and comforting friend, providing advice, guidance, and support in quiet, personal ways. In her own modest way, she once described how she would like to be remembered: "That she worked very hard, she was a reasonably good administrator. She was a thoughtful and fair judge and she made some small contributions towards pushing the law forward as an effective means of solving human and social problems."[10]

She is indeed remembered as all that—and so, so much more.

---

[10] Jeffrey Lubbers, *Administrative Law as Seen from the DC Circuit: An Interview with Chief Judge Patricia M. Wald*, 34 FED. BAR NEWS & J. 15 (1987).

BIO

Marcia D. Greenberger

Described as "guiding the battles of the women's rights movement" by the *New York Times*, and by *USA Today* as one of "100 Women of the Century Who Changed America," Marcia Greenberger is the founder and Co-President Emerita of the National Women's Law Center. With her creation of the Center fifty years ago, she became the first full-time women's rights legal advocate in Washington, DC.

A recognized expert on women and the law, particularly in the areas of education and employment, health and reproductive rights, and family economic security, Ms. Greenberger has been a leader in securing the passage of major legislation, counsel in landmark litigation establishing new legal protections for women and girls, and the author of numerous published articles. Examples include the Lilly Ledbetter Fair Pay Act, the Pregnancy Discrimination Act, the Civil Rights Act of 1991 providing critical protections against sexual harassment on the job, and Supreme Court victories strengthening protections for students and teachers against sex discrimination in schools and in the workplace.

Her leadership and contributions are reflected in the professional honors she has received and the numerous boards on which she has served, including her induction into the National Women's Hall of Fame in Seneca Falls, New York. Ms. Greenberger received her BA with honors and JD *cum laude* from the University of Pennsylvania. She practiced law with the Washington, DC, firm of Caplin & Drysdale before she founded and became Director of the Women's Rights Project of the Center for Law and Social Policy, which became the National Women's Law Center in 1981.

BIO

Sarah E. Wald

Sarah Wald is a lawyer and educator whose career has been in government and higher education. She is currently Senior Policy Advisor and Chief of Staff to the Dean at the Harvard Kennedy School, as well as Adjunct Lecturer in Public Policy at the Kennedy School.

Sarah has co-taught the seminar on Gender and Public Policy at the Harvard Kennedy School, and she is one of the faculty who teaches in and oversees the joint MPP/JD program between the Harvard Kennedy School and Harvard Law School. At Harvard, she is active as a member of several university-wide committees, and the Committee on Faculty Conflict of Interest and the University Trademark Policy Committee. She has also been Dean of Students and Lecturer on Law (class: The Government Lawyer: Public Enforcement of Consumer Rights) at Harvard Law School, Assistant Provost for Policy and Planning at the University, and a member of the Harvard University Task Force on Sexual Assault Prevention and the Advisory Committee on Title IX Policy.

She is a former Assistant Secretary of Consumer Affairs and Business Regulation and former Assistant Attorney General in Massachusetts. She has also been at the University of North Carolina, where she was Special Assistant to the Dean at UNC School of Law and Assistant Dean for Academic Affairs at UNC School of Medicine. She served as President of the Massachusetts Women's Bar Association, and teaches seminars on gender communications to practicing lawyers around the country.

Sarah is a graduate of Brown University and Yale Law School and her legal publications have appeared in the *Harvard Women's Law Review,* the *Administrative Law Journal,* and the *Widener Law Review.*

He Sensed a Story and Cancelled the Party

6

Esther Moellering Tomljanovich

*I*t is hard for any young lawyer or law student today to imagine the pervasive hostility that a woman matriculating in the 1950s experienced from her male classmates and law professors. Outright bias was inescapable and, as Justice Tomljanovich writes, part of the culture.

Women were gaslit by an alternate reality of senseless rules that served only to reinforce privilege. Justice Tomljanovich offers a glimpse into what it was like to try to navigate this reality, and describes the crucial role of allies in the slow process of successfully implementing change. Her stories provide useful insights for addressing the pervasive, unconscious biases that still exist today.

Lauren Stiller Rikleen, Editor

Hiring a woman lawyer is like teaching a dog to walk on his hind legs, you can do it, but why bother. So said a prominent Minneapolis attorney when I entered law school in 1951.

In the 1950s and 60s, "Why Bother" was the customary theme with regard to women in the law.

Despite the small number of women law students in the 1950s, there were a number of women lawyers—most of whom had entered the profession shortly after women got the vote, believing that everything would be equal. Of course, nothing was equal. After being admitted to practice law, many of the women continued in the jobs they had held before law school, be it teaching, legal secretary, or another clerical job. Those who practiced law often did so with a husband, father, or brother, doing the routine office tasks, while their male colleagues did the "real practice of law." A very few practiced on their own, even fewer—only two or three—were in large firms.

There were no women law professors, no women judges. In the Minnesota State Bar Association, no women served on a committee, except perhaps the committee to provide entertainment for the law-yers' wives during the annual convention.

Women were largely ignored in the legal profession. Worse, we were invisible.

In society in general, discrimination against women was a part of the culture. Laws and ordinances often restricted the kind of jobs women could hold, the hours they could work, the amount they could lift. Women were often prohibited from working as bartenders where they were safely behind a bar, but not as cocktail waitresses, where customers could, and often did, touch or fondle them.

In some cities, women were prohibited from working as report-ers in newsrooms after midnight, but not barred from working as cleaners in the very same newsrooms. Union contracts had different rates of pay for women and men for the same job. Very few women were employed outside the home after they married. To be pregnant and employed was unthinkable.

Against that backdrop, challenging gender discrimination would have been counterproductive in the 1950s. In general, we just accepted discrimination because "that's the way things were."

The position of women actually made my law school experience easier. I was the only woman in my class. I was no competition to any of my classmates. My classmates knew that upon graduation I would not get the job they wanted. I would not even get an interview for the job they wanted, so they were free to treat me as the class pet or mascot.

One of the professors did say often, and in my presence, that there was "no place in law school for women." But he knew too, that I was no competition for the men, so he didn't bother to discriminate against me. Discrimination seemed passive to me.

My first brush with more aggressive discrimination came upon graduation. My husband (then my law school classmate) and I were invited to a dinner honoring law school graduates at the St. Paul Athletic Club, a private men's club. We walked in the front door and sat down in the lobby to await the arrival of our host for the evening, whereupon I was told that I was not permitted to come in the front door, nor was I permitted to sit in the lobby. I was shown to the side door, the "ladies' entrance," and directed to wait in a rather dingy Ladies Waiting Room. I didn't object or complain. I was so humiliated at not knowing the rules, at having committed such a social error, that I didn't tell anyone about that for at least fifteen years.

Years later I was to discover that a number of other women had had a similar experience. They had reacted as I had, blaming themselves for not knowing the rules.

While being barred from the private men's clubs might seem trivial, it was a significant problem for women. The private clubs were the places where contacts were made, where deals were made, where jobs were offered. In St. Paul, many lawyers went to their offices on Saturday morning and at noon adjourned to the more exclusive Minnesota Club for lunch with other lawyers and business and community leaders. Women were completely excluded from that world.

Our reaction to discrimination in the workplace was often avoidance. I went to a night law school and worked at a life insurance company during the day. After graduation, I discovered that I was paid less than my male colleagues with similar experience. Many of our policies also had a disability clause, where disabled policy holders would be paid a small amount during the term of their disability. From time to time a colleague of mine would be assigned to investigate the disability claims, and to check personally on the claimants.

Since my colleagues were young lawyers, who had had very limited opportunities to travel, the disability investigation trips were highly prized. After I was admitted to practice law, I requested one of the disability investigation assignments. I then learned that I was barred from business travel, because "women are not allowed to travel." No reason was offered other than that I was a woman.

When I inquired about my future with the company, my supervisor acknowledged that he liked me and my work was satisfactory. But my salary was lower, my opportunities limited, and I would never be considered for the position of General Counsel because I was a woman. My only remedy was to seek employment elsewhere.

In 1957, I was hired to be an Assistant Revisor of Statutes for the state of Minnesota. At the time, the office drafted most of the proposed legislation for the legislators, the Governor's office, and for other state departments. In addition, the office published and indexed Minnesota Session Laws and Minnesota Statutes. A man was hired to head the bill drafting function. I was hired to index and edit the Session Laws and Statutes. My new boss said, often and publicly, that he had hired me because "women do boring work so well."

I did with the Boring Job what women did: you took the job you could get, often because it paid less, was less prestigious, or was boring. You dealt with discrimination by working hard, doing whatever tasks there were to do, even if not in your job description. You made yourself indispensable. Soon you might find you had the job you wanted.

In my case it turned out that I did the bill drafting better than the boring work and I related well and made friends with legislators, department heads, and those in the Governor's office. I found myself doing the bill drafting work.

The Revisor of Statutes office was a great place for anyone with political ambitions. At any given time, there might be a future U.S. Senator, maybe a future Congressperson or a future Governor in the Legislature. It is where I met and became friends with Senator Rudy Perpich who later became Governor and appointed me to the District Court in 1977. I had the great good fortune to have him be Governor again in 1990 when he appointed me to the Minnesota Supreme Court.

It was the early 1960s before I ever spoke out against gender discrimination. I was a member of the National Association of Business and Professional Women, which advocated for women's equality and the Equal Rights Amendment. When a particularly egregious discriminatory ordinance or law was proposed, I might tip my toe into the pool of gender discrimination and write a letter to the editor of the local newspaper.

The Business and Professional Women's Clubs (BPW) of Minnesota made bold to aggressively push for Equal Pay for Equal Work at the Minnesota State Legislature in the early 1960s. We secured an author who introduced a bill. The BPW had a statewide network of clubs, so we had the laboring oar in our lobbying efforts. The women's service clubs of Zonta and Altrusa were supportive, but lacking as extensive a statewide network, they played a somewhat minor roll. Many of the BPW members across the state lobbied their local legislators. Several of us in the St. Paul BPW made numerous speeches to local service clubs and organizations, and to whoever would listen.

Our main opposition was the Minnesota Chamber of Commerce. The CEO of the Chamber of Commerce often appeared with us, and he was a worthy opponent. He had the backing and resources of most of the major businesses in the state. At the meetings, we each presented our arguments for our position. Our arguments generally focused on simple justice. Among arguments against the legislation were: It would be bad for business; women were less reliable employees; there was more absenteeism, always subtle hints of monthly absences and emotional instability during "that time of the month"; businesses spent time training women, then they got married or pregnant and quit work; women worked for what was termed "pin money," not to support families.

Even ridicule of the legislators supporting the bill was used. Two of our main supporters, Representative Peter Popovich (later Chief Justice of the Minnesota Supreme Court) and Representative Don Wozniak (later Chief Judge of the Minnesota Court of Appeals), were ridiculed for being "mama's boys" supporting women. But fair play finally prevailed and, in 1964, the Equal Pay for Equal Work bill became law in Minnesota.

In the early 1960s, the Kennedy administration established a Federal Commission on the Status of Women and encouraged states to do likewise. Governor Rolvaag established the Minnesota Commission on the Status of Women in 1964. I served on that Commission, and we set about trying to educate women and the public about the rights of women, highlighting those areas where gender discrimination existed. In furtherance of that goal, I authored a pamphlet on the rights of women that was widely distributed to women's organizations throughout the state.

The Commission operated in a low key and always "lady like" fashion, but often our attempts were met with ridicule. For example, consider the offenses of adultery and fornication. Fornication was a misdemeanor and applied if a married man and a single woman were involved. Adultery was a felony and applied whenever a married woman was involved. We suggested that married men and married women be treated equally. The local newspaper carried the headline "Women Want Equal Rights to Commit Adultery."

The Minnesota Commission on the Status of Women didn't change many laws, but its reasoned and nonconfrontational views did set the stage for real attitude change to come later.

As the 1960s movement for equal rights for women began to gain momentum, it brought forth a wave of "anti-woman" feeling. The editor of the St. Paul newspaper wrote a number of editorials explaining why women could not compete in the workplace. The newspaper carried multiple articles about women bosses—usually concluding that women did not make good bosses; the majority of workers would not work for a woman. They were petty and unpleasant.

Meanwhile women were reminded every day of our second-class status. Although we focused on jobs and employment discrimination, it was there in social and everyday matters. For example, when I was President of the local Business and Professional Women's Association, our club was asked to cohost a reception for new citizens along with the local chapter of the Jaycees. Hosting required us to choose a speaker and provide refreshments.

When I met with the President of the Jaycees, I was informed that they had chosen the speaker and our group could provide refreshments. I objected that the Business and Professional Women's Association preferred to choose the speaker rather than provide the refreshments.

The Jaycees president was perplexed; he said he didn't know why we objected to providing refreshments, that their wives liked to be in charge of the food. I suggested that he invite the wives to do just that, because the BPW would not participate.

These young, inexperienced men just assumed that an organization of mature professional women would bring the cookies, because they were women. While this incident was not important in itself, it illustrates the constant reminder of our status as the coffee makers, never the policy makers.

In the 1960s, the legislature established an interim commission to study reorganization of the court system. Various groups, including the Young Lawyers of the Minnesota State Bar Association, were asked to submit nominations for membership on the commission. The President of the Young Lawyers Association sent a letter to members, requesting nominations. They were to be "Movers and shakers and Men, our wives will take care of the Ladies."

He assumed that only men would know the legal system and add value to the commission. I believe he thought a woman or two would be added, not for what they knew but just for appearance's sake. (I long have suspected that a woman was needed to make coffee and to take notes.) I objected, saying I knew a number of movers and shakers but, unfortunately, they were women, so I would not propose any members. These kinds of responses, though subtle, often hit the spot and made other lawyers rethink their preconceived notions.

In 1974, I finally had the job I wanted: the legislature named me Revisor of Statutes. Now, I assumed, discrimination was behind me.

This was a time when lobbyists spent money lavishly entertaining legislators and staff. Lobbyist-sponsored parties and lunches were the order of the day. The railroad lobbyists gave one of the grandest luncheons. Invitations were issued and all my male assistants were invited, but there was no invitation for me.

I called the lobbyist to remind him that I was now the Revisor of Statutes so he must have made a mistake in not inviting me. He answered that there was no mistake, he had not intended to invite me as the party was for his old friends. I acknowledged that I could understand his attachment to old friends, especially two of my young male assistants who had worked for me for several months and had been invited. But still no invitation.

I tried humor and asked if he intended to have a naked lady jump out of the potato salad and if that was why a woman would hinder the enjoyment of the party. Still no invitation. This was a time when the so-called "Society Page" of the St. Paul newspaper was beginning to have stirrings of gender equality. I called the editor of the Society Page; she sensed a story and called the lobbyist. He sensed a story and cancelled the party. I don't know if that was a successful conclusion or not, but it did make a lot of disappointed luncheon guests aware of gender discrimination.

In 1977, I was appointed to the Minnesota State District Court. I was the second woman District Court Judge in the state, and the first in a semi-rural district. It was an eight-county District and in at least six of the counties, lawyers had never seen a woman lawyer, much less a woman judge. Because of the power of a trial judge, there was little overt discrimination. Again, it was the small things—not being able to join clubs like the Lions Club and the Rotary, not being able to join the local golf club. Those contacts and interactions that made it easy for men to fit in were not available to me.

In the early 1980s, I decided to challenge the exclusion from those clubs when I was invited by one of the members of the Lions Club to attend their annual picnic, held at the riverside home of a member of the club. The host was also the oldest and a highly respected member of the Washington County Bar Association.

When I arrived, the picnic was in progress. Members and their guests appeared to be having an enjoyable time, but as I stepped out of the car, the lively conversation stopped, and I was greeted with complete silence. The men, many of whom were lawyers who appeared regularly in my courtroom, seemed not to believe such a breach of protocol as a woman attending their picnic could occur.

At that moment the host of the evening approached; he gave me a kiss on the cheek and welcomed me. The kiss was probably inappropriate. But it showed the attendees that he welcomed me, and the party resumed. I was reminded of a documentary I had seen on television where children in an isolated part of Africa were confronted by two white men. Having never seen a white person before, the children ran away in terror. The difference was that those men had seen a woman before, a woman sitting on the bench in a courtroom, and still they thought their way of life was in jeopardy.

One incident may illustrate the atmosphere at the time. A judge from an adjoining district was invited to address our district meeting. I was still the only woman judge in the district and our guest was a talented and entertaining speaker. His speech drifted into sexually inappropriate stories. After the meeting I quietly reminded him that judges' meetings were not stag parties anymore. He cleaned up his language and stories for future presentations.

One of the most difficult areas to deal with were gestures that were well meant, but in fact were discriminatory. For example, soon after my appointment as a District Judge, the support staff began calling me "Judge Esther." It was meant as a sign of affection, but I felt it diminished me as an equal to the men judges. I told the staff that when the men became Judge Jack, Judge Howard, and Judge Ken, then they were free to call me Judge Esther. Until then, I was Judge Tomljanovich.

Even harder to deal with was a greatly loved, retired judge who often was assigned to our courthouse. When he arrived in the morning, I would often be meeting in my chambers with attorneys, sorting out the day's work. He invariably poked his head into my door and called out "Morning Honey." Because I knew there was no ill will, he truly thought of me as Honey, and he was a product of a bygone time, I never found a way to deal with that greeting. I continued to be "Honey," not even "Judge Honey," as long as he lived.

During my time as a trial judge, there was one matter where I think in retrospect that my response to discrimination was wrong. When I was appointed to the District Court in 1977, a woman judge was a novelty. When people discovered I was a Judge, they would almost invariably ask if I was a Family Court Judge or a Juvenile Court Judge. Despite the importance of family and juvenile law, the people I met seemed to think it wasn't "real law," so it was okay for a woman to be assigned to those courts.

At the time of my appointment, neither family nor juvenile law was assigned to the District Court. I usually answered the inquiries about my role by saying that I only handled large civil cases, gross misdemeanors, and felonies, explaining that felonies were things like rape and murder. Later, when the District and County Courts were merged, each judge, both District and County, was assigned their share of juvenile and family cases.

I took advantage of what was termed a "grandmother clause" that exempted me from Family and Juvenile Court. In retrospect, I believe that I should have taken my share of Family and Juvenile Court cases and should have helped people to understand that they are some of the most complex and important cases in our legal system, important not only to the parties but to the larger society as well.

I always tried not to criticize an attorney in open court. On occasion, there were challenges that I found necessary to address immediately and openly. For example, during a hearing, I told an attorney that the evidence he was offering would not be accepted. He responded, "This is my case, I will do it my way," whereupon I responded, "This is my Courtroom, you will do it my way." In that case, I felt that his challenge being made in open court had to be responded to in open court.

In another instance at the Supreme Court, when I asked an out-of-state lawyer a question, rather than answering, he posed a question to me. I simply responded that I didn't know how things operated in his home state, but in Minnesota the Justices asked the questions and the attorneys answered the questions. He answered the question.

In both of those instances and in others like them, I felt that the challenges to me were based on my gender. In those public cases it was often necessary to admonish promptly and publicly because those challenges threatened the integrity and dignity of the Court.

The incidents I have mentioned illustrate only a few of the challenges that were confronted every single day, but they illustrate my way of dealing with the slights, the insults, the unfair treatment that women face.

In the 1970s, when women were entering the mainstream legal world, women lawyers often wore little blue suits, with white blouses and fluffy ties. They looked, for all the world, like little men. To try to emulate and do things like a man was a mistake. Women have so much to offer the legal profession. We experience the world differently than men. We need the experiences of both men and women to make this a truly great profession.

As I look back on my career, I realize that my response to discrimination and negative feelings about my, or any woman's, ability to do the job was simply to work harder and do a better job than a man would do and prove the doubters wrong. I wonder if I should have been more aggressive in setting out my views and responding to the everyday slights and insults. Did I let things slide when I should have responded with anger? My conclusion is that given the times and the culture, a polite, sometimes humorous response was most effective.

My advice to young women is to pick your battles carefully—be logical and polite. Admonish privately. If you are going to change attitudes and behavior, nothing is to be gained by publicly embarrassing your adversaries. Acknowledge that you will have to be smarter and work harder than your male counterparts to achieve the same result in your career.

And finally make time every day to enjoy and celebrate being a part of this really great legal profession.

BIO

Esther Moellering Tomljanovich

Born on November 1, 1931, Esther Moellering Tomljanovich was raised in rural northern Minnesota.

Justice Tomljanovich graduated from Itasca Community College in Grand Rapids, Minnesota, in 1951. She then moved to St. Paul, Minnesota, to enroll in law school, even though she had never met a lawyer nor did she know if there were any women lawyers. But she did know a radio soap opera character named Portia who was a woman lawyer in the soap opera *Portia Faces Life.*

With Portia as her inspiration, she enrolled at St. Paul College of Law (a predecessor of Mitchell Hamline School of Law), the only woman in her class. She graduated and was admitted to practice law in 1955.

Justice Tomljanovich was employed as Assistant Revisor of Statutes for the state of Minnesota from 1957 to 1966. When her son Bill was born in 1966, she opted to be a full-time mom, doing whatever legal work was available to a stay-at-home mom.

During the stay-close-to-home years, she was active in her community, including a term on the local School Board and membership on the Lake Elmo City Planning Commission.

In 1974, Justice Tomljanovich returned to full-time work and served as Revisor of Statutes until 1977, when she was the second woman to be named a Minnesota State District Court Judge. She served as a District Court Judge until 1990, when she became the third woman to be named to the Minnesota Supreme Court, where she served until 1998.

In 2001, she joined the Board of Directors of Medica Health Insurance Companies and retired from that Board on January 1, 2022.

Among her many professional activities, Justice Tomljanovich has served as a member of the Governor's Judicial Selection Committee and as a member of the William Mitchell College of Law Board of Trustees.

She has received a number of awards during her career, including the Minnesota Women Lawyers' Myra Bradwell Award and the American Bar Association's Margaret Brent Women Lawyers of Achievement Award. The William Mitchell College of Law named her one of "100 Who Made a Difference," and *Law and Politics Magazine* named her one of the "100 Most Influential Attorneys in State History."

Justice Tomljanovich lives with her husband of 65 years in Lake Elmo.

Confronting Challenges

Ruth Cooper Burg

7

*L*ike many other personal stories shared in this book, Judge Burg offers a richly detailed account of how biases intersect—in her case, facing gender discrimination and anti-Semitism. Her overt examples of both help demonstrate that what we see today as unconscious bias has deep roots in outright individual and institutional discrimination.

Judge Burg shares insights into significant times in her life when she felt compelled to stay silent because she feared punishment if she responded to the biases she experienced. Her story should inspire every organization—including higher education institutions as well as workplaces—to have in place meaningful policies by which victims of bias can report in safety and with support.

Lauren Stiller Rikleen, Editor

"We would normally obtain a judicial clerkship or a position in a major law firm for the person graduating first in the class but in your case, you realize that is not possible. We will be happy to write a letter of recommendation for any position YOU can find."

These were the words with which the Dean of George Washington University Law School greeted me in May 1950. I do not know whether today I am more shocked with what he said or the fact that I sat there and agreed with him. Certainly, such words would not be said today. With this experience, I began my postgraduate career in law.

I graduated high school in June 1943, just after the United States entered World War II. As valedictorian, I was awarded a four-year scholarship by George Washington University (GW). My hope had been to attend Radcliffe College. However, my father was concerned that his "little girl" might be stranded in Cambridge—there was a prevailing fear then that the East Coast would be shelled from German submarines off the coast.

My parents were way ahead of their time and were determined that their two daughters always be able to support themselves. We were not wealthy and, while my father had a senior-level position as an electrical engineer with the Navy, his income was not great. Knowing his concern about me being away from home and concerned about future costs since I planned to attend medical school, I decided to accept the scholarship. This decision was the first turn in my lifetime yellow brick road.

The original position of the GW medical school counselor was that I should major in a "woman's major." I never went near his office to discuss my future because he had invited me to visit him there so he could "paint my organs on my body." (This was not my first or last experience with sexual harassment.) After I had taken his advanced biology courses, he decided I was capable of handling medical school. Despite my failure to visit his office, with his recommendation I entered GW medical school after my junior year.

I again lived at home. It was because I never had the opportunity to experience the independence of being responsible only for myself that I was determined that my children live away from home when attending college. I never had that opportunity, and I believe it is important, especially for a woman.

For the first time in my life, I met strong antifeminism and anti-Semitism as a freshman medical student. While I enjoyed my classes and made good grades, it was quite unpleasant. The major problems I encountered were with the anatomy professor. I became a butt of his prejudices. There were 10 women in our class of 120. Many of the men were veterans of World War II and many were married. I was very involved with my future husband so had no sexual interest in any of my colleagues. I did enjoy associating with them.

One Saturday after class we listened to the Army-Navy football game on a radio one of the men had brought with him and had a good time cheering for the team we were supporting. We suddenly realized the professor was spying on us and for some reason was not pleased that we were having a good time. He had insisted that all the women in the class be separated from our male colleagues during the lab and placed all the women together at one cadaver. It was obvious he was angry that we were spending time together even on our free time.

He was also quite sadistic and if you missed an exam because you were ill, would allow a make-up only if you had an excuse from a doctor. Shortly after the episode concerning the football game, I missed one of the three neuro-anatomy examinations for the course because I was running a high fever due to the flu. While he was not the instructor in that course, he refused to let me take a make-up exam although I obtained a written excuse. A zero in the exam potentially meant I would fail the course. The entire class as well as the instructors were outraged by his action, but he remained adamant. I worked very hard in the lab and received top grades so managed to pass the course.

On another occasion while the professor was handing out exam bluebooks, I held out my hand when he called my name. He pulled the blue book back and said, "I thought you were Cohen." I sat next to June Cohen, who was not Jewish but carried her father's name. It was quite evident what his remark indicated. Since the various anatomy courses were a major part of the freshman curriculum, this matter seriously concerned me. I had never really met anything like it before.

I had met my first husband just before entering medical school. Because we wanted to get married and because of my dislike for the experiences, I requested a leave of absence. Many years later, while sorting through my father's papers after his death, I found a letter from GW Medical School stating that while it was unusual to grant a leave of absence, I was such an excellent student they would do so. That the letter was sent to my father, and not to me, would not occur today.

After leaving medical school, I took a job at the Naval Research Laboratory, indexing and abstracting the Manhattan papers (the story of the development of the atomic bomb). Many of the documents were still classified. Protecting classified information is always a problem. Only persons with security clearance can be present when classified material is not under lock. Later, as a judge, I had cases involving secret information. This meant that everyone in the court-room had to have a secret security clearance, and nobody could enter the courtroom without one even to deliver a message. Documents had to be placed under lock at the end of the day or when everyone left the courtroom. If I was using the documents in my office, I could not leave or allow anyone to enter without security clearance and the documents had to be locked up at night or whenever not in use. I made every effort to have the parties stipulate relevant facts and avoid classified information. This was often successful.

I always intended to continue my education, and my husband was quite supportive of my doing so. His parents had sent him to this country from Germany in 1937 when he was seventeen because of Hitler's treatment of Jewish citizens. While his family had been quite wealthy in Germany, he arrived in the United States with almost no money, so he could not continue his education. He worked up from a stock boy at a major department store to a buyer in one of the departments. After we met, he decided to return to college under the GI Bill and was studying to become a CPA when we married.

I spent two years deciding whether to return to medical school and finally decided not to do so. I had found working with sick patients or even performing healthy examinations was very difficult for me. While I had been told that one became accustomed to treating patients, I had severe concern about my doing so. I considered earning a graduate degree in biochemistry but there was not a good university near Washington for this degree. I knew no knowledgeable person with whom I could discuss all of this. While my family was supportive of whatever decision I would make, that was not very helpful.

I decided to take an aptitude test with a psychologist at GW. The results indicated that law was my highest aptitude, with medicine and other biological sciences also quite high. I was not surprised that housecleaning came out the lowest of all aptitudes. I really disliked doing it immensely.

Because I preferred to stay in Washington where my husband was starting his career, I applied to GW Law School and was admitted. Georgetown did not accept women at that time. I enjoyed my classes. Several of my professors learned that I had indexing experience and asked me to index textbooks they were writing. It was interesting work, and the one dollar per hour that I was paid was welcome. Some of my male classmates were able to get part-time jobs with law firms, but that opportunity was not available to women in our class. I also received a scholarship for the final two years of law school, which was quite helpful for our very limited budget. We were living on the GI Bill allowance, and it barely covered the rent. My husband had a part-time bookkeeping job and that helped.

I enjoyed law school. I was first in the class, and according to custom I should have been editor-in-chief of the *Law Review*, but the professor in charge did not appoint me to that position. Since he appointed the woman who was second in the class, I assume it was because I was Jewish. Classmates spoke to me about his decision, and I considered speaking to the dean but felt it might do more harm than good and result in a lower grade since I was taking a course that the professor was teaching. I was taking a graduate law course in taxation, so he created a new position of taxation editor and appointed me to it instead of as editor-in-chief.

As noted at the start of this article, I graduated first in the class in May 1950. The day before graduation, at the award ceremony, I received the John Bell Larson Medal. At the completion of the ceremony, I was interviewed by several reporters since the university apparently thought this was good publicity.

The next day, several of the Washington papers carried a story in their local sections that a woman had graduated first at GW Law School. I was so naive that, when asked by the reporters what I intended to do after graduation—since I had no offers and had not had any time to look for a position—I said I would take the summer off and decide in the fall. I never told them that the school was making no effort to help me.

With the help of a friend who was horrified when she learned of the Dean's attitude, I was told to send my resume to three recently appointed judges at the U.S. Tax Court. Judge Stephen Rice called me for an interview and offered me a position. Each judge had two positions for tax advisors. While some of the judges used the positions for law clerks, other advisors remained for their entire careers and were experts on federal taxation issues. Judge Rice agreed to keep his predecessor's senior tax advisor who had been there for many years. The junior advisor, also an experienced tax advisor for many years, was employed by another tax court judge.

As the first and only woman tax advisor, I was not "one of the boys." I never was invited to lunch with them, although on rare occasions I was invited to join them for coffee. I kept my distance, worked on cases, attended trials by Judge Rice, and learned a great deal.

The senior advisor did not want to share his office with a woman, so I shared the office of the second advisor of Judge Rice's predecessor, who had also been at the court for many years. Judge Rice's offer to me had been on the condition that this advisor would be asked to be the senior advisor of another member of the court, and in fact he was asked to be the senior advisor by the only woman judge on the court. She was not at all interested in helping young women in the law, was very difficult to work for, and had frequent staff turnover.

She quickly decided she did not want him on her staff, which put me in a very difficult position. Luckily, another judge decided to ask for his services, so he remained employed, but it did not help my situation. While I had nothing to do with his transfer, I was resented by the other tax advisors since they thought I had taken his position. They completely ignored me or addressed me as if I was a secretary. No one spoke to me directly about the situation, but Judge Rice told me that the rumor mill was busy making comments blaming me. I really believe that had I not been a woman, there would not have been the resentment that I encountered.

After two and a half years with Judge Rice, I inquired about a position with the tax division at the Department of Justice (DOJ), but was informally told by a friend who had a top position at the DOJ not to even bother filing an application because I was a woman. It was not until many years later that I learned that a woman was a senior attorney in the tax section. Had I known, I would have tried to talk to her. It is for this reason that I advise young women to seek out senior women to discuss their future. I also have mentored many younger women and am proud of their achievements.

I was never contacted by any law firm about a position and no one, including the school, made any suggestions about how to go about looking for one. In 1953 I set up a sole practice specializing in federal tax law. My husband had become a CPA and some of his colleagues and friends began calling me to meet with clients who had legal questions.

In those days I looked quite young, so I wore large dark-frame glasses and braids coiled on my head to appear older. Still, some of the clients (all men of course) were shocked to see me as the tax law expert. I could always sense the moment in the meeting when they stopped seeing me as a woman and began to recognize me as an expert who was advising them. Some became long-time clients.

My practice grew and became quite successful. It was primarily tax law and estate tax law. This led to also handling estates of deceased clients. I worked from home and saw clients in the office my husband shared with an attorney.

My son was born in 1955 and my daughter in 1956. I worked while they were asleep, and when they got older, I worked when they were in school. In 1962 I had rented the "rear entrance" of an international law firm. I would dictate to my secretary from home, so I was available for my children. The firm had a double door entrance in a well-located office building. They also had a rear entrance around the corner with a separate number on it. That opened on to two rooms that they were not using at that time. I rented the rooms and had a separate entrance through this "rear door."

These were the days before computers. I would go to the office after the children were in bed at night and review the documents my secretary had prepared. There was some consideration of my becoming associated with the firm, but I was unwilling to make any commitment while my children were young.

The challenges of having a family and a profession still exist today. I made the choice to limit my practice and make raising my children my primary concern. Once my children were in school all day, I spent more time in my office, but I was always there to see them off to school and I was there when they came home unless there was an emergency for a client that I had to resolve.

My husband, Max, was now a partner in a CPA firm in Washington, DC. In 1961 he had open-heart surgery to replace the aortic valve in his heart. Although he played tennis and other sports, the doctors felt he would be better off if the valve was replaced. This was in the early days of valve replacement and the artificial valve began to fail a few years after the surgery. He died in 1964, leaving me with two children aged seven and eight.

My practice had become quite large and not at all "part time," but I just did it at odd times of the day. My children, suffering from the loss of their father, desperately needed my attention. Thus, when I saw the sad expression on the face of one of my children, who I was trying to quiet while on the telephone with a client, I closed my practice in 1966. I discussed my decision with one of the partners in the law firm from whom I rented space, but really felt I had no choice since the welfare of my children was paramount and I felt they needed me.

About that time, Mary Bunting, Dean of Radcliffe, had just been appointed a Commissioner at the Atomic Energy Commission (AEC). Concerned that the country suffered a loss from the unwillingness of professionally educated women to work full time, she persuaded the AEC to start a pilot program of hiring such women on a part-time basis. While most were for scientists, I was offered one of the two legal positions.

In 1965, I became legal assistant to Paul Gantt, the chair of the AEC Board of Contract Appeals (AECBCA). I knew nothing of public procurement law, but Paul was an excellent mentor and teacher, and during the next seven years I learned this arcane area of the law. I participated in the hearings and worked on most of the cases.

Since the docket was not large, the AECBCA used a part-time panel of private practice attorney experts in the subject to serve as judges. Not only did I learn procurement law by participating in the appeals, I also advanced my experience with nonjury trial procedures and the Federal Rules of Evidence that I had used as a clerk at the Tax Court. I attended seminars on the subject and even coauthored several articles with Paul. It was an excellent postgraduate course on federal government procurement. Paul Gantt was one of the giants in the field at that time and was quite active in local and national organizations. I attended meetings with him and became acquainted with leaders in the field in addition to those who served as part-time judges to our board. Some of them became lifelong friends.

In 1967, Maurice Burg (Moe) and I married. He was a widower with two children, almost the exact ages as mine. When we married, all our children were between the ages of nine and twelve. We became and remain a wonderful family with three marvelous grandchildren. It was not easy. In fact, at times it was sheer hell.

Our children all had lost a parent and grief counseling did not really exist. Our rabbi was helpful in working with the children and I spent many a sleepless night comforting one or another of them. We worked hard at combining the family and were successful. We did realize that it was important for the two of us to get away alone and used meetings and speaking engagements to try to do it together.

Moe was a physician doing research at the National Institutes of Health and is world-renowned for his kidney research, for which he was elected to the National Academy of Sciences. Upon his retirement after fifty-seven years, an annual lectureship was established in his name. This is only one of many honors and awards he received in recognition of his outstanding work. We enjoyed fifty-five years together.

I continued working at the AEC on the twenty-hour-per-week part-time program, although I often worked up to thirty-nine and a half hours each week. As the children became older, I worked even longer hours.

In 1972, I was appointed as a judge on the Armed Services Board of Contract Appeals (ASBCA). While the United States is the largest contractor in the world, contractual disputes with the government cannot be heard in federal district courts. Over the years, there have been many attempts to tweak the process for trying and resolving these disputes.

When I became an ASBCA judge in 1972, many federal agencies had boards of contract appeals, and many of those had only a few disputes and only three judges, but the ASBCA had many disputes and thirty-eight judges. Today the Boards have largely been consolidated so there are only two, the ASBCA and the Civilian Board of Contract Appeals (CBCA). Disputes before the Boards often involve intricate technical issues, and hearings are nonjury. Appeals are to the Court of Appeals for the Federal Circuit and from there to the United States Supreme Court.

I was the first woman appointed to the ASBCA and remained the only one for the next eight years. I found the work challenging. With my science degree and my construction experience from my law practice, however, I was particularly well equipped to rule on the many technical issues that were involved in the disputes, a fact that was not acknowledged at first by the military personnel and attorneys involved in these appeals.

While my male colleagues were not challenged when blueprints were involved, I was doubted on many occasions even though I could read them and some of my male colleagues could not. Years later, after this came up during an award ceremony, a gentleman came up to me and identified himself as someone who I had taught to read blueprints when he was a young Army captain serving as a clerk to our Board.

I had other interesting experiences involving attorneys who doubted my ability to understand factual technical issues, and at times they were quite humorous. On one occasion, an Air Force sergeant insisted that it took no longer to polish stainless steel kitchen equipment so it had no streaks than it did to wipe down white kitchen appliances. Since I was still the only female judge on our Board, I called counsel to my chambers and told them they had the wrong judge. I told them I had polished too many stainless steel kitchen items to believe such nonsense, and I told them to settle the case. They did. Eventually my reputation eliminated doubts about my competence.

I had become a member of the American Bar Association Public Contract Law (PCL) Section at Paul Gantt's suggestion and began to attend meetings. It was a great way for me to enjoy discussions about procurement law in a way that was not possible from the bench. I served and then chaired various committees, was nominated to the PCL Section Council, and then became chair of the Section in 1985.

I was the first woman to chair the PCL Section; at that time there were very few women who were even members. It was really a man's world. Some of the men welcomed me, mentored me, and were very helpful, while others openly or behind the scenes opposed my advancement and leadership roles. When I was Vice-Chair, there was a concerted effort from some of the active members (including several past-Chairs) to nominate another member (male) to be Chair instead of me. Other active members (also including past-Chairs) worked hard to thwart this and were successful. To avoid this problem ever again developing, the PCL Section subsequently made it automatic for the Vice-Chair to become Chair.

I made every possible effort to have women be given a larger role, and I encouraged participation of women at every opportunity. For example, I was well known for always asking how many women had been invited to speak as experts and panel members, and to express my dismay in early years that all the speakers were men. I was successful. Program chairs would frequently approach me to tell me how many women they had invited to participate in panels or be nominated for office.

Several years ago, I asked for a point of personal privilege at a seminar to say how thrilled I was to see a panel composed of seven women who were legal counsel to major corporations or major divisions (including Lockheed and Northrop). The panel had one white male who introduced himself as the "token male" of the panel. Several of the women took the opportunity to publicly acknowledge the help my mentoring and encouragement had given them.

I believe it is the obligation, indeed the responsibility, of every woman attorney to mentor younger women, and I have been fortunate to receive many awards for doing so. One of which I am very proud is the Margaret Brent Women Lawyers of Achievement Award given by the ABA Commission on Women in the Profession. It is a pyramid filled with glass shards representing breaking the glass ceiling. I am grateful to the many women and men who supported my nomination for this award.

Today there are many successful women practicing public procurement law. I am proud of the achievements of many I have mentored. When women complain of long lines at the women's rest room at meetings, I tell them how pleased I am to see such lines. I remember when I was the only woman there and it was very lonesome. At least today we have seen changes in the number of women participants. Many have worked hard and become chair of the PCL Section, and recently the entire slate of officers was all women.

I remained at the ASBCA for twenty-three years. I was interviewed for various Federal Article 3 appointments but never had the necessary support to be nominated. In those instances where I was interviewed, it was because of unsolicited recommendations by counsel who had appeared before me. This was the case for other competent women of my generation. It was the reason for creation of the National Association of Women Judges, which created a useful network like the existing "old boy network."

Progress, although slow, continues to be made. We now have women on the Supreme Court. I look forward to the time when Justice Ruth Bader Ginsburg's wish for nine women on the Court comes to pass. My own ASBCA is about 50 percent women, and until recently the Chair of the CBCA was a woman.

Following my retirement, I served as a mediator or arbitrator where the parties preferred to use alternative dispute resolution. This has become a very popular way to resolve disputes. Because of the complexities of arcane public procurement law, many contractors and subcontractors prefer to use an alternative dispute procedure to resolve these disputes. I was flattered by the number of instances where I was asked to serve. I have always believed the best way to resolve contractual disputes is by settlement, and I was able to settle many cases on my docket. No judge will ever be aware of all the circumstances surrounding a dispute; the parties are in a far better position to resolve the matter. I especially enjoyed several instances where I was asked to serve as judge in a mock trial (a so-called red trial) when the company was preparing for a major trial. It gave me the opportunity to make helpful suggestions concerning a trial that I could never express while on the bench.

As I reflect on my ninety-five years, one of the things my career has lacked the most was a network of leaders to whom I could turn for help and advice. Certainly, helpful advice, whether taken or not, would have made some decisions less stressful.

I am pleased with the many young persons I have mentored along the way and thrilled with their achievements as judges, practitioners, and in academia. Today, more assistance exists for young women, and I hope it becomes even more readily available. I believe all of us who have attained some degree of success have the responsibility to help others do so. I was quite thrilled when, several years ago, GW Law School established a scholarship in my honor. I have tried to mentor each young woman who has been a recipient and hope to continue to do so. They and other young women and men I have mentored are really my legacy.

I recognize that there has been progress and some success for women in the law. As I have indicated, one of the major difficulties that I encountered was the lack of women to whom I could turn for help and advice. Today, more women in law school and during their early years in practice have access to older women who are willing to encourage and advise them.

I had many turns in my road. Whether any would have been different or easier had there been someone other than parents or male colleagues to help me will never be known. My career has been fun and successful. Like many successful women of my generation, I have many "firsts" in my curriculum vitae. Some have been recognized by others and I am flattered by the awards that I have been given over the years.

My life has not all been work. My family remains an important part of my life; I have watched my children and grandchildren develop and have made wonderful friends along the way. Moe and I traveled both professionally and for enjoyment. We enjoyed family vacations to interesting parts of the world and spent many vacations fly fishing at our home in Montana or on trips to New Zealand, Chile, and Argentina. My yellow brick road has had bumps and surprising detours leading me in directions I never thought I would follow. My life has been interesting and rewarding. I hope that those who read this can say the same as they reflect on their lives.

My decisions to accept the scholarship to George Washington University, to leave medical school, to study law were all critical decisions in my life. As I reflect upon them, I am not sorry about the ones I made. I have a wonderful family, two successful marriages, an interesting career, and I helped make cracks in the glass ceiling.

BIO

Ruth C. Burg

After twenty-two years as an Administrative Judge at the Armed Services Board of Contract Appeals, Ruth C. Burg currently acts as a neutral in alternative dispute resolution matters, serving as a mediator, neutral advisor, or arbitrator on contract matters, public and private, or as an expert witness or consultant on public contract matters. She is a recognized expert in complex cost accounting and major construction issues.

Appointed to the Armed Services Board in 1972, she retired in February 1995.

A graduate of George Washington University Columbian College, she received her Juris Doctor *cum laude* from that University's School of Law, graduating first in her class. Early in her career, she specialized in Federal Taxation, serving as a law clerk to Judge Stephen E. Rice of the Tax Court of the United States, the first woman to serve in a Tax Court clerkship.

After leaving the Tax Court, Judge Burg practiced tax law in the District of Columbia and Maryland. In order to give more time to her children, in 1965, she became the part time legal assistant to the Chairman of the Atomic Energy Commission Board of Contract Appeals and continued in that capacity until her appointment to the Armed Services Board of Contract Appeals.

She is the recipient of many honors, including the DC Bar Association Beatrice Rosenberg Award for Excellence in Government Service, the George Washington University Law Alumni Association Fulbright Distinguished Public Service Award, and the Margaret Brent Women Lawyers of Achievement Award. She was also the first recipient of the American Bar Association Public Contract Law Section Fellows Spirit of Leadership award. The Public Contract Law Section of the American Bar Association created an annual Ruth C. Burg Luncheon Honoring Women in Public Contract Law.

In 2019, GW surprised her with the Ruth C. Burg scholarship at GW Law School, also affording her the privilege to meet and mentor the recipients.

Judge Burg has been active in legal and community organizations. For example, she was founding president of a chapter of B'nai B'rith Women and served as

International President of Phi Sigma Sigma Fraternity, one of the first sororities founded and open to women of all religious and ethnic backgrounds. She served on the Board of Advisors of the Federal Contract Reports and on the Court of Federal Claims Advisory Council and is presently a member of their Friends of the Court.

Her major bar activities have been with the American Bar Association, where she is a Past Chair (1984–1985) and a Fellow of the Public Contract Law Section, a Life Fellow of the American Bar Association Foundation, and a former member of the Standing Committee on Judicial Selection, Tenure and Compensation. She has written and lectured extensively, primarily in the area of public contract law.

BIO

We Couldn't Say "No" to Vaino

8

Consuelo Bland Marshall

*E*ven trailblazers need role models. Judge Consuelo Bland Marshall, herself a pioneer in the profession and on the bench, benefited greatly from the mentorship and sponsorship of the first Black woman judge in California.

Judge Marshall's anecdote about the way in which her relationship with her mentor began is also instructive. Her worried response to her mentor's initial expression of interest reveals a common pattern of behavior among women, yet overcoming that fear was the first step in developing a crucial relationship in Judge Marshall's life.

Her story makes clear that both mentor and mentee did something very right, and Judge Marshall has been paying it forward ever since.

Lauren Stiller Rikleen, Editor

I grew up in the segregated South. My family's life experiences were separated from the experiences of white families in Knoxville—our church, our schools, indeed, every aspect of our lives. We moved to Los Angeles when I was in high school, my first experience in an integrated environment. I had always wanted to be a lawyer, inspired by the civil rights movement and the opportunity to achieve change.

When I graduated from law school, I went to law firms, resume in hand, looking forward to beginning my career. I recall entering elevators which, back then, were always run by Black elevator operators. I also recall elevator rides where skeptical operators would dampen my optimism with their more realistic assessment of the likelihood of my job search ending successfully. I would leave those elevators, optimism intact, only to be told by the receptionists at the firms that any appointment I had was not able to go forward, or that they would review my résumé and call back. They never did. I also recall elevator rides back to the lobby where the operator had an I-told-you-so look.

I applied for an opening at the City Attorney's Office and was told that they didn't hire women lawyers. I ultimately had an opportunity to meet with the City Attorney, who told me that the reason they did not hire women was because they would be exposed to unseemly people and experiences in the role. By the time I got home, however, I was the recipient of a job offer.

It was in that first job at the City Attorney's Office where I was appearing daily at the Los Angeles Courthouse that I first saw Vaino Spencer. I was so impressed. She was beautiful, tall, stunning, and immaculately dressed. I did not introduce myself because I was a young lawyer, and she was a judge.

I was later assigned to her courtroom for a hearing. After my appearance, her bailiff approached me and invited me into her chambers. I thought I had done something terribly wrong, but I learned she wanted to get to know me.

That was my first formal meeting with her, and I will never forget that day. She served tea in a sterling silver tea service with China cups and saucers. I later learned that she reached out to many young lawyers, especially young women lawyers.

Justice Vaino Hassan Spencer was the first African American woman appointed as a judge in the state of California. Born and raised in Los Angeles, as a teenager she appeared as a dancer in two movies, along with her father, Abdul Hassan.

Instead of dance, Vaino Spencer pursued a career in the law. She graduated from Polytechnic High School in 1938, was an undergraduate at Los Angeles City College, and earned her JD from Southwestern Law School in 1952. Vaino Spencer was the third African American woman in California to pass the state bar examination and the third to open a law practice in Los Angeles.

But it was in 1961 when Governor Edmund G. "Pat" Brown appointed Vaino Spencer to the Los Angeles Municipal Court bench that confirmed her status as a true pioneer, because she became the first African American woman judge in California and the third in the nation. At the time, she had not yet reached the tenth anniversary of her graduation from Southwestern Law School. She was later appointed as a Los Angeles Superior Court Judge in 1976 and named as Presiding Justice of the California Court of Appeal, Second Appellate District, in 1980. She retired in 2007, after a distinguished forty-six-year career on the bench.

As one of the longest serving judges in California, Vaino Spencer was truly a trailblazer for women, and particularly African American women, in the legal profession. She was active in the Civil Rights movement and a leader in the community. She was also recognized for her groundbreaking efforts in support of gender equity in the legal profession and efforts to increase the number of women appointed to the bench.

In the 1970s, she founded the Black Women Lawyers Association, and cofounded the National Association of Women Judges (NAWJ) with Justice Joan Dempsey Klein. Years later, the NAWJ awarded the first Justice Vaino Spencer Leadership Award in her honor.

Beyond the courtroom, Vaino Spencer was dedicated to community service. Throughout her career, she served in numerous leadership positions, such as the California Law Revision Commission, National Judicial Council, Judicial Council of California, and Attorney General's Advisory Committee on Constitutional Rights, and as an officer and director of the Los Angeles County Commission on Justice. She also held leadership positions in over two dozen professional and community organizations and was the recipient of many honors and awards.

To the many fortunate young lawyers who crossed her path, Vaino became our mentor, advising us of job opportunities, career goals and objectives, and planning our next steps. She invited us to attend bar functions and encouraged us to serve on committees and boards so we would be better known in the community.

And we were willing participants because you could never say "no" to Vaino, and I never did. Through the years, she would tell me about job opportunities and positions for which I should apply.

There were times when I felt I was not ready. It was early in my career. I had a young family and was trying to balance family and career. Flexibility was so important that I left the City Attorney's Office when I was asked to join a colleague—Johnnie Cochran—who was leaving the city to set up his own law firm. He was willing to give me whatever flexibility I needed, so I accepted his offer.

Within a few years, I was encouraged to apply for a position in the Juvenile Court that sounded like a wonderful opportunity but lacked flexibility. Vaino, however, provided the encouragement I needed to be willing to accept the position. With the active support of my husband, who used his greater flexibility to step into additional responsibilities with the children, I began my career in the court system.

With each opportunity to advance, I was again encouraged by Vaino and others to garner the confidence to accept the role. They encouraged me to respond affirmatively when I questioned whether I could do the job and made me realize that these were opportunities that might not be available later.

I continued to advance in my legal career. I became a California Superior Court Commissioner, California Municipal Court Judge, California Superior Court Judge, and finally, United States District Judge.

Vaino Spencer attended my swearing-in ceremonies and spoke at my enrobing ceremony for the U.S. District Court. I knew she was not just doing this for me, but for many of the young lawyers including women who were appointed to the bench.

Now, I am a mentor applying the teachings of Justice Spencer to my mentees—a role I especially enjoy. My mentees are former law clerks and judicial externs, and others I meet along the way who are from diverse backgrounds. Like Vaino, I advise them about career paths, ask them to serve as diverse law representatives to circuit conferences, apply for positions within the judiciary, and become active in bar associations. They are ambitious and I am glad they have more opportunities today than were available to me early in my career, as they serve in a wide variety of legal positions. One is even going through the confirmation process and hopefully will be appointed to the U.S. District Court on which I serve.

They have sought my advice on a wide range of challenges that demonstrate that we still have a long road ahead, as much as significant progress has been made. They worry about whether biases will impact their opportunities for promotion, they question their ability to manage their work-life responsibilities well, and they fear for their future when considering how to confront sexual harassment in the workplace. With their concerns, however, they have all made wonderful contributions to the law and community and I enjoy watching them pierce the glass ceiling.

I also enjoy mentoring young people who are interested in a career in law. A few years ago, I participated in a career day program at a local college where I met a high school student whose school was nearby. She introduced herself and we talked about the law, and she told me she was going to be a judge. We talked, she asked if she could visit in chambers, I agreed, and she came to visit.

It was during that visit that I learned she was only fourteen. She spent the summer at our courthouse, meeting judges and lawyers and thinking more about her career as a lawyer. This year she received her Master's Degree in Public Policy and is presently attending law school. She became one of my mentees and we continue to talk often as she makes career decisions. I have no doubt she may one day achieve her goal.

As I learned from Justice Spencer, to be a good mentor one must be a good listener, develop a relationship with others, be available to give advice when asked but also give the mentee someone with whom they are comfortable reaching out and talking not just about career planning but about life in general.

I am glad to be able to share my life experiences with my mentees and, in turn, I have learned much from them about their cultures, their lives, and the paths they have walked. This has been helpful in decision making as a judge and has enriched my life.

Support from other women and supporting other women has been transformative in my life and career.

BIO

Consuelo Bland Marshall

Consuelo B. Marshall is a Senior District Judge of the United States District Court for the Central District of California. She attended Howard University Law School where (as one of three women) she graduated third in her class and was an editor of the *Howard Law Journal*. She began her legal career as a Deputy City Attorney in Los Angeles. She was the first woman hired as a lawyer by the Los Angeles City Attorney's Office. She later entered private practice at the law firm of Cochran & Atkins. She left private practice for the bench, serving as a Los Angeles Superior Court Commissioner, Inglewood Municipal Court Judge, and Los Angeles Superior Court Judge.

Judge Marshall was appointed to the United States District Court for the Central District of California in 1980 by President Jimmy Carter. She became the seventh woman of color to serve as an Article III judge in the country. In 2001, she became the first woman to serve as Chief Judge of the Central District of California. Throughout her judicial career, she has been an inspiration and mentor to hundreds of lawyers and judges who have followed her into the legal profession.

Judge Marshall has received many awards, including the Criminal Bar Association Judicial Excellence Award, induction into the Langston Bar Association Hall of Fame and the City of Los Angeles Hall of Fame, Los Angeles County Bar Association Criminal Justice Section Career Achievement Award, Los Angeles County Bar Association Outstanding Jurist Award, California Women Lawyers' Joan Dempsey Klein Distinguished Jurist Award, and the American Bar Association Margaret Brent Women Lawyers of Achievement Award.

Judge Marshall has long been active in the legal community—locally, nationally, and internationally—chairing and participating in committees and boards for the Ninth Circuit, the Federal Bar Association, and the Association of Business Trial Lawyers. She has been a faculty member for The Rutter Group and the Trial Advocacy Workshop at Harvard Law School. She has lectured in Nigeria, Ghana,

Zimbabwe, Yugoslavia, Italy, and Greece. Judge Marshall has also been active in the local nonlegal community, serving on the Board of Directors for the Weingart Center, a nonprofit facility for the homeless, and the Legal Aid Foundation of Los Angeles. She served on the RAND Institute of Civil Justice Board of Overseers and on the Board of Directors of Equal Justice Works. Judge Marshall chaired the Ninth Circuit Pacific Islands Committee from 2006 to 2017. This committee oversees judicial training for the Pacific Islands of Guam, Saipan, Palau, American Samoa, the Federated States of Micronesia, and the Republic of the Marshall Islands. Judge Marshall serves on the Ninth Circuit Fairness Committee and participates in the Court's community outreach programs: Just the Beginning Summer Institute for high school students, Teachers' Institute, and the American Bar Association's Judicial Internship Opportunity Program.

BIO

Challenging the Status Quo

9

Irma S. Raker

*C*ountry *clubs that exclude all but privileged white men perpetuate systems of inequality. Such social clubs are where deals are quietly made and business relationships develop and grow. Exclusion from these opportunities means exclusion from all the professional benefits that emanate from the privilege of belonging.*

In describing her role in a case that challenged these bastions of exclusivity, Judge Irma Raker demonstrates how the impact of one court decision can reverberate throughout the country. Her legal reasoning drew a line in the sand for clubs that denied admittance to women while enjoying their state's financial support for their activities.

The Burning Tree Club may remain a bastion of exclusion and an anachronism of the past, but Judge Raker's pioneering decision had an indelible impact and led to the doors of many social clubs finally opening to women.

Lauren Stiller Rikleen, Editor

My legal career might be considered traditional today, but back then in the 1950s, law was unorthodox and unusual for women, although it seemed normal and natural to me at the time. From the time I was a child, watching my father and uncle practice law, I wanted to be a lawyer.

I graduated from college in June 1959, and planned to attend law school at New York University School of Law in September. I attended a wonderful summer program at the Hague Academy of International Law at The Hague, the Netherlands, on a scholarship from the Maxwell School of Citizenship of Syracuse University, my alma mater.

Ah, "the best laid plans of mice and [wo]men often go awry." Instead of law school, I became engaged to my current husband, got married, moved to Washington, DC, and raised three children.

At the age of thirty-two, when the youngest child was three years old, and the oldest eight years old, I enrolled at the Washington College of Law of the American University, and while juggling child-care, motherhood, wife, and community activities, I received my law degree and entered the practice of law.

In 1973, when I graduated from law school, there were few women in my class and hardly any women practicing criminal law. I was fortunate to be hired as the first woman Assistant State's Attorney for Montgomery County, Maryland. At the time, there were no women judges in the county, no women public defenders, no women sheriffs, hardly any women police officers, and certainly no women prosecutors. Happily, all those numbers are different today, and the prosecutor's office has more women than men attorneys.

I was appointed to the bench in 1980 and served as a trial judge from 1980 until 1994, when the Governor of Maryland appointed me to serve as a judge on the Court of Appeals of Maryland, the State's Supreme Court. At the time of my appointment, again, like the prosecutor's office and the trial bench, I was the only woman judge out of a seven-member court. And again, happily, the numbers today are different. Maryland's Court of Appeals has a majority of women judges, and until recently, the Chief Judge was a woman.

As a judge for over forty years, I have ruled on many precedent-setting cases, and as a judge sitting on the state's highest court, I have participated in many cases challenging the status quo. Interestingly, however, if asked to choose to write about one particular case, I would focus on a case when I was a trial judge—a case that had widespread impact beyond what one would think in regard to a lower court opinion. That case was *Bainum v. Burning Tree Club.*

Why, when I have sat on cases ranging from the death penalty to redistricting to contributory negligence versus comparative negligence to de facto parenthood, would I pick a case where I was a lone circuit court trial judge? The answer to me is easy. It is to emphasize that each case we hear is very important to the litigants but can have ramifications and ripples far beyond the individual parties, no matter the level of court.

My "little" case was reported in the *International Herald Tribune, New York Times, Washington Post,* the local newspapers, and the national golf magazines. As a result of my trial court opinion, which was affirmed on appeal, golf clubs around the country voluntarily changed many of their sexist rules, such as requiring women to tee off only during the week because the working men needed the tee times on the weekends. And men-only grills were often abolished. Many private social clubs changed their policies and began admitting women, and indeed, permitting women to enter the club from the front door instead of the back or side doors.

A little background. Burning Tree Club is an established men-only golf club located on Burdette Road in Bethesda, Maryland. It has long enjoyed the reputation as a high-end golf club where United States Presidents, United States Senators, and Congressmen play golf. Membership was (and still is) open only to men. The Club is described online in Wikipedia as follows:

> Burning Tree Club is a private, all-male golf club in Bethesda, Maryland. The course at Burning Tree has been played by Arch Manning, numerous presidents, foreign dignitaries, high-ranking executive officials, members of Congress, and military leaders. The course was designed by architect Alister MacKenzie.

In a 1983 article by Ben A. Franklin, Special to the *New York Times,* titled "Problem at Burning Tree That Won't Go Away," the Club "problem" became national news. Mr. Franklin noted that the Club, founded as an all-male club in 1922 on 225 acres, was "founded by men impatient over the Sunday morning queues, probably of women, on the greens at the Chevy Chase Club," noting that the problem was women, and that they will not go away. Franklin noted:

> A good measure of Burning Tree's cachet stems from its mixed membership of corporate chairmen, influential lawyers and public officials. The club has long made a practice of extending honorary memberships to the loftiest layers of Washington officialdom, from Presidents to members of the Cabinet and the Supreme Court. Presidents Eisenhower and Kennedy were frequent players. . . . President Reagan, a nongolfer, is not a member. But Vice President Bush is. So are Richard M. Nixon, Gerald R. Ford, Warren E. Burger, Spiro T. Agnew, Barry Goldwater, William Randolph Hearst Jr., Edmund S. Muskie and Donald T. Regan, to name a few.

Maryland treasures green, open spaces and the state property tax code provides a tax benefit for preserving open spaces, including "open space" for country clubs. The clubs receive a tax deferral from the annual real estate tax, as the tax due is calculated on an open-space agricultural basis rather than on the best and highest commercial use. Franklin reported, back then, that the club pays only $13,600 of what otherwise would be an annual assessment of $165,600.

The 1965 Maryland tax exemption law provided for the tax exemption. Interestingly, in 1972, the Maryland General Assembly proposed an amendment to the State Constitution, which was passed by the voters—Article 46 of the Maryland Declaration of Rights, the State's Equal Rights Amendment barring sex discrimination. Thereafter, the tax exemption statute was amended in 1974 to include bans on discrimination based upon race, color, creed, sex, or national origin.

But a provision stated that the sex discrimination ban did not apply "to any club whose facilities are operated with the primary purpose, as determined by the attorney general, to serve or benefit members of a particular sex . . . ," sometimes referred to as the "Burning Tree Loophole."

Needless to say, many women organizations and women taxpayers resented the tax benefit to a club that would not admit women but enjoyed the benefit of tax exemptions supported by women taxpayer money. Legislation to withdraw the tax advantage to the club failed in the early 1980s, and a lawsuit was filed by State Senator Stewart Bainum Jr. of Montgomery County and his sister, Barbara Bainum Renschler, in the Circuit Court for Montgomery County, Maryland.

The lawsuit challenged the "loophole" and asked that Ms. Renschler's application for membership at the club be considered as well as a declaration that the club not receive the tax exemption if it did not admit women. Former Attorney General Benjamin Civiletti represented Burning Tree Club.

With that as a backdrop, I was a relatively new Circuit Court Judge and the only female judge on the court. I was probably the only judge who did not play golf at Burning Tree Club. And I was the only judge on the court that did not recuse. All the other judges disqualified themselves. I got off the bench at 4:00 p.m. one day and saw on the docket for the next day a motion for summary judgment in the case of *Bainum v. Burning Tree Country Club*. Little did I realize the magnitude of the case.

I heard magnificent arguments from both parties, took the matter under advisement, and issued a written opinion sometime later, knowing full well that my court was only a weighing station before the case was heard by the Court of Appeals. My ruling: The Club, as a private club, could maintain the membership policy of its choice but it would have to reverse its "men only" rule if it wanted to continue getting a break on its state and local property taxes. Violative of the state's Equal Rights Amendment, Maryland could not continue to grant tax breaks to the Club as long as it denied membership to women. The Court of Appeals of Maryland ultimately affirmed the Circuit Court ruling. *Burning Tree Club v. Bainum*, 305 Md. 53 (1985).

The Club had a choice. As Senator Bainum stated, "Either admit women or pay your taxes like the rest of us." UPI Archives, Sept. 14, 1984. What did the Club choose? The answer to that question is the Club chose to maintain its all-male membership and forgo the tax break. And so it is today. But that is not the end of the story.

Even though the Club remains an all-male club today, the Circuit Court ruling had wide ramifications, beyond the borders of Montgomery County. Aside from extensive media coverage, the case has been explained, quoted from, and cited before Congress during Congressional hearings on the impact of the Equal Rights Amendment.

The case, in my mind, shows the challenging of the status quo, and the importance of every court decision at each level of court. Senator Stewart Bainum, Jr. and his sister challenged the status quo of a prestigious and powerful club. And as a Circuit Court Judge, my ruling changed the status quo as well. It shows that every court decision has ramifications beyond the immediate case and can change society and mores.

BIO

Irma Raker

Judge Irma Raker began her legal career in 1973 as an Assistant State's Attorney for Montgomery County, Maryland, as the county's first female prosecutor. In 1979, she joined the law firm of Sachs, Greenebaum & Taylor as a partner, and in 1980 she was appointed by the Governor of Maryland to serve as a judge in the District Court of Maryland. Two years later, the Governor appointed her to serve as an associate judge in the Circuit Court for Montgomery County, the general jurisdiction court, where she served until she was appointed in 1994 to the state's supreme court, the Court of Appeals of Maryland.

In 2008, Judge Raker took senior status from the Court and currently sits by designation as a judge on Maryland's two appellate courts.

Judge Raker was very involved in the American Bar Association (ABA), the Maryland State Bar Association (MSBA), the Maryland chapter of the National Association of Women Judges (NAWJ), and judicial activities. A few of her notable activities are Chairperson of the Pattern Jury Instructions Committee of the MSBA from 1981 through 2008, Chairperson of the Maryland Access to Justice Commission, and Chairperson of numerous Task Forces of the ABA Criminal Justice Standards Committee.

Her numerous awards and honors include the ABA Margaret Brent Women Lawyers of Achievement Award, Maryland Daily Record Leadership in Law Award, Outstanding 100 Women, and the Maryland Bar Foundation Vernon Eney Award.

Judge Raker has been engaged as mediator, arbitrator, neutral case evaluator, and Claims Adjudicator in class actions. Since retiring in 2008 from the Court of Appeals, she has mediated over 1,000 cases involving construction disputes, employment disputes, breach of contract, defamation, motor torts, medical, legal, and dental malpractice, invasion of privacy, and sexual assault.

Living the Life of the Moment

10

Rosemary Barkett

*J*udge Barkett's story about her parents' decades-long journey to America is a quintessential immigration story, reminding us how much families will sacrifice to provide a better, safer life for their children. Like so many others—in history and continuing today— leaving the country of one's birth requires fortitude and resilience that becomes a part of the family legacy passed down to each generation.

Judge Barkett also describes the role that luck has played in her life, while recognizing the importance of two other factors that are foundational to good luck: hard work and a loving family that always supported her dreams and the paths that she pursued. And while we know that also having a support network can be essential, she demonstrates that such a network is developed by a willingness to accept a variety of opportunities and the confidence to say yes when that network pushes you forward.

Finally, her description of her own confirmation and retention challenges reinforces the need for lawyers to speak out to preserve the independence of our courts and keep politics out of the judicial system.

Lauren Stiller Rikleen, Editor

When I was initially contacted to contribute to this project, I must confess I initially rebelled against my usual reflexive response to say "yes" to every ask. I rebelled because this project envisioned chronicling personal life experiences and reflections, which was a much harder task than writing about some legal problem. Since you are reading this, you can see I gave in, and I will start by telling you that the overarching theme of my life has been extraordinary luck. That is not to say that I have not worked hard, but hard work alone without luck would never be enough.

Start with being lucky enough to be born to a family that loves you, cares for you, and supports you in all your endeavors. One surely cannot take credit for where and to whom one is born. Nor is that to say one cannot overcome any kind of adversity and that many do. I am simply saying that my path was a lucky one just in terms of its beginning.

I am often asked to name my "role models" and I always feel the expected answer is some Justice, or perhaps a lawyer or other public figure. But the traits I always want to emulate are those I observed daily in the people closest to me, starting with my parents, whose lives, and the extraordinary way they lived them, have always been role models.

Our parents were born in Syria in a small farming community around the turn of the last century. They were—when I stop to think about it—wildly independent and adventurous, even for those days.

Their marriage was arranged in accordance with the custom of the times. She was around fourteen, he was nineteen. Mom told us she tried hard to get out of it because she only knew him as the guy who stole her chickens. Fortunately for us, she did not get out of it. They were together for more than seventy-six years, after which they died eighteen days apart.

Approximately five years after their marriage and the birth of their first son, they attempted to leave Syria to join my father's brothers, who had recently left for America, as the family farm could not support all the brothers and their families-to-be. But the immigrant quota from Syria into the United States for that year had been filled and they were told to apply for entry the following year. With the impatience which I now know to be a pervasive family trait, they were not about to wait a whole year.

So, they somehow ascertained how best to leave Syria, cross Europe, reach Marseille, find a ship bound for Mexico, and arrive there with their baby somewhere in the early 1920s when they themselves were only in *their* 20s.

However, upon arrival, they found they would be unable to continue their journey to America because Mexico's quota of immigrants to the United States was also filled for *that* year. This time it was even harder to wait—for they had little money, no family, knew no one except other immigrants, could not speak the language, and were not familiar with the customs of the country.

The quota system precluded them from traveling into the states initially for several years and then my mother's pregnancies and World War II delayed it further. At the beginning of their sojourn in Mexico, my father began work as a peddler selling goods in the mountains of Mexico to support his family. By the time I was born, my parents were owners of a successful small department store. But, notwithstanding being successful merchants, the goal of reuniting with family was never lost. Our parents, with all my sisters and brothers in tow, ultimately managed to join my father's four brothers and their families in Miami, Florida, in approximately 1946 when I was six years old. They had lived successfully in Mexico for twenty years, during which I and all my siblings, with the exception of my Syrian-born eldest brother, were born.

I could write pages and pages more of the wonderful family stories about their adventures in Syria and then in Mexico, including how my mother's grandfather in Syria, as Mayor of their village, converted the entire village to Roman Catholicism, and my father's various escapes from bandidos in the mountains of Mexico, but will leave those stories for other days.

My point is that there is no better example for living a life than theirs. They worked hard in Syria as youngsters; they were brave enough to leave a country and family they knew and end up in a second country with a new language and new customs to learn; they succeeded there but left twenty years later to start all over again in a third country, having to learn yet another language and different cultural norms. And beyond examples of family unity, of incredible bravery, of endurance, of perseverance, of continuing good humor, and so much more, I was also lucky to have been exposed to the mixture of Mexican, Syrian, and American languages, food, cultures, and heritage.

Our experiences of being welcomed in both Mexico and America, and of making contributions to both countries, make it hard to understand the fear and rejection of immigrants that exist today. I have addressed that subject a lot over the years and will continue to try to remind us of the place of immigrants in our history, and more importantly, how much richer a country or an individual becomes by embracing, rather than fearing, "others."

At any rate, we arrived in Miami, Florida, and I was enrolled in Gesu School and went on to high school at Notre Dame Academy, both operated by the Sisters of St. Joseph. We spoke no English when I enrolled in first grade, though I don't think it took us long to learn as we were the only people that spoke Spanish. It would not be until many, many years later that we saw the influx of other Spanish speakers from Cuba into Florida.

In those days, Miami was a simple small town. On arrival, my parents purchased a small corner grocery store with a house next door, a few blocks from the Orange Bowl, and my sister and I would deliver groceries on our bikes throughout the neighborhood.

Then, during my last year of high school, although I had been accepted to Catholic University in Washington, DC, where I intended to study theater arts (another story for another time), I decided I had a vocation for service. So, upon my graduation from high school, instead of college, I entered a religious order, the Sisters of St. Joseph of St. Augustine. My family was not happy about this turn of events, but a seventeen-year-old on a mission is not easily deterred, and, although not too happy, they were ultimately, as usual, supportive.

I served for several years, and much was happening during the years I taught as a member of the Order—the civil rights movement, the Vietnam war, the murder of President Kennedy. After much soul searching (sorry for the overused phrase) for several years, I ultimately left the convent, feeling that I could serve in a different and perhaps more directly relevant way.

There were many experiences while a member of the Order for which I am grateful. I know I have benefited from the richness of that experience. I also credit my time in the convent with the development of two useful attributes that have served me well throughout my life. First, I think that as a result of the deference always shown to a "woman of the cloth," I started my "lay" life with a sense of self-confidence, which certainly helped as I navigated a primarily male professional world. Second, I had developed the belief and expectation that people would always treat you fairly, decently, and well.

After a year of teaching in a public school in my first year as a "lay person" (an interesting contrast to my years of teaching in Catholic schools as a nun), I entered law school at the University of Florida. Why? Although I loved teaching and have continued to do it in some fashion all my life, I wanted independence from the constraint of a classroom, and I also had become inordinately curious about why certain laws existed. (OK, some family members said I simply loved arguing and so I should become a lawyer.)

There were very few women, of course, enrolled in law school in 1968 or 1969. And it was there, and later in my professional life, that my convent experiences and attitudes, I think, served as a shield from much of the direct discrimination suffered by many of my sisters. As I said earlier, I think my naive self-confident expectation of fair treatment perhaps shielded me from perceiving the discriminatory nature of some behavior, which I recognize now.

I went to work for a small trial firm in West Palm Beach and discovered that trying cases to juries was sort of like teaching school or directing a play. After a few years, our firm broke up, as firms are wont to do, and I was lucky enough to be appointed to the Fifteenth Judicial Circuit Court in Palm Beach County. After a few more years, I moved to the Fourth District Court of Appeals and then was appointed by our Governor, Bob Graham, to the Florida Supreme Court in 1984.

I guess at this point I should digress to explain a bit better about what I mean by "luck" as I certainly do not want to deny the importance of hard work. Louis Pasteur has been quoted as saying that "chance favors only the prepared mind." Thus, the importance of being open to and ready to accept any challenge cannot be underestimated. But one must be realistic enough to acknowledge that there are many "prepared minds" and the right "chance" does not favor every one of them. Thus, it is silly not to acknowledge the role fortune plays in being chosen for a particular position while at the same time being prepared when the opportunity arises.

With reference to the "preparation" part, I think each person's path will be different. Mine was more reactive. There really was nothing in my background to suggest to me that I could be a judge, so it never occurred to me to seek the position. The opportunity was presented by a few members of the trial bar on the Judicial Nominating Committee who asked me, as a trial lawyer, to submit my name for the trial bench.

When asked (as in this article) what factors account for having been approached and then appointed to the bench, I would say that it was trying to live a life in accordance with what I had been exposed to at home, in school, and in the convent. That meant replicating my parents' work ethic: that is, working as hard as you can at every job you are given and persevering until it's done or you recognize that it cannot be done. It meant being willing to always do more than the job called for by participating in committees or extracurricular activities or projects.

It meant trying to be kind to everyone you meet and keeping an open mind about everything. It also meant enjoying life by taking advantage of opportunities that broaden your interests and make you a more complete human being, like travel or music or sports or all of the above. When these attributes are inherent in your lifestyle, these traits are noticed and considered by others.

So, when asked to submit my name for consideration for the trial bench I said yes. I will add that my family kept me grounded with the understanding that there are others as capable and equally "prepared" who could have been chosen instead, and that any heights you might achieve professionally might not be the most important thing in life.

Which reminds me of one of my favorite stories about my mother during my tenure on the Florida Supreme Court. Florida employs a merit retention system for all appellate judges. The system required Supreme Court justices to win the approval of voters in the first state election after their appointments and every six years after that. (More about merit retention later.)

During my first election cycle, my sister was taking my mother to vote, and my mother was complaining that I had not been home very often after my appointment. My sister explained that Tallahassee, where the justices resided, was much farther away from Miami than West Palm Beach where I had lived before my appointment. Also, she pointed out that my workload was much greater and so "she [me] was not able to come home to visit as often." My mother's very serious reply was "then, why are we voting for her?" (I am still not sure whether I received my own mother's vote.)

At any rate, I ultimately retained my seat, and I cannot be more grateful for the opportunity to serve in the judiciary. Both the trial and appellate courts were extensions of my trial practice and I continued to learn and love the law (at least as it used to be then).

My experiences on the Florida Supreme Court, however, brought much different challenges. Although I knew how to go about deciding cases, I was surprised by how much more the Florida Supreme Court had to do besides simply deciding cases. And being Chief Judge was quite an education. Besides the tedious administrative work of preparing the judicial budget for the legislature and deciding how many new judges were warranted by the state, there was also the rulemaking responsibilities and the other work in conjunction with the Florida Bar.

What made life a bit more interesting was the correspondence I received as Chief Justice. One example resulted from an opinion I wrote on behalf of the court, disbarring a lawyer who then sued all the members of the court. In the caption he listed the full names of every male justice and then added "and that bimbo Barkett." Or the surprising (but really sad) letter Justice McDonald received while he was chief from a lawyer saying that he had been a witness when Justice Barkett killed a World War II pilot; that she should be removed from the court and that he was prepared to take my place because he really needed the money. (Justice McDonald forwarded the letter to me with a note saying: "have you been lying about your age!")

A gentler letter was the one telling me that the writer disagreed with an opinion of mine and ending with the words: "You have slipped off the path—in time you will return, please hurry." There were so many more, but you get the gist.

And then there was my Merit Retention Campaign. Until the nineties, it seemed that members of all political parties, although disagreeing about policies, were civil to one another. The Court worked with the legislature on administrative matters and both were respectful of the other. In 1990, however, Florida's merit selection of judges was distressingly politicized and Justice Leander Shaw, the Court's first and only Black justice, was challenged, allegedly as a result of his vote in the Supreme Court's ruling that struck down mandatory parental consent for minors who seek abortions. He fought successfully against the single-interest group that challenged him, but they returned with a vengeance to challenge me in 1992.

I will say that was not my favorite part of the Supreme Court experience. However, yet again, my family (whether or not they agreed with all my decisions), my friends, and all the people I had met and worked with along the way lent the support that made my first ever "political campaign" endurable and, sometimes, even funny. I survived the challenge and I thought that was the end of having to deal with this one issue group who used very disagreeable tactics to try to achieve their goal. Sigh. It was not to be.

President Clinton was elected during my tenure as Chief Justice and, again, I was fortunate enough to be the one asked to serve on the Eleventh Circuit Court of Appeal. The group that had challenged my retention in Florida, however, reprised their attack through their representatives in Congress and I again had a bit of a fight on my hands. (Many funny stories and many lessons learned during this experience.)

The confirmation process was indeed eye opening and astonishing in many ways. I will confess to having been incredibly naive about the role politics plays in the process. I was fortunate to have had then-Senator Joe Biden chair the Judiciary Committee. He referenced his own Catholic education by asking me at the beginning of my hearing if I intended to revert to my convent days and rap any knuckles that day. Before I could stop myself, I responded that it would depend on whether the Senators behaved themselves. (I could hear the sighs of my Justice Department "handlers.") I survived, but again learned a lot, although it was a bit difficult to suffer the indignity of being criticized so publicly, even though it was for policy and legal choices rather than for personal traits.

My nomination resulted in a debate on the Senate floor and my mother again broke the tension. Every time a Senator spoke against me arguing that I was too liberal, my mother would glare at C-Span and mutter "desgraciado."

After a lot of years on the appellate bench and while I was ruminating about taking senior status, I was asked by the State Department to join the Iran-United States Claims Tribunal in the Hague as an Arbitrator-Judge. This, again, I think, was partly due to having met so many people as a result of having been willing to work on various educational and other committees, including as a liaison between court programs and the American Society of International Law, of which I am a very proud member.

Although I did stop to think about it for a small minute, I again said yes, and moved to The Hague, where I would live part time and continue to have another wonderful experience. There are nine judges on that court, three appointed by the United States, three appointed by Iran, and three third-country members.

We are presently deliberating the case we have recently heard, and deliberations are like an *en banc* hearing on steroids. Instead of a usual three-judge panel, the nine judges on the Tribunal engage in deliberations on every issue in every case. It is like an en-banc conference every day, with the additional twist that the nine of us come from different legal systems, different cultures, different methods of legal analysis, different levels of knowledge. And our controlling document consists simply of the Treaty that was signed over thirty years ago in the midst of an international crisis. The cases we hear involve the government of Iran and the government of the United States and range from procedural matters to evidentiary principles to contract issues and to property issues, all in an international context.

Presently, I have been serving on that Tribunal since 2013. In addition, I have been occasionally serving as a private arbitrator in commercial arbitration and other domestic matters. And yet here again, I cannot tell you how much I have learned about the world of international arbitration, about its tempo, and compared to the federal court, in my view, its less disciplined pace and structure. At the same time, learning from other perspectives, other legal systems, other methodologies indicate how very many ways there are to solve the problems of the world.

So, in a bit of a whirlwind, that's my story. Even with a thesaurus, I cannot find a word big enough to encompass how lucky I have been. I feel like I am part of a sci-fi movie where you jump from Mexico to teenage years in Florida to life in the convent, then out, and then into the crazy hectic world of trial lawyering followed by the peaceful world of trial judging where you have control again. That would have been a good stop, but my sci-fi jump did not stop, and I was able to look into the world of appellate judging, of administratively running one of the largest judiciaries in the country in Florida, of seeing the world of the federal courts and now the international courts and arbitration tribunals.

I would say that the theme of my life is living the life of the moment; being open to whatever opportunity of any kind presents itself, leading to so many experiences that were formative. I am thankful that I said yes to the convent, to being a teacher, a trial lawyer, a state trial and supreme court justice, a federal judge, and an international arbitrator and judge. And I am thankful for saying yes to the enjoyment of so many other things in life: music and sports and travel and making and keeping wonderful friends.

As I have said, everybody's path through life is different. I am grateful that someone with the unconventional background that I have can have the life I've had so far. Without the help, the encouragement, the support, the hand holding, and the pushing of so many I am sure it would have taken many different turns. I am looking forward to the next opportunity that comes along.

BIO

The Honorable Judge Rosemary Barkett

Born in Mexico to Syrian parents, Judge Rosemary Barkett immigrated to Florida as a young child. After serving as an elementary school teacher, Judge Barkett went on to study law and practice as a trial attorney in Florida before being appointed to the bench. Since October 2013, Judge Barkett has served as a Judge on the Iran-United States Claims Tribunal in The Hague. Judge Barkett is the only individual to have served as a State Trial Court judge, a State Appellate Court judge, including on the State's Supreme Court, a Federal Appellate Court judge, and now also a judge on an international tribunal.

Judge Barkett's judicial career began in 1979 when Florida's Governor appointed her as a state trial court judge, later elevating her in 1984 to the state's intermediate appellate court, before ultimately appointing her to the Florida Supreme Court, making her the first woman and Hispanic woman Justice in the Florida Supreme Court's history. On July 1, 1992, her colleagues elected her as Florida's first woman and first Hispanic Chief Justice. In 1994, Judge Barkett was appointed by President William J. Clinton to the United States Court of Appeals for the Eleventh Circuit. Judge Barkett served on that Court for two decades prior to her present appointment on the Iran-United States Claims Tribunal. In 2015, President Barack Obama appointed Judge Barkett to the Panel of Conciliators for the International Centre for the Settlement of Investment Disputes.

During her thirty-year judicial career beginning in 1979, in addition to authoring many landmark opinions across all areas of the law, Judge Barkett has been engaged in improving the administration of the courts, access to justice, and promoting judicial education. Judge Barkett has served on the faculty of Florida's Judicial College, the National Judicial College, the Institute of Judicial Administration's New Appellate Judge Seminar, Aspen Institute's Justice and Society Seminars, and various other Appellate Judges Seminars and law courses. She has also lectured and participated in seminars on Constitutionalism and Human Rights, the rule of law, access to justice, and court structure and administration throughout the world.

Judge Barkett has received many honors and awards for her work as a judge and as an individual committed to improving justice. In 2017, she was honored with the Prominent Woman in International Law Award at the American Society of

International Law's Annual Conference. The recipient of seven honorary degrees from institutions of higher learning, Judge Barkett has also earned many prestigious honors and awards from national and state professional, civic, and charitable groups. She has received the Margaret Brent Women Lawyers of Achievement Award, presented by the ABA Commission on Women in the Profession, the Latin Business and Professional Women Lifetime Achievement Award, and has been inducted into the Florida Women's Hall of Fame. She is a member of the International Women's Forum and the American Society of International Law (ASIL) and served on ASIL's Judicial Outreach Program Advisory Board. She has been the National Association of Women Judges Honoree of the Year. Awards are given in Judge Barkett's name annually to outstanding lawyers and she has been honored by the naming of the "Rosemary Barkett Inn of Appellate Law" in Miami, Florida.

In 2016, Judge Barkett was elected as Honorary President of the American Society of International Law. In 2015, President Barack Obama appointed Judge Barkett to the Panel of Conciliators for the International Centre for the Settlement of Investment Disputes.

VAWA and the Art of Listening

11

Mary M. Schroeder

*J*udge Schroeder offers a behind-the-scenes look at the passage of the critically needed Violence Against Women Act (VAWA). Her role in securing the required support for this law demonstrates that, to achieve results that can change lives, it is important to develop a clear strategic focus and build a powerful coalition of committed stakeholders.

Her description also reveals how a great role model can inspire people to work hard and make a difference in the lives of others.

Judge Schroeder also provides an example of an attack on judicial decision-making that reinforces the importance of an independent judiciary. Her story supports the need to protect the judiciary from political interference.

Lauren Stiller Rikleen, Editor

Mid-century America did not offer women vistas of opportunity or independence. I grew up in the Midwest, the daughter of a university professor father and a homemaker mother. My mother had university teaching positions before her marriage, but due to nepotism rules dating back to the Great Depression, she was barred from employment at the university so long as her husband was on the faculty.

My mother was, nevertheless, active in community affairs, a pillar of the League of Women Voters, and with twin gifts of empathy and common sense. Because we lived near the town's shopping district, women in the community, including neighbors and other faculty wives, often dropped by to chat, and, over coffee and mother's chocolate chip cookies, would talk to mother about their problems.

It was at my mother's kitchen table that I learned a lot about life; children were not always a blessing and husbands were not always loving. More than one of these visitors, I later came to understand, were victims of domestic violence, although that was not a term used then, and violence was not expressly discussed in my presence. I only saw the occasional bruises and sensed the frustration some of the women felt.

Women who grew up in the 50s were not taught leadership skills. They were not supposed to know about social ills much less do something about them. Marriage and children were the goal. A career in nursing or a job as a teacher before marriage, maybe, but a lifelong career in the law was out of the question. Thank goodness there were exceptions, and my friend Brenda Murray is one of those exceptional women.

Brenda married only briefly, went to law school, and had an extraordinary career spanning more than fifty years at the Securities and Exchange Commission, becoming the Chief Administrative Law Judge. Her day job brought her into contact with wealth, avarice, and regulatory mazes. Her passion, however, was helping women in trouble.

A consummate believer in networking, Brenda was an early member of the National Association of Women Judges (NAWJ) that was founded in 1979, and, over the following decades, fought to help women in prison, often enlisting the assistance of influential friends like Professor Judith Resnick at Yale Law School and the late, legendary Patricia Wald of the United States Court of Appeals for the D.C. Circuit.

Brenda successfully opposed the relocation of a federal women's prison to a site far from the women's families, fought for the creation of prison nurseries so incarcerated women would not be separated from their newborn babies, and, even after her retirement, met with generations of Directors of the Federal Bureau of Prisons to improve the lot of women prisoners. She understood that women in prison were themselves often victims of violent and nonviolent crimes.

In 1992, Brenda was the incoming president of the NAWJ, when she spotted a problem the NAWJ should try to address. Senator Joseph Biden had introduced far-reaching legislation intended to help prevent women from becoming the silent victims of violent crimes. Entitled the Violence Against Women Act, and known as VAWA, the legislation would provide resources for law enforcement and the courts, shelters for the victims of domestic violence, and a permanent office for administration and public education.

The legislation was also meant to send a message, over and above the typical Washington ploy of throwing money at a problem. At the heart of the bill was a civil rights provision, a recognition that women have a civil right to be free from violence on account of their gender. It created a cause of action in federal court for victims to sue perpetrators of violence against women for the violation of their civil rights. It was this provision that was creating deep trouble for the legislation. Both state and federal judges were opposing VAWA.

Brenda Murray recognized immediately that the NAWJ had to respond. The strength of the NAWJ has always been the range of expertise of its members. They include judges at every level of the judiciary, administrative law judges, tribal judges, state court judges from the municipal courts through to state Supreme Courts, and the federal courts from bankruptcy judges to Justices of the Supreme Court of the United States. It is a national organization with national meetings that enable judges like myself, for example, in the relatively isolated federal courts, to understand the problems that beset judges in state trial courts overwhelmed by cases of domestic abuse and sexual assault.

Brenda must have made many calls to her friends when she heard of VAWA's plight, and one of those calls was to me. As Brenda liked to say years later, rescuing VAWA was a job above her pay grade and someone with the constitutional job security of Article III had to be enlisted. Brenda had a plan that, at its core, had her inspired understanding that the NAWJ was the only organization that could communicate with all the VAWA players: the women's organizations that supported the legislation, the state and federal judicial organizations that opposed it, and its principal sponsor, Senator Biden, the Chair of the Senate Judiciary Committee.

In order to understand why the judges opposed VAWA, I had to do some digging. The state judges' opposition came through the Conference of Chief Justices. At least as I came to understand their position, they feared that the civil rights provision could be used as a weapon to delay, and thereby interfere with, the conduct of marriage dissolution proceedings in the state courts. The federal judges, through the Judicial Conference of the United States, and led by no less than the Chief Justice of the United States Supreme Court, William Rehnquist, opposed the bill out of concern that the civil rights provision would clog the federal courts with matters that belonged in state courts. "We do not want purse snatchers in federal court" was the phrase I recall hearing from one prominent attorney who was convinced the bill was a bad idea.

The Administrative Office of the U.S. Courts had tried to calculate the potential number of cases that could be filed in federal court and had come up with some staggering figures. These figures were based on what seemed to me to be the almost fanciful assumption that every victim of sexual assault in the country was likely to use the provision to file a suit for damages in federal court.

VAWA appeared to me to be good legislation directed at serious problems of gender-based violence, ranging from street crime to domestic abuse, and where the overwhelming majority of victims were women. I wondered what the NAWJ could do about it, but Brenda Murray had a strategy. The NAWJ would create a committee to draft a resolution the organization would then adopt. The Committee Chair could speak for the NAWJ in Washington to try to reconcile the proponents and opponents so the bill could pass.

I was to be the Chair, and because the NAWJ would be the only national judicial organization that supported VAWA, Brenda believed our voice would be heard. After some thought, I got on board with the idea that I could occupy such a role, because I had been a member of NAWJ almost since its founding, and I was not a member of the U.S. Judicial Conference, which had taken a stand against the legislation, nor was I a member of any of its committees that might have had a part in formulating that opposition.

Drafting the NAWJ resolution was tricky, however, because some of our members supported the civil rights provision and others feared, not without reason, that the provision was drawn so broadly that it could clog the federal courts. The solution that won the day was for the NAWJ to endorse all the provisions of the bill except the civil rights provision, and to support that provision "in principle." I was given the task of representing the organization in seeking a way to make that provision more "narrowly tailored."

I had a surprising ally. The Chief Justice had appointed a committee to review VAWA, and one of its members was a United States District Judge from Florida, Stanley Marcus, who also chaired the influential Judicial Conference Committee on State Federal Jurisdiction. Judge Marcus contacted me, and it soon became clear that, while we may have come from different directions, we ended up on the same page. The NAWJ was committed to recognizing the rights of women to be free from gender-based discrimination, and Judge Marcus believed that judges should not oppose civil rights legislation. We both read all of the Supreme Court cases we could find that might provide helpful language. We spoke on the phone often, and Judge Marcus would begin every call with: "Let's talk about Violence!"

I also spoke often with Victoria Nourse, Senator Biden's very able staffer. She had drafted the original bill, and with the Senator's blessing, was looking for ways to reduce the opposition. I spoke more than once with the brilliant young lawyer for the NOW Legal Defense and Education Fund, Sally Goldfarb, who deftly deflected some of my ideas that were less than inspired.

The culmination of all our efforts came at a meeting that included Nourse, Goldfarb, and veteran Washington lobbyist Pat Reuss, as well as Judge Marcus and Judge Barbara Rothstein, a member of his Judicial Conference VAWA Committee. We met in the only available room that Nourse could find for us, a poorly lit cubby hole in the basement of the Capitol, or perhaps it was the basement of the Senate Office Building, since we did a good bit of wandering through dark halls.

The upshot of the meeting was general agreement that the civil rights provision should create a civil remedy only for serious felonies that were motivated, at least in part, by gender-based animus. Those concepts were embodied in the final legislation that was signed by President Clinton in September 1994. Judge Marcus had, miraculously in my view, managed to convince the members of the U.S. Judicial Conference to withdraw their formal opposition.

Sadly, Chief Justice Rehnquist had the final word. In *United States v. Morrison*, 529 U.S. 598 (2000), the Supreme Court struck down the civil rights provision. The vote was 5-4. In his majority opinion, the Chief Justice ruled the provision was not a valid exercise of Congress' authority under either the Fourteenth Amendment or the Commerce clause. *Id.* at 627.

Yet, as the proponents of the legislation agreed when they gathered for an anniversary celebration years later, the civil rights provision fashioned in the Capitol basement accomplished what it was intended to do. It constituted Congressional recognition of gender-based crime as a national problem. It brought domestic violence out in the open. It enabled the passage and successful operation of the rest of the legislation, which has been repeatedly re-authorized, to focus public attention and develop programs to combat violence, in addition to annually providing hundreds of millions of dollars for law enforcement agencies, and, importantly, for nonprofit organizations offering shelter, education, and emotional support for victims of domestic violence.

Of course, without the unwavering support of Senator Biden, none of that would have happened. He spoke on the occasion of that anniversary celebration, when he was then Vice President of the United States. As I recall, he went to some lengths to explain why he supported VAWA. He said he was often asked whether he came from an abusive home, and he would answer no, not at all, but that the lesson he learned from his father was to "stand up against the abuse of power."

Abuse of power is what the fight for VAWA was about. It is also what the NAWJ is about, what the Declaration of Independence is about, and what the principle of separation of powers and the Bill of Rights in our Constitution should continue to be about.

The lessons for me were more personal and direct. I learned how important it is to listen to all sides of a disagreement in order to understand the differing interests and fears. I also learned how one's voice is magnified by participation in an organization whose members have concerns similar to yours and experiences that they can share. I learned the importance of forming alliances when help is available. And I learned that my friend Brenda Murray is a very smart lady–because she knew these things all along.

These lessons stood me in good stead when, as Chief Judge of the Ninth Circuit, I had to defend our courts from attacks on their independence.

Criticism was not new. The Ninth Circuit, comprised of the nine western states and a large expanse of the Pacific Ocean, had for decades been the object of faultfinding in Congress. Such discussions were generally prompted by environmental decisions affecting the region of the Pacific Northwest and were always about whether the Circuit should be divided into smaller units. Little ever came of the discussions because there was never any agreement on how to divide it and most of the country didn't care.

Near the beginning of my tenure as Chief Judge, however, a panel decided a case that drew national attention. It was about a cold war–era California statute that required teachers to lead the Pledge of Allegiance daily so students could declare we are a nation "under God." The panel majority held that the California statute was unconstitutional as an establishment of religion in the schools.

Unfortunately, the public perception was that our court had struck down the Pledge of Allegiance itself. Attacks on the court and our judges came from everywhere. Half a dozen bills were introduced in Congress to split the court's geographic authority into various configurations. There were multiple hearings in the House and Senate. It was said we were "too big" but the true, though unspoken, purpose was to punish us for an unpopular decision. The threats thus went to the core principle of judicial independence.

We fought back. Our circuit, district, and bankruptcy judges made their opposition known. So did local, state, and national bar associations. More than 500 law professors signed a petition opposing division and supporting judicial independence.

And we prevailed. How? By listening to what was being said and then answering, with tools not generally associated with courts: alliances, organization, and public communication. This was the combination I had years earlier come to know as the "Brenda Murray Principle." The key to its success was the art of listening, something gleaned from my experience with VAWA as well as from the women having coffee around my mother's kitchen table.

BIO

Judge Mary M. Schroeder

Judge Mary M. Schroeder was the Chief Judge of the United States Court of Appeals for the Ninth Circuit from December 2000 through November 2007 and has served on that court since 1979. She previously served on the Arizona Court of Appeals and practiced law in Phoenix.

Judge Schroeder is a graduate of Swarthmore College and the University of Chicago Law School. After graduation she was a trial lawyer in the Civil Division of the U.S. Department of Justice. She has also taught at Arizona State University Law School and been an adjunct lecturer at Duke University Law School. Judge Schroeder has published articles and lectures in various law reviews and is a member of the Council of the American Law Institute.

She is a recipient of the Arizona State Bar Association's James A. Walsh Outstanding Jurist Award, the American Bar Association's Margaret Brent Women Lawyers of Achievement Award, presented by the Commission on Women in the Profession, and the Joan Dempsey Klein NAWJ Honoree of the Year Award. In 2006 Swarthmore College awarded her an Honorary Doctor of Law degree. She has her chambers in Phoenix, Arizona.

She and her husband, Professor Milton Schroeder, have two daughters and two grandchildren.

Dealing with Criticism

12

Beverly McLachlin

*J*ustice McLachlin offers insightful advice for avoiding *the traps that others set. Her strategies for responding to criticisms that we inevitably face in life are instructive for discerning when a critical comment may be helpful, notwithstanding the sting. She also helps us recognize when negative remarks that serve only to undermine self-confidence should be ignored.*

Justice McLachlin's observations about the damage caused by the myth of perfectionism are deeply relevant in a world driven by false illusions of perfection and happiness on social media. Similarly, her wise advice about authenticity is helpful at every level of one's career.

Lauren Stiller Rikleen, Editor

No matter how well you conduct yourself, how well you do your job, you will face criticism. To engage in the world—to do things and sometimes change them—is to attract criticism. It is therefore essential for lawyers and jurists to learn how to deal with criticism.

Women face more criticism than men, given stereotypical views on how women should present themselves to the world. How should they dress? How assertive or docile should they be? Are they up to the really tough cases? We have all heard criticisms like this—criticisms that have little or nothing to do with competence or ability to get the job done. Every professional person faces criticism, but women tend to get more than their fair share. I was no exception. Let me share some thoughts on what my journey through life and law taught me about meeting criticism constructively.

I. RESPONDING TO CRITICISM

Looking back over a career spanning sixty years, I realize that at different stages of my professional life I responded to criticism in different ways. Some of my responses, particularly in the early years, had negative impacts on my self-esteem and confidence. As I gained experience, I found positive ways to respond to criticism, allowing me to learn and grow and become stronger. In the end, I arrived at a considered response involving four elements:

1. View criticism objectively not personally.
2. Separate valid from invalid criticism.
3. Avoid the perfection trap.
4. Adopt a consistent approach to when to ignore criticism and when and how to respond to criticism.

A. View Criticism Objectively

As a young lawyer, I found it hard—indeed impossible—to view criticisms objectively. Everything hurt. Criticisms that had some foundation made me feel inadequate and doubt my ability. Criticisms with no validity—like when I was chastised for wearing too short a skirt to court when in fact the so-called offender was a different woman—stung with unfairness and left me feeling angry. Both ways, I felt diminished, with my self-confidence—already in short supply—battered.

One day, after a particularly debilitating and completely unfounded criticism, I found myself in court fighting paralysis; I simply couldn't do this. On a recent occasion, I had been accused of being too aggressive in my cross-examination of a witness. A few days later, leading counsel asked me, without warning, to cross-examine a different witness. I found myself paralyzed. Looking back, I see the criticism as sexist. A man would never have been accused of being too aggressive. But because I was a woman, my attack was seen as unseemly. As it turned out, just as I was struggling to my feet, my co-counsel, sensing my distress, took over. At the time, my temporary paralysis was a frightening experience.

Upon reflection, I later realized that I had been wrong to let the criticism affect me. I remembered the rule I had learned as a child on the ranch—if you fall off the horse get right back on and ride it. The next day I applied the lesson to my work as a lawyer. I vowed to find a better way to deal with criticism.

That way was the conscious application of objectivity.

Objectivity about myself. I wasn't stupid. I could formulate an argument and present it as well as or better than many lawyers.

Objectivity about the content of a particular criticism. Perhaps, viewed from the perspective of others, there was some basis for it. I could have handled a particular moment or issue better. I reflected on the criticism and tried to learn from it. Perhaps, on the other hand, the criticism was unfair and off the mark. In that case, the criticism said more about the person criticizing than about me. I dismissed it and moved on.

B. Separate Valid from Invalid Criticism

Viewing criticisms objectively taught me an important lesson: Some criticisms are positive, pointing to things we could do better. The professional life is a life of constant growth—or should be. One of the catalysts for growth is criticism. We see ourselves through the eyes of the critic. We think about how we can do better next time. We learn.

Valid criticism should not be confused with kind criticism. The nicest form of criticism is the criticism of a mentor—someone who likes and respects you and is offering insights into how you can do better. But nasty or angry criticism can also be valid. It stings, but it can teach us as much as kind criticism. Don't dismiss criticism just because it comes in a negative package. If you respond objectively, you can learn as much from negative criticism as from positive.

I recall watching a young woman argue a motion. The issue was one of jurisdiction, and difficult to explain simply. The young woman, immersed in her learning, did her best, but the judge—another woman as it turned out—either could not or would not understand. The judge kept saying things like "I can't understand your reasoning," "You're not making sense." The comments were personal to the point of being offensive.

The young woman was crushed. Her opposing counsel tried to comfort her. "I understood your arguments perfectly," he told her at the break. Later, the young woman told me she had been crushed by the judge's comments. "Don't be," I told her. "First, the judge was wrong to couch her concerns in terms of personal criticism of you. But second, accepting the judge was rude, ask yourself what went wrong. Could you have asked her to consider the problem in a different light and bring her along? And even if that might not have been possible, learn from the experience. Sometimes judges have bad days. Go along with it. The judge may find for you in the end. In any event, such behavior is the judge's problem, not yours."

Invalid criticism is criticism that is wrong, not based on facts, or the product of ill-founded judgments and bad logic. You are doing something new and different—ergo it is wrong. Or, you dress too loudly, your hair is bad, you are too aggressive or too passive. Dismiss this kind of criticism. Don't waste a moment on it. To succeed in law as in life you must be yourself—be authentic. Criticisms that demand inauthenticity are never helpful.

C. Avoid the Perfection Trap

No one is perfect. Yet girls of my generation were brought up to be perfect. The perfect outfit, the perfect hairdo, the perfect length of skirt or cut of bodice. The perfect way of behaving—not too aggressive, not too docile. I carried this ideal of perfection into adulthood and my professional life.

As a result, I became my own biggest critic. When I didn't win a case, it was my fault. When a potential client went to another lawyer, it was my fault—something I had said or not said. Self-examination

is a good thing. But self-examination based on the demand for perfection can undermine one's self-confidence. The best is never enough,
because it is not perfect.

At a certain point in my career, juggling motherhood with a
job and a million miscellaneous duties in a haze of striving confu-
sion, I realized I would never, could never, be perfect. A late-running
meeting might make me late to pick up my child from daycare. A
fitful night might take the edge off a stellar performance in class or
court the next morning. So be it. I could only do my best. I put it this
way in my memoir, *Truth Be Told* (fn p. 150):

> In my early years in law, I strove for perfection and flag-
> ellated myself when I fell short, as inevitably happened.
> Sometimes the quest for perfection almost paralyzed me . . .
> Years later, it came to me that the singular obsession with
> perfection that had bedeviled me for so long was a uniquely
> female trait. The men around me never obsessed about
> whether they were perfect—they just got on with the job at
> hand. Women of my generation had subliminally absorbed
> a message—we were allowed into a man's world by grace,
> but to keep our place we had to be perfect. The inference
> was lethal: If we were not perfect, we were not worthy. If we
> were not perfect, we deserved to fail.

Once I recognized that I could not be perfect, the load on me
lightened. Joy returned to the execution of tasks, small and large.
I would do my best. And that would have to do. As it turned out it
did. I made peace with myself. And as a result, I became a better lawyer and a better teacher.

I realized that there is no such thing as perfection. The idea one
should be perfect is a terrible trap—and a trap that snares women
more than men. Men around me did not suffer from this affliction.
They didn't flagellate themselves for minor slips, they didn't go
through life in a perpetual attitude of apology. Most of them simply
did the best they could and moved on.

I decided to do the same. I would not let the chimeric pursuit
of perfection make me my own worst critic. It saved my career, my
family, maybe my life.

D. Adopt a Consistent Approach to When to Ignore Criticism and When and How to Respond to Criticism

How you respond to criticism can have an important impact on your life and your career. You can become angry and reject the criticism. Or, at the other end of the spectrum, you can take it on to the point that it undermines your self-confidence and paralyzes you. You can lash out at your critic and denounce her. Or you can decide simply to let it go and move on. Behind these different reactions lie different personality traits. Some people are more sensitive to criticism than others.

Early in my career, I was debilitatingly sensitive to criticism. As I gained experience and confidence, I realized that I had a choice. I could accept the criticism and learn from it. Or I could reject it as unfounded. Either way, criticism could not hurt me.

Viewing criticism objectively rather than personally and considering the context in which it is made will help you find the right response to a particular criticism. Before responding to criticism, I learned to ask myself a simple question: will any good come of this?

During the almost four decades I sat as a judge—almost three of them on Canada's highest court, it was my job to make difficult decisions on matters that divided the population. Same-sex rights, assistance in dying, indigenous rights, the right of a Province to secede from the country, cross-examination of the victims of sexual assault—these and many more issues were my daily fodder. Not infrequently, I faced strident criticism for making a particular decision or authoring a particular set of reasons.

Judges must make their decisions on the facts and law in the case before them. They cannot be swayed by public opinion or the fear of criticism. For this reason, judges are guaranteed independence. No matter how heated the criticism of their decisions, they cannot be fired or demoted. Criticism comes with the job.

The judge accepts this when she dons her robes. Generally, she does not respond to criticisms. She does not lash out against her critics. She does not write letters to the editor explaining her side of the story. It can be difficult for a judge to sit silent while press and populace rage about the wrongness of her decision. But the general rule is that after delivering their reasons, it is best that judges not descend into the public arena and enter into a debate with their critics. It is a rule that has, by and large, served the judiciary well.

Yet every rule has its exceptions. As Chief Justice, I woke one morning to a headline stating that the Prime Minister had accused me of interfering with the appointment of a particular judge to my Court, the Supreme Court of Canada. It was a serious charge, which if true would have required me to resign and would certainly have undermined public confidence in the Court.

I weighed whether to respond or not. Should I follow the judicial protocol of silence? Or should I respond? I decided that I should respond at least by setting out the facts relating to the allegation of misconduct, but no more. The public, I decided, had the right to know what had happened. Then they could judge for themselves. I issued a brief statement the same morning. *I have done nothing wrong. These are the facts.*

My account of the facts was not refuted, and the Prime Minister's criticism was dismissed as groundless by national and international legal bodies who studied the matter. Public confidence in the Supreme Court emerged unscathed.

Sometimes, it is necessary to respond to criticism. But there must always be a good reason.

II. CONCLUSION

Criticism is always with us. As lawyers and as jurists we cannot escape it. How we respond to it is important, for our well-being, for our careers, and for the maintenance of public confidence in the legal system and for the rule of law.

Approach criticism objectively, distinguish between valid criticism and invalid criticism, avoid the perfection trap, and consider carefully how and when to respond to criticism—these are the lessons that my journey through the law have taught me. Thank you for allowing me to share them with you, as you follow your own journey.

BIO

Beverly McLachlin

The Right Honourable Beverley McLachlin served as Chief Justice of Canada from 2000 to mid-December 2017. In the summer of 2018, Ms. McLachlin became a Member Arbitrator at Arbitration Place.

Ms. McLachlin works as an arbitrator and mediator in Canada and internationally. She brings to those forms of dispute resolution her broad and deep experience for more than thirty-five years in deciding a wide range of business law and public law disputes, in both common law and civil law; her ability to work in both English and French; and her experience and skill in leading and consensus building for many years as the head of a diverse nine-member court.

Ms. McLachlin also sits as a Justice of Singapore's International Commercial Court and the Hong Kong Final Court of Appeal.

Her judicial career began in 1981 in the province of British Columbia, Canada. She was appointed to the Supreme Court of British Columbia (a court of first instance) later that year and was elevated to the British Columbia Court of Appeal in 1985. She was appointed Chief Justice of the Supreme Court of British Columbia in 1988 and seven months later, she was sworn in as a Justice of the Supreme Court of Canada.

Ms. McLachlin is the first and only woman to be Chief Justice of Canada and she is Canada's longest serving Chief Justice.

The former Chief Justice chaired the Canadian Judicial Council, the Advisory Council of the Order of Canada, and the Board of Governors of the National Judicial Institute.

In June 2018 she was appointed to the Order of Canada as a recipient of its highest accolade, Companion of the Order of Canada. She has received more than thirty-five honorary degrees from universities in Canada and abroad, and numerous other honors and awards.

Ms. McLachlin is an Honorary Bencher of The Hon. Society of Gray's Inn, The Hon. Society of Lincoln's Inn and The Middle Temple; Vice-President of The Law Society, University College Dublin; and an Honorary Fellow of the American

College of Trial Lawyers, the American College of Construction Lawyers, and the International Academy of Construction Lawyers.

Throughout her judicial career, Ms. McLachlin has been involved with count-less areas of the Canadian legal system, both common law and civil law, and both private and public law, in English and French. In addition to working in those languages, she has limited fluency in German.

Ms. McLachlin is the author of numerous legal articles and publications, as well as a mystery novel, *Full Disclosure*, published in 2018.

The 2,094 Supreme Court of Canada judgments in which she participated—of which she wrote 442—and her legal writings and speaking, include a wide range of subjects in corporate, construction, financial services, taxation, contract, tort, other areas of business law, as well as arbitration and mediation. Her legal texts include, as lead coauthor, the first and second editions (1987 and 1994) of *The Canadian Law of Architecture and Engineering*. It is generally recognized that the judgments of the Supreme Court of Canada during her tenure have affirmed Canada as a jurisdiction that is very supportive of arbitration.

The former Chief Justice received a BA (Honours) in Philosophy in 1965 and both an MA in Philosophy and an LL B in 1968 from the University of Alberta. She was called to the Alberta Bar in 1969 and to the British Columbia Bar in 1971. She practiced law in Alberta and British Columbia. Commencing in 1974, she taught for seven years in the Faculty of Law at the University of British Columbia as a tenured Associate Professor.

BIO

Never Remain Silent in the Face of Injustice | 13

Judith McConnell

*J*ustice McConnell describes her lifetime involvement *in efforts to secure rights for women, including the fight to pass the Equal Rights Amendment in California. Her examples of hard-won gains remind us where women's rights would be today if women of her generation had not worked for change.*

These reminiscences are a lesson for younger generations about the struggle for opportunities now taken for granted. The strategies she and her colleagues employed then still have resonance for today's ongoing challenges to protect rights that prior generations worked to secure, as well as rights thought secure, but are no longer.

Justice McConnell's key point is that women continually need to speak up in the face of wrongdoing. The painful experiences she shares from her past teach us all that we must act courageously to end the silence that protectively shields misconduct.

Lauren Stiller Rikleen, Editor

I grew up in the small city of Lincoln, Nebraska. My early life consisted in playing outdoors in all kinds of weather, fighting with siblings, and attending an elementary school two blocks from home. My father was a Pulitzer Prize–winning newspaper man, so I was aware of the professional world from an early age. Both he and my mother always wanted to live on a farm. So we moved to the country outside of town for a few years, where I attended a two-room school, with students of all ages.

In those days, athletic girls were referred to as "tomboys"—I loved having my own horse, riding in the fields around our home, and participating in 4-H. That life came to an end when we moved to Beverly Hills and my father became the editor of another newspaper.

Since I was a good student, my only challenges growing up were those of a typical teenager. During high school, I went to Tokyo as an exchange student and lived with the family of a newspaperman, learning some Japanese, and having my eyes opened to the larger world. It was a life-changing experience, since I arrived at a time when there were intense anti-American demonstrations in the streets of Tokyo. At the same time, I made good friends with Japanese kids my own age.

Back in California, I spoke frequently at school assemblies and service clubs and became comfortable with appearing in public. Until law school I never felt disadvantaged by being female, although, like most women, I experienced what I now recognize as sexual harassment on the job.

Little did I know when I began law school in 1966 the challenges I would face as a woman. I had always been a good student and successfully navigated a variety of jobs, including being the first female "copy boy" at the *Pasadena Star News*. But law school was definitely a man's world. This was made clear to me on the first day of classes, when a student sitting in front of me turned and said, "What are you doing here?"

To this day, I have no idea how I responded, but my memories of law school are mixed. When I graduated and began looking for jobs, one firm wrote me that they were "sticking with the boys." Another actually interviewed me and asked me what birth control I used. I walked out of that interview.

Nonetheless, I was referred by a former classmate to interview with the law office of the California Department of Transportation and hired to be a trial lawyer. Before I could officially start the job, however, I had to be interviewed by the State Personnel Board in Los Angeles. I walked into the room and faced four white men in suits. At one point, one panel member asked how I would choose between being an attorney and being a wife. I turned to him and asked whether he had been asked how he would choose between being an attorney and a husband. He turned brick red and said he wasn't, and I responded that I declined to answer his question on the ground it was discriminatory. I am happy to say I got the highest score in the state.

I was the first woman lawyer hired by the Department of Transportation. I was lucky to have a supervisor who fully supported me, despite the fact some in Sacramento were averse to hiring what they called "hen" attorneys. I was immediately put to work trying cases before juries and loved being in the courtroom.

The challenges I faced as a woman didn't end there. One judge didn't like the way I wore my hair. He took me into chambers to show me a photo of his granddaughter and told me I should wear my hair like hers. Fortunately, the bailiff charged into chambers and told the judge to leave me alone, so I knew I had allies.

Jurors were uniformly supportive in all the years I was in trial, both as a lawyer and as a judge. It was customary for trial lawyers to talk to jurors after a verdict. It is always interesting to hear what they thought of the case and of the way we tried cases, especially since I often tried cases with a junior colleague—a woman who later also became a judge. Many jurors started by saying they had a daughter and hoped she could grow up to be a lawyer. One juror decided my colleague should go home with her and meet her son. Some jurors cautioned me to be careful when posting exhibits since when I raised my arms up to display a map, they could see my underwear. I relished their comments and, by the way, always wore two-piece outfits after that last comment.

My biggest challenge as a lawyer was keeping busy, since between trials I found myself bored. My boss said there is no excuse for being bored since there is much to do in the community and I should go out and get to work. Inspired by his support, I became a founding member of the National Organization for Women in San Diego and began a long career of public speaking in support of feminist causes.

I was invited to debate Phyllis Schlafly about the Equal Rights Amendment (ERA) on public television. At the time, Schlafly was the leader of a movement opposed to feminism; she advocated women should stay home and raise children, although she herself was a lawyer and always on the road and on a soapbox. I was astounded that her main objection to the ERA was that women would have to use the same toilets as men.

Because there were few women lawyers in San Diego, we gathered to support each other, sharing lunch and ideas for jobs. The ERA had not been ratified by the California Legislature and we used it to help mobilize women and men to form a feminist bar association, which we called the Lawyers Club of San Diego. I became its first president.

Our local state senator was firmly opposed to the ERA and called it a "Mickey Mouse" piece of legislation, but we pressured him to change his views. He was the president pro tem of the California State Senate, which made him ex officio chair of the Senate Rules Committee, and he blocked all efforts to bring the ERA to the floor of the Senate. We finally persuaded him to set up a special "Blue Ribbon Advisory Committee on the Equal Rights Amendment," and he appointed me and others who supported the ERA to serve. The "committee" met for about five minutes and unanimously agreed to recommend that he change his position to support passage of the amendment. He followed our recommendation.

We had many challenges to fight: in California, husbands had sole management and control over community property; women could not get credit in their own names without a husband or father's signature; women could not engage in financial affairs on their own. We were constantly challenged to prove our worth. I always felt we had to be better than the men to make any progress.

I also learned that becoming a mother placed additional burdens on women. When I had my first child, I didn't want to leave him, so I took him to work with me. My boss was supportive, and I was able to do my job. Yet when the local newspaper ran a story about my taking the baby to work, I received death threats from people who were angry that a woman would bring her baby to the office.

When the baby became too active for the office, the struggle to find good care began. I appreciate that parents still have that difficulty. I was fortunate that my husband and I had good incomes, but finding someone I could trust to care for my precious children was a huge challenge. The best advice I received was to spend whatever it took to get good care. I followed that advice, but I know most working women often spend a large part of their pay on childcare.

After my years in the courtroom, I decided a judicial career would be interesting. Fortunately, Jerry Brown was Governor. He was determined to diversify the bench and I was appointed to the court in 1977.

Sad to say, judges themselves were not immune from sexual harassment. When I began my service on the Superior Court, it was the practice in California to assign a "mentor judge" for each new judge. I quickly learned my mentor was literally "hands on," so every time he came into my chambers, I stood up and moved to keep the desk between us. He finally stopped visiting. To this day, women judges report harassment by their male colleagues and one judge was recently removed from the bench for his mistreatment of female judges and lawyers.

I decided early on to do whatever I could to improve the judicial system and I started by joining the Personnel Committee of the court. In those days, interviews of prospective court employees were conducted by the judges, who asked questions of women about their birth control practices. I recall one interview where a judge asked such a question and I kicked him under the table and told the applicant not to answer the question. After the interview concluded, I told the judge such questions were discriminatory, and he couldn't ask them.

I was always interested in improving the way courts were run and when I was elevated to the Superior Court I ran for and was elected to the Executive Committee. My interest in court administration led me to many challenging supervisory assignments and ultimately, I was elected the first woman presiding judge of the San Diego Superior Court. As the first woman to be Presiding Judge of a major metropolitan general jurisdiction court in California, I enjoyed broad support from my colleagues who had elected me.

One of the worst tasks of a Presiding Judge is assignment of courtrooms, and our court was facing a critical shortage of facilities. We dealt with it by building temporary courtrooms in an old hotel, but many judges resisted going there to work. One judge even came to my chambers late in the day to complain. No one was around and he grabbed my throat and started squeezing it, leaving a circle of bruises. I saved his twenty-page letter of apology in case he tried to move up in the judiciary, but he never did.

To this day, the memory of the assault is painful for many reasons, but above all because I didn't do anything about it. I never complained to the state disciplinary officials, I didn't discipline him myself, and, to my surprise, I didn't knee him in the groin. I deeply regret my inaction.

When I was a new judge, I joined in founding the National Association of Women Judges. Our goal was increasing the number of women on the bench and improving the courts for the benefit of all vulnerable populations. To that end, I helped prepare the first judicial education program on gender bias in the courts. We developed the program because we felt education was the key to changing judicial and attorney behavior. Our focus was on the most obvious bias: treatment of women attorneys, treatment of victims of rape and domestic violence, family law court treatment of women in child support and spousal support disputes, and use of gender-biased language.

Putting that program together was a challenge, in part because judges uniformly deny they have any biases. When we first presented the course, many of the student judges were quite hostile when we discussed issues like the treatment of rape victims in the court or judicial decisions on child and spousal support. Nonetheless, once the ice was broken, elimination of bias in the courts became a regular part of judicial education in California.

We next presented the program at the National Judicial College in Reno, where several of the students—all of whom were judges—threw spitballs at the faculty. We persisted, and eventually persuaded most Chief Justices around the country that elimination of bias in the courts should be a top priority. That work is ongoing, and the educational programs have become more diverse and sophisticated.

After twenty-three years as a trial judge, Governor Gray Davis—whose Chief of Staff had been a co-founder with me of the Lawyers Club—appointed me to the Court of Appeal as an Associate Justice and later as Presiding Justice. When I joined the ten-justice division, I was the third woman justice; now seven of the ten justices are women.

I am still working to improve diversity on the bench as a whole and seeking out new talent to join the judiciary. Professional organizations such as the Lawyers Club and the National Association of Women Judges have been critical in this work. The American Bar Association was originally resistant and was viewed by many women as simply another "old boys club," but now it provides support for women in the profession and has had a remarkable series of women presidents.

Reflecting on my experiences, the most important advice I can give is always to speak up and never remain silent in the face of injustice, even if it may appear to put you at risk. Failure to confront inequities wherever we find them will only allow them to persist.

For young people entering the profession, you can always find support in those of us who have come before you. The greatest honor is to be asked to lend a hand.

BIO

Judith McConnell

Administrative Presiding Justice Judith McConnell was appointed to the Court of Appeal, Fourth Appellate District, Division One, in August 2001, and took office upon her confirmation on October 3, 2001. On September 25, 2003, she was confirmed as Presiding Justice of the Court. On September 29, 2003, she was appointed by the Chief Justice as Administrative Presiding Justice of the Fourth Appellate District.

She served for twenty-three years as a trial judge in San Diego. Her colleagues on the Superior Court twice elected her Presiding Judge. She also served as Presiding Judge of the Juvenile Court and Supervising Judge of the family, appellate, and civil law and motion departments during her tenure on the Superior Court.

During Justice McConnell's judicial career, she has worked to improve the court system through better case management and to make the courts more accessible to the public. Justice McConnell served on the California Judicial Council and the Commission on Judicial Performance, the judicial disciplinary agency. She was a member of the Blue-Ribbon Task Force on Jury System Improvement, the Commission on the Future of the Courts, and the Advisory Committee on Gender Bias in the Courts.

She is a recipient of the 2001 Judicial Council Jurist of the Year Award and, in 1999, the first recipient of the Benjamin Aranda Access to Justice Award presented jointly by the Judicial Council, the California Judges Association, and the State Bar of California. In 2019, she received the American Bar Association's Margaret Brent Women Lawyers of Achievement Award.

Justice McConnell was a founder and first president of the Lawyers Club of San Diego and founder and president of the National Association of Women Judges, and has worked to eliminate all forms of bias in the courts.

Women Workers/ Women Lawyers: Three Foremothers

14

Marsha S. Berzon

Judge Marsha Berzon is an extraordinary pioneer who has influenced countless lawyers over the years. Here, she shares the remarkable stories of three women lawyers who left an indelible influence on her own early career.

In her detailed descriptions of these influencers, Judge Berzon teaches an important lesson. She demonstrates that we are always serving as role models to others who are anxious to learn and excel. Simply by the way we present ourselves and treat others, we impact people in ways both intended and unintended.

Just as Judge Berzon was influenced and, in turn, continues to be an influence, she wisely shows us that it is never too early to think about our own legacy and the importance of supporting others.

Lauren Stiller Rikleen, Editor

Women lawyers much younger that I sometimes ask me for advice about how to live their future lives—mostly, how to balance legal careers and parenthood. (For whatever reason, I have never gotten these questions from young men.) How did I manage an active legal career while raising two children, the first born at the end of my second year of law school? Should they have their children right after their clerkships (often, the questioners are women law clerks) or five years into their legal careers? Is it time to slow down for a while and take a less challenging job when the stress of litigation carries over into day-to-day parenting? And, on a different subject, if they want eventually to become a judge, what should they do and not do as lawyers?

In answering these questions, my theme tends to be that planning one's life too far in advance and too rigidly is both futile and unwise. As to the parenting questions, I usually first quip that I have amnesia as to the career/childrearing conflicts, which is not entirely true—I certainly remember, for example, the time I missed an event in my daughter's class to go to an important meeting, although, tellingly, my daughter says she has no memory of that. Then, I observe that for me, avoiding working in a large institution while my children were young—in my case, founding with my husband and a friend a very small firm, originally Altshuler and Berzon, provided a measure of flexibility and pacing (although no respite from deadlines for filing briefs or from flying across the country for oral arguments).

As to the judge question, I usually answer that structuring one's career with an eye to a judicial appointment will usually lead to a much less interesting career—and you probably won't become a judge anyway, as the process is something of a lottery. Better always to do work that matters to you as well as you can do it and be open to new opportunities to do what comes your way, whether through serendipity or active search.

Whether the young women seeking advice will remember what I told them—who can tell? One never knows which encounters in life are determinative of life's direction and habits and which prove incidental. I do suspect, though, that examples of other women's lives interwoven with one's own are likely to be more influential than words of advice from senior women lawyers.

For me, that has certainly been the case. I have carried with me for more than forty years conversations with and images of Ruth Weyand, Beatrice Rosenberg, and Judith Vladeck, all women lawyers who remade their careers to challenge sex discrimination in the workplace. And I have called upon those conversations and images as I, decades younger than them and working in a legal community into which many more women lawyers were finally admitted, tried to carry on their work.

For much of my legal career before joining the judiciary as a Ninth Circuit judge, I represented labor organizations and women workers. Often, it was both, as several labor organizations in the 1970s and 1980s were interested in bringing groundbreaking cases on behalf of women members challenging entrenched employment practices that disadvantaged women workers. Pregnancy discrimination, discrimination in pay, pension, and insurance, family leave, and sexual harassment—I was involved in trailblazing cases and legislative efforts in all of these realms, most often with the support of the federation of labor organizations for which I was Associate General Counsel, the American Federation of Labor-Congress of Industrial Relations (AFL-CIO).

After I began practice in 1975, I soon met Ruth Weyand (1912–1986), Beatrice Rosenberg (1908–1989), and Judith Vladeck (1923–2007), woman lawyers a generation or two older whose careers by the time I met them were largely devoted to the advancement of the interests of working women. I'd like in this chapter to memorialize these three women who inspired and supported me as their legal work intersected with mine.

By different routes, by the 1970s, as I was starting out, Ruth, Bea, and Judith had each come to devote their careers to advancing equality of women in the workplace, working on litigation, administrative guidelines, and legislation under Title VII, the Pregnancy Discrimination Act, and the Equal Pay Act. They were women of courage, brilliance, and independence; strong, funny, and quirky. And each of them took the time to encourage me in my early endeavors, as well as to provide a sense of continuity across generations by storytelling about their own lives and legal careers. I believe that all knew each other—I know that Beatrice and Ruth did, and I believe Judith knew the other two, although she was a bit younger and, unlike the other two, never worked for the Equal Opportunity Employment Commission (EEOC). I'll discuss them in the order that I met them, Ruth first, then Beatrice, and then Judith.

I.   RUTH WEYAND

I clerked for Justice William J. Brennan on the United States Supreme Court in 1974–1975, his first woman clerk. How I came to do that is a women's rights story in itself, told in detail in the biography of Justice Brennan written by Seth Stern and Stephen Wermiel, *Justice Brennan: Liberal Champion.*

The short version is that Justice Brennan initially would not hire me when I sought a clerkship in December 1973, just as he had not hired another woman graduate of my law school, now Berkeley Law, several years earlier, because he was not comfortable having a woman clerk. Justice Brennan had in the May 1973 case, *Frontiero v. Richardson,* proclaimed that sex discrimination "put women not on a pedestal but in a cage," and that statutory sex discrimination thus should be subjected to strict scrutiny, as "the sex characteristic frequently bears no relation to ability to perform or contribute to society."

The law professor who had chosen me for the clerkship position on Justice Brennan's behalf, Stephen Barnett, either wrote a letter or visited the good Justice in person—the stories vary—and pointed out the contradictions between his ideals, as enunciated in his plurality opinion in *Frontiero,* and his refusal to hire me because I am a woman. So Justice Brennan reversed his position and took me on— for a wonderful year, in which he could not have been more gracious and supportive.

It was at the end of that year at the Court that Larry Gold, a professional acquaintance of my husband's, offered me a position he was vacating to become General Counsel of the AFL-CIO. The job was at a small firm that represented the AFL-CIO, mostly in the Supreme Court, and also advised some international unions. I knew from my Supreme Court clerkship that the Justices thought extremely well of the work Larry and his colleagues did at the Supreme Court on behalf of the labor movement. And I had become interested in representing workers when studying in law school with David Feller, himself a Supreme Court advocate and labor lawyer before becoming a law professor. So I accepted the job, expecting to learn a great deal about appellate and Supreme Court advocacy as well as about labor and employment law, which I did.

A week or two after I started, I was asked out to lunch by Ruth Weyand, then Associate General Counsel of the International Union of Electrical Workers (IUE). Ruth's career and personal trajectory until that point was both fascinating and disturbing.

Ruth had tried to enroll at the law school at the University of Chicago in 1929, but was not allowed to do so, because the faculty thought young women wanted to go to law school only to find husbands. So she enrolled in the School of Social Service Administration but took all the first-year law school classes. After she finished the first quarter with higher grades than any of the men in the law school class, she was permitted to stay in law school and graduated.

After some years of private practice, she became a lawyer for the National Labor Relations Board (NLRB) in Washington. Ruth argued for the NLRB before the Supreme Court in nine cases, including several landmark labor law cases. But when, in 1950, it became known that she had married Leslie Perry, a Black lawyer who was head of the NAACP's Washington office, she was asked to leave the NLRB.

When I met her, she had been working with the IUE for some time, at a desk strewn with papers, surrounded by four walls of books. Ruth, with IUE General Counsel Winn Newman, was working on a Supreme Court case, *General Electric Co. v. Gilbert*, that concerned whether, under Title VII, employers could refuse to provide disability benefits for women disabled during pregnancy or after childbirth—benefits that were provided to other temporarily disabled employees.

Ruth poured her heart and considerable intellect into the case, filing a brief more than two hundred pages long (probably the reason the Supreme Court shortly thereafter imposed page limits on Supreme Court briefs for the first time). The brief—drawing on the papers on Ruth's desk and on the books that lined her walls—recounted the history of discrimination against working women at General Electric and industrial plants generally and tied that history to the exclusion of and lack of support for women when they became pregnant and gave birth.

The AFL-CIO was interested in filing an amicus brief supporting the IUE's position that General Electric's disability policy disfavoring pregnancy was sex discrimination under Title VII. I thought that potential brief would be the subject of our lunch. But in fact, Ruth was more interested in celebrating my hiring as the first woman representing the national labor federation.

Ruth told me that she had a personal reason for her interest. Some years before, the then-General Counsel—whose name I do not remember—of the AFL-CIO had promised her a position similar to the one I was embarking upon. Ruth was preparing to start in that job when the man who hired her suddenly died. His successor was not about to have a woman—even a woman who was an experienced Supreme Court advocate and labor law expert (which I at that point was not)—representing the (then mostly male) workers in AFL-CIO unions, and he withdrew the offer. So Ruth was delighted, she told me, that I was now to do the work she was not able to do.

The class of workers Ruth represented lost in *Gilbert*, and both she and I became embroiled in an effort to amend Title VII to declare that discrimination based on pregnancy was sex discrimination. We worked closely on that project, which became the Pregnancy Discrimination Act, along with a loose organization of primarily women lawyers (and, as I recall, one man), and then both toiled on the EEOC enforcement guidelines that helped implement the new statute.

By that time, Ruth had switched hats—she had become Equal Pay Act counsel at the EEOC and was assigned—along with Beatrice Rosenberg—to help draft the new guidelines. Once again, Ruth was indefatigable, committed, deeply knowledgeable about the on-the-ground situation of working women—and willing to listen closely to the ideas of a novice like me, who was just starting her legal career in the field of employee representation.

By this time, there were still relatively few women lawyers but there were now some male lawyers supportive of attacking discrimination against working women, as well as a union movement now willing to litigate and support legislation forwarding the interests of women workers. Ruth was instrumental in forging that change, and in continuing to foster it.

II. BEATRICE ROSENBERG

I first heard of Beatrice Rosenberg from Justice Brennan. The two of them were the same age, had grown up in Newark, New Jersey, and were in the same high school class. Bea had been a Justice Department lawyer for most of her career after attending NYU Law School at night, often appearing before the Supreme Court as Deputy Chief of the appellate section of the Criminal Division. On behalf of the government, she argued thirty times at the Supreme Court and worked on landmark cases, including *Miranda v. Arizona* and *Terry v. Ohio*. It was her Justice Department criminal law work on the side of the prosecution that Justice Brennan knew about and, although he spoke of her with respect (albeit a bit quizzically, as a female criminal appeals lawyer appearing before the Court was quite a novelty), I'm not sure he was all that fond of the positions she was taking in the Court.

By the time I met her, though, Bea had switched gears and, in 1972, become the head of the Appellate Division of the fairly new EEOC. Why she made that major career change I never learned from her. But it does not seem a coincidence that someone who had been one of very few women in her profession throughout her career would gravitate toward a new government agency dedicated, in part, to challenging workplace discrimination against women, including professional women.

So Ruth and Bea, coming from very different backgrounds, were both at the EEOC when, in 1978, the Pregnancy Discrimination Act was enacted by Congress and signed into law by President Carter. And, together, they became the primary lawyers at the agency working on EEOC enforcement guidelines for the new statute. It was in that capacity that I encountered Bea, as I tried to provide the agency with thoughts about the direction those guidelines might take.

Bea, as I recall her, was a chain-smoking, supremely confident, somewhat intimidating woman. She once remarked of her smoking that she was not going to stop because, after all, she was not going to die young. (She was about seventy when I knew her, an age that, much as I hate to say it, does not seem old to me now). And, unlike me, she had experience not only in Supreme Court representation, but also in drafting legislation—she had drafted while in the Justice

Department proposed legislation for preventive detention and "no knock searches."

Although those subjects were, of course, far from the sex discrimination issues she was now addressing, and EEOC guidelines are not legislation, the task of capturing in relatively few words the principles of a complex subject with the clarity and foresight needed to be useful for enforcement and compliance was similar to legislative drafting. Yet Bea—and Ruth—listened closely to what I had to say as we worked through the new legislation, line by line, trying to provide context and meaning to its provisions. Working with them early in my legal career on a project we all cared deeply about provided me with a tie simultaneously to the past and the future of women's rights lawyering, a reassuring connection across generations.

III. JUDITH VLADECK

For me, Judith Vladeck's reputation, both as a formidable employment discrimination lawyer and as a tough but effective role model for women lawyers, preceded her.

After graduating from Columbia Law School in 1947, one of twenty-six women in her class, she became, some years later, a partner in the labor law firm her husband, Stephen Vladeck, founded in the late 1940s. (Their grandson, also named Stephen Vladeck, was my law clerk some years ago and is now a preeminent law professor at the University of Texas, well known to those who watch CNN legal commentary or read newspaper op ed pages.)

Before I met Judith, I was told by others that she was a strict task mistress in the law firm she had taken over after her husband's death, particularly for young women lawyers. She insisted that women lawyers had to dress in carefully curated business attire as she always did, telling them that they had to do so to be taken seriously as women lawyers, and also had to speak forcefully, not reticently. And Judith practiced and taught courtroom flair combined with careful factual analysis, brooking no mistakes and no backing down.

To me, Judith was unfailingly kind and supportive. Like Bea, Judith was a chain smoker and an intimidating figure. At meetings of union lawyers, we were often the only two women lawyers in a room full of men, including in the early days of an organization that became known as the AFL-CIO Lawyers Coordinating Committee. It was at one of those meetings that Judith, dressed impeccably as usual, first introduced herself to me as the oldest living woman union labor lawyer—perhaps Ruth Weyand was no longer alive (Ruth died in 1986, in a car accident), or, more probably, was no longer practicing labor law. And she always was sure to speak up forcefully and with assurance at those meetings, challenging male attorneys she had known much longer than I had. The example resonated, and, over time, I was able to thrust aside my own reticence and speak my mind.

Like Ruth and Bea, with the advent of Title VII, Judith switched gears, in her case from union labor law, and dedicated herself almost entirely to challenging sex discrimination in employment. For her, that meant representing mostly women professionals—academics, engineers, and doctors—but also women construction workers.

Judith sued formidable employers—the City University of New York, Union Carbide, Chase Manhattan, New York Hospital-Cornell Medical Center. She became known by her opponents as a lawyer not to be trifled with—she traced salary histories for thousands of female faculty members at the City University of New York to prove a pattern of unequal pay, for example, and on one occasion waved before a judge a demeaning sketch left on a female client's desk. And she was known by her clients as an attorney entirely on their side. My own efforts in employment discrimination law were less colorful, as I rarely appeared in trial courts and instead appeared for the parties or amici in cases on appeal or in the Supreme Court, relying on records made by courageous lawyers like Judith Vladeck in the trial courts.

* * *

I have on the wall in my chambers a Department of Labor Women's Bureau poster featuring the stylized silhouette of several striding women and the caption "Women's Work Counts." These three women lawyers strode against barriers, and their work certainly counted. As a believer in conveying stories of meaningful lives—more meaningful than advice—to new generations, I am grateful to Ruth, Bea, and Judith for their life's work, and have tried to convey that gratitude by telling their tales, however briefly.

BIO

Marsha S. Berzon

Judge Marsha S. Berzon is a graduate of Radcliffe College and the law school at the University of California (UC), Berkeley, where she was Articles Editor of the *California Law Review*. She served as a law clerk to Justice William J. Brennan, Jr., of the United States Supreme Court and for Judge James R. Browning of the United States Court of Appeals for the Ninth Circuit.

Before joining the United States Ninth Circuit Court of Appeals, Judge Berzon was an appellate and Supreme Court advocate at Altshuler, Berzon, Nussbaum, Berzon & Rubin, a San Francisco law firm. She presented cases in most of the federal circuit courts and the appellate courts of California and several other states. She filed briefs in dozens of cases in the United States Supreme Court, appearing four times as an oral advocate before the Court. Among the cases in which Judge Berzon participated were many setting important precedents in the fields of labor and employment, environmental law, women's rights (including the landmark employment discrimination case, *UAW v. Johnson Controls*), and free speech law.

While in practice, Judge Berzon served as Associate General Counsel of the AFL-CIO; as a member of the Executive Committee of the Bar Association of San Francisco's Labor and Employment Law Section, co-chair of the Appellate Courts Committee of the Bar Association of San Francisco, Treasurer of the Labor and Employment Law Section of the State Bar of California, member of the Board of Directors of the AFL-CIO Lawyers Coordinating Committee, member of the Board of Directors of the Legal Aid Society of San Francisco, Vice President and member of the Board of Directors of the ACLU of Northern California, and member of the California Commission on the Future of the Legal Profession and the State Bar.

In the fall of 1994, Judge Berzon was practitioner in residence at Cornell Law School, where she taught Supreme Court litigation. In the fall of 1998, she was a practitioner in residence at Indiana University Law School, and in the fall of 2003, she was the Alvin B. and Janice Rubin Lecturer at the Paul F. Hebert Law Center of Louisiana State University. She has taught at Berkeley Law and currently teaches

Current Constitutional Cases as an adjunct professor at the UC Hastings College of the Law. Judge Berzon received the Faye Stender Award from the California Women Lawyers' Association for her contribution to establishing the legal rights of women, the American Jewish Committee's Learned Hand Award, the American Bar Association's Margaret Brent Women Lawyers of Achievement Award, and the Berkeley Law Jensen Award for Public Service for 2022. Judge Berzon gave the Madison Lecture at New York University Law School in 2008, and the David Feller lecture at the UC Berkeley School of Law in 2003. She has written many law review articles and book chapters.

Judge Berzon was confirmed as a judge of the Ninth Circuit on March 9, 2000. She is currently a Fellow of the American Bar Foundation and a member of the American Law Institute, and has been a member of the Board of Advisors to the Center on Law and Information Policy at Fordham Law School.

BIO

A Judge's Journey

15

Nancy Gertner

*F*ormer Federal District Court Judge Nancy Gertner
writes with heart and humor about her very nontraditional path to the bench. Her honest depiction of the
experience, including the uncomfortable compromise
seemingly struck between two senators to move her
nomination forward, reveals both her own tenacity
and courage as well as the political side of the Senate
confirmation process.

    Judge Gertner also demonstrates that it is possible—
indeed critical—to rule with impartiality as to outcomes
while judging with clarity, purpose, and heart. Her
words offer a wise lesson at a time when Americans are
losing trust in the judiciary.

Lauren Stiller Rikleen, Editor

Mine was not the usual path to the bench. In fact, my confirmation trajectory was described in my memoir, *In Defense of Women: Memoirs of an Unrepentant Advocate* (Beacon, 2011). I describe a panel at the Yale Law School in the 1990s sponsored by women students. They wanted to know how one becomes a judge.

There were two panelists: Judge Sonia Sotomayor and me. I had been a judge of the U.S. District Court in Massachusetts for only a few years. Sonia was then on the Second Circuit Court of Appeals in New York City. We were both Yale Law graduates—I in the class of 1971, she in the class of 1979.

Sonia went first, speaking deliberately as is her wont: How does one become a judge? You graduate this fine institution with a stellar record. You work as a prosecutor in the Manhattan DA's office and then in private practice. You have clear principles, but you take care not to be publicly associated with controversial causes. You demonstrate in every way, in word and deed, that you can be a neutral, temperate jurist. And then you become a judge.

It was my turn. How does one become a judge? Yes, you graduate from this fine institution with a stellar record. But then, I said, pausing for effect with voice getting louder, the cadence quicker: You represent the first lesbian, feminist, radical, anti-Vietnam War activist accused of killing a police officer you can find; that would be your first major case in prime time. You take every abortion case in Massachusetts; you speak out on the major hot-button legal issues of the day in rallies on Boston Common or on television, or on the editorial pages of newspapers. You represent defendants of all kinds, from those in political corruption cases to high-profile murder cases, and, for the final coup de grace, you marry the legal director of the American Civil Liberties Union (ACLU) of Massachusetts. In short, after doing everything that, at the time, should disqualify you for the position, you become a judge!

It was, of course, a funny presentation—but true. For twenty-four years I had been a high-profile civil rights and criminal defense lawyer. I had practiced law at a time when there were few women lawyers, fewer still women *trial* lawyers. Like many of my generation, I had endured: judges' snide remarks like the one who, when I asked to have a woman law student accompany me at counsel table, said, "I thought one woman in a courtroom was bad enough"; or the comments of potential employers who insisted that women were not cut out to do trial work; or of opposing counsel who regularly wrote to my male partner whenever I wrote to him (even though I was lead counsel); or lawyers who thought that a single woman lawyer was open season to harass; and on and on.

Then there was my family. I was born on the Lower East Side of Manhattan, the second daughter of Moishe and Sadie Gertner. The four of us lived in a tenement until I was seven, sleeping in the same room—me in a crib because there was no space for another bed. Flushing, Queens, where we next moved, was a step up—to a lower-middle-class community in the flight path of LaGuardia Airport.

They were bewildered with their daughter. My father urged my older sister to take the commercial rather than the academic courses at Flushing High School; an academic course, he said, would be "wasted" on a woman. We were not permitted to leave town for college. "Girls are supposed to live in their father's house or their husband's." She didn't listen; I wouldn't either.

I had tried to ignore my family's reaction to my chosen career, and worse, to the fact that I did not marry or have children until I was 39. My mother literally said to me when I got into Yale Law School, that I had "priced myself out of the male market!" Her aims for me were, I suppose, as high as her own aspirations went, to hearth and home and no further.

But I persisted—trying criminal and civil cases, appeals at all levels, state and federal courts, and for good measure, teaching and writing on the side. (I never needed much sleep, which stood me in good stead when I finally did become a mother.)

At thirty-nine, I married my dear friend and co-counsel, John Reinstein, the legal director of the ACLU, and had my first child, Stephen. (I like to say that menopause and birth were neck and neck but that was an overstatement.) Less than two years later came Peter, who joined my stepdaughter, Sarah, in a new composed family. True there were new challenges, but having a family when my career was well established enabled me to call the shots in ways that many women cannot—with my partners, with judges, with clients. To clients, I would say: You want me? Then wait until I have finished nursing Peter.

And I loved trying cases when I was pregnant. During the other lawyer's closing argument, I would rub my belly and moan softly. It seemed only fair; Clarence Darrow was fabled to put a wire in his cigar (when you were permitted to smoke in court), so that the ash would linger and linger without falling off. The jury, they say, was transfixed. For all the years that male trial lawyers took advantage of their sexual stereotypes—the booming voices, the insider advantages, the presumption of competence—now I would take advantage of mine.

I recall once, long before marriage and children, in a study group I was in, arguing vehemently against any special relationship between mothers and children. It was mythological, I said, hype in order to socially construct motherhood and keep women tied to the home.

Then Stephen was born. John took a paternity leave. He had been at my side at the birth and would stick by me for two weeks. One morning, when I was still in bed, with Stephen nursing, John announced that he would go into his office for a bit. It occurred to me that I could not. Whatever its source—nature, social construction—I was entangled and in love with this child. I would not venture far from him.

Still, I was surprised when everyone asked: Would I return to work now that I had a child? Return to work? This lawyer identity had been mine for over thirteen years. It was the mom part that was new. Of course, I would go back to work.

Sex harassment cases, murder cases raising battered women defenses or tied up with racism, white collar and blue collar, discrimination against women in the academy and private industry, high-profile and unknown—my usual mix continued in my not-so-usual career.

Then Bill Clinton was elected President. Bill and Hillary were classmates at Yale. Many of my friends were getting jobs in the government; I thought that if I did not make a move then, the opportunity would pass me by. I doubted if they would be happy with my nomination as a judge. Hillary, with whom I was quite close, knew me as a radical in law school. I was far from the risk-averse choice.

The nomination papers were extensive. I went over every case I had ever done. "What are the cases you are proudest of?" the application asked. My reply was *Moe v. Secretary of Administration and Finance,* the Massachusetts case establishing the right to choose abortion under the Massachusetts constitution. And so it went.

Fact is, I did not expect to be a judge. I only expected to try. Senator Ted Kennedy, however, had other ideas. He nominated me for the bench and put his considerable, considerable influence behind me. One of my partners, Tom Dwyer, assembled an extraordinary packet of letters in support. Somehow, someway, after all my controversial work and cases, literally everyone that had opposed me in court—U.S. attorneys, District Attorneys, the Attorney General—agreed that while they parted company with me on some issues, I would make a superb judge.

Of course, it wasn't easy. It never is. In November 1993, my confirmation hearing was scheduled. While the press response to my nomination had been overwhelmingly favorable, a week before the hearing, a local columnist for the *Boston Herald,* Don Feder, whom I did not know, attacked me in print. He compared me to Lorena Bobbitt, the woman who had just been arrested for cutting off a piece of her abusive husband's penis. "Judge Gertner," he said, "would do to justice with her gavel what Lorena did to her husband with a kitchen knife."

Perfect. Scratch the surface of any woman's image and come up with a stereotype—here the castrating bitch—whether it remotely fit or even made sense.

And it worked—nearly. Four Massachusetts nominees were presented to the Senate Judiciary Committee, three were voted out of committee; I was not included. Senator Jesse Helms had objected to me based on the Don Feder piece. All my work reduced to this caricature. It seemed absurd, but also déjà vu.

Four months later, John and I were eating breakfast when I read in the paper that Kennedy had voted for a Helms-sponsored school prayer amendment. I called the Senator and insisted I was not worth it. By that afternoon, I was confirmed.

When Clarence Thomas was confirmed to the Supreme Court, his metaphor for the kind of judge that he would be was "stripped down like a runner," "without entangling opinions or prejudgments." Absurd, in my view.

We pick judges in their forties and fifties presumably with life experience. We understand that they are likely to have opinions, feelings, positions. Everyone who decides he or she is going to be a judge must move to neutral. And that move should be no more difficult for a civil rights lawyer than for a prosecutor or a corporate lawyer, for a woman than for a man. I have always been suspicious of the juror who said (especially in a high-profile case): I know nothing, I read nothing, I have no opinions. I have always felt more comfortable with the juror who acknowledges his or her opinions, who is committed to struggling with them.

I knew who I was, who I had been, what I believed in. A passion for justice. A determination to work and work to all hours of the night until I found an answer. Looking at the people before me in court as people I might have grown up with or represented. Feeling empathy, and yet learning detachment.

And then there was this: I had been a judge for a week when I got a call in the middle of a proceeding. My clerk said, "Peter is on the phone." "Can't be," I said. "He doesn't know how to dial. He is only six." "But judge," she insisted, "Peter is on the phone." I announce solemnly to the lawyers in front of me that I have a very important call to take. I go into my lobby and pick up the phone. "Peter," I say, "what's the matter?" "Mama, there's no chocolate pudding in my snack!" Melting at the sound of his voice I say, "Sweetie, it is in the paper bag in your pack." "Oh," he says, "Bye."

I ascend the bench. The world has come back in perspective.

BIO

Nancy Gertner

Judge Nancy Gertner is a graduate of Barnard College and Yale Law School, where she was an editor on the *Yale Law Journal*. She received her MA in Political Science at Yale University.

She has been an instructor at Yale Law School, teaching sentencing and comparative sentencing institutions, since 1998. She was appointed to the bench in 1994 by President Clinton.

In 2008 she received the Thurgood Marshall Award from the American Bar Association, Section of Individual Rights and Responsibilities, only the second woman to receive it (Justice Ginsburg was the first). She became a Leadership Council Member of the International Center for Research on Women the same year. In 2010 she received the Morton A. Brody Distinguished Judicial Service Award. In 2011 she received the Massachusetts Bar Association's Hennessey Award for Judicial Excellence, and an honorary Doctor of Laws degree from Brandeis University. In 2012 she received the Arabella Babb Mansfield Award from the National Association of Women Lawyers, and the Lelia J. Robinson Award from the Women's Bar Association of Massachusetts. In 2014, Judge Gertner was a recipient of the Margaret Brent Women Lawyers of Achievement Award from the American Bar Association Commission on Women in the Profession.

Judge Gertner has been profiled on a number of occasions in the *Boston Globe,* the *ABA Journal, Boston Magazine,* and the *Wall Street Journal.* She has written and spoken widely on various legal issues and has appeared as a keynote speaker, panelist, or lecturer concerning civil rights, civil liberties, employment, criminal justice, and procedural issues throughout the United States, Europe, and Asia.

Her autobiography, *In Defense of Women: Memoirs of an Unrepentant Advocate,* was released on April 26, 2011. Her book *The Law of Juries,* coauthored with attorney Judith Mizner, was published in 1997 and updated in 2010. Her most recent book, *Representative Opinions of Ruth Bader Ginsburg,* which she edited and for which she provided commentary, was published in 2022. She has published articles, and chapters on sentencing, discrimination, and forensic evidence, women's rights, and the jury system.

In September 2011, Judge Gertner retired from the federal bench and became part of the faculty of the Harvard Law School, teaching a number of subjects, including criminal law, criminal procedure, forensic science, and sentencing, as well as continuing to teach and write about women's issues around the world.

BIO

Angels, Mentors, and Friends

16

Peggy Quince

*J*ustice Quince provides a richly detailed description *of her segregated childhood in rural Virginia, and the racism she and her family regularly encountered. Her story shows how the nation's deeply engrained institutional biases presented barriers to an equal education long after* Brown v. Board of Education *offered the promise of integrated schools.*

The Justice's reflections are a reminder that American history is based on facts and lived experiences that are not altered by contemporary efforts to deny that reality.

Justice Quince also offers poignant insights into her father's loving guidance and its foundational importance to her strength and resilience. And she demonstrates how the kindness and compassion of those who cross our paths—friends and strangers alike—can change lives.

Lauren Stiller Rikleen, Editor

As a Negro, African American, Black girl growing up in rural Virginia, a part of the Jim Crow South, I learned from an early age that Black people, at least Black people of African descent, were treated differently from white people.

My first real perceived experience with exclusion occurred on a visit to a doctor's office. During this time of my life, I lived in a neighborhood with other Blacks and did not give much thought to the fact that everyone in the immediate neighborhood, except the person who owned the corner store, was Black.

My younger brother and I had dermatitis and would have to visit a doctor when it got too bad. On my first visit to the doctor's office when I was about six years old—at least it was the first doctor's appointment that I remember—we were told to go to the waiting room where other Black people were sitting. I could plainly see that there was another room where only white people were sitting. I noticed that some of the white patients who came in after me were seen by the doctor before me.

This meant that I had to wait a longer time beyond my scheduled appointment time before I saw the doctor. From that day forward my eyes were open to racism, and I began to see that Blacks and whites were treated differently in many ways.

When I was in the second grade, my parents' marriage ended when my mother left our home for the last time. There had been several occasions when my mother had gone away for a week or two, but she had always returned eventually. However, this time there was no return, and my father was left with five children, Mary, Peggy, Barbara, Solomon, Jr., and Michael—the youngest of us was still in diapers.

But as far as I could determine at the age of six or seven, my father, after becoming a single parent, did not miss a beat. He continued to make sure we were fed and clothed. I must say, however, that I did not like having to help change diapers. Luckily, my little brother was soon potty trained, and diapers became a thing of the past.

My father also soon realized that he needed to hire someone to take care of his children during the day; only two of us, my older sister and I, were school age. There were three children who needed supervision and guidance on weekdays. Thus, for several years we had a housekeeper who lived-in during the week; she went home to her family for the weekends.

My father was not well educated; he had not finished high school. However, he had the wisdom of his namesake, Solomon. He understood and appreciated the fact that education was the key to upward mobility in America, so he made getting an education mandatory in our household; it was the number one priority.

As an example, we lived for years in an agricultural area of Virginia. Many Black people in this area did the planting and harvesting for the white landowners that were around us. Often, some of the Black children were taken out of school for several weeks to help their parents with the planting and harvesting. My father would not allow us to miss school for this reason.

Although we did not miss school to "work in the fields," my now deceased older sister, Mary, and I did this type of agricultural work sometimes in the summer. This was a way to get spending money, since my father could not afford allowances. We also used the money to buy back-to-school clothing. It was exhausting work, but worth the effort so we could have some of the "luxuries" that other children had. But doing this kind of manual labor reinforced my desire to get an education.

My father would only allow us to be out of school when we were sick. In fact, if one of us said he or she was too ill to go to school, that person had to spend the entire day in bed, no getting better after the school bus had left. Of course, the only way to get to school was on the school bus because my father would have already left in the car to get to work. As you can imagine, staying in bed all day was no fun, so we were only sick if we really were. Because we did not live near our friends, school was also our in-person social opportunity, another reason to get on that bus and go to school.

"School is your job." This short sentence was my father's favorite saying, and it became my mantra. This was not just a saying. The rule in our home was you could not watch television until you had completed your homework. We needed to do our homework early because bedtime was 8:30 pm (we could stay up until 11:00 pm on Fridays and Saturdays only). This bedtime was ironclad, Sunday through Thursday, with the only exception being an excessive amount of homework. So, if we wanted to watch television at all, it paid to do homework as soon as we got home from school.

My father believed in the honor system, so he believed us when we said we either had no homework or had finished it. We, at least for the most part, were truthful on this issue because we did not want to face the consequences if Daddy learned that we had not been truthful. He was a firm believer in the adage, "Spare the rod and spoil the child." I saw the rod enough to try to spare myself additional such experiences.

We tried to follow his teachings and my father experienced some success in his rearing of five children without the presence of a mother. He made us understand that as Negroes, we had to work hard, do well, and stay out of trouble.

We took his messages of working and studying to heart. We also took to heart his message of staying out of trouble; not one of his five children was ever in jail or prison. Of his five children, four attended college, three completed undergraduate school, and one completed law school. The one who did not complete college, because she said it simply was not for her, nonetheless lived a fulfilling life both personally and professionally. The one sibling who did not attend college at all was in the military for twelve years and obtained a position with the federal government after he left the military.

In addition to the love and discipline I learned from my father, I was blessed to have teachers who believed in my ability to succeed. I was six years old when the United States Supreme Court decided *Brown v. Board of Education*, 347 U.S. 483 (1954). Despite this ruling that basically required the desegregation of the public schools, I attended segregated schools from kindergarten through the twelfth grade.

In response to the *Brown* decision, some of the Virginia schools closed to avoid having to comply. Others simply continued to operate in the same manner as they had before—separate and unequal. In fact, in response to Senator Harry F. Byrd's call for "massive resistance" to the integration of schools, some schools in Virginia closed from one day to five years to prevent school integration. Because of this white resistance, I continued to attend segregated schools.

I believe there were some personal benefits, however, from attending my segregated schools. Despite their extremely low salaries and having to operate with used textbooks and poor facilities, I had Black teachers who cared about the future of the students. I was not allowed to be a goof-off. Not only was I punished in school for a failure to perform "up to my potential," but my teachers would call my father, resulting in punishment at home also. My teachers genuinely cared about me and my future. This caring manifested itself inside and outside of the classroom.

Several teachers encouraged me to participate in activities that were available to students who excelled academically. I have a scrapbook from my elementary and high school days (no junior high or middle schools then). My scrapbook was literally falling apart, and I recently replaced it, trying to arrange each page in the same way that the original was arranged. In this scrapbook are the many certificates and awards I received for participation in scholarly competitions. I was a good science and math student, which led to my decision to major in Zoology in college. Some of these certificates were for participation in math and science fairs. Other certificates were received for Humanities, Government, History, Geography, Biology, and Chemistry. But again, all these opportunities for participation were fueled by teachers who cared about my future.

A couple of my teachers invited me into their homes to spend nights and/or weekends with them and their children. While visiting with them, I was often exposed to ideas and concepts that were not discussed at my home. Many times, during these weekend stays, we visited places that I had not been to before.

Because we were poor, we often did not attend events or visit places that were normal for people who were not living on or below the poverty line. For example, my schools would sometimes go on field trips to some of the historic sites in Virginia—Williamsburg, Jamestown, Yorktown, Luray Caverns, etc. On several occasions I had to tell my teacher(s) that I could not go on the trip because my father could not afford to pay for it.

My teachers, who were overworked and underpaid, would pay for me to go on the excursion, making it possible for me to visit places I might not have been able to otherwise. They did not want the fact that I was poor to hamper my learning experiences. What loving Angels! Thank you to all my elementary and high school teachers; I love you!

Even when I went off to college, they stayed connected and got reports on my progress. I loved them for their care and concern.

The idea that others believed in me served as additional motivation for me to succeed.

Because I had been a good student, I received numerous scholarship offers to both historically Black colleges and universities as well as to some prestigious majority schools, such as the University of Pennsylvania and Grinnell College. I chose to attend Howard University in Washington, DC, an essentially Black university.

Two factors motivated my decision—I did not want to be too far away from home, and second, and more important, at the age of eighteen I was not yet ready to be thrust into a basically all-white environment. I knew that I was not mature enough or savvy enough to be able to effectively deal with the discrimination and hostility I would face. Additionally, Howard offered me a scholarship and a grant that would and did more than cover tuition as well as room and board.

So off to Howard I went, and it was one of the best decisions of my life. I could not have chosen a more maturing and loving environment in which to come of age.

A good friend from high school also decided to attend Howard, and we requested an assignment as roommates. We got that assignment, but it also included a third roommate. Our room contained a single bed, bunkbeds, two built-in closets, and a moveable closet. I don't remember if I was the last of the roommates to arrive or not, but I had the top bunk and the moveable closet.

The third roommate was a girl from Chicago, Illinois. The day we meet her, she swaggered into the room in a leather jacket, and what I unfairly and prejudicially considered a tough-girl attitude. She was a confident person, proved to be a good friend, and introduced me to some people who became life-long friends. From this experience, I learned the meaning of the phrase, "You can't judge a book by its cover."

This was but the first of the many lessons I learned at Howard. The most important of the lessons was to have confidence in myself and to take people as you find them. As a poor country girl, I came to school with little. The clothes I had were either bought at the discount stores or gotten from Goodwill. Some of the students at Howard came from affluent families, and they had beautiful, expensive clothes. In fact, during my third year, I had a roommate who was beautiful, with wonderful clothes, and money from her parents. She was a good person, and because we were the same size, she allowed me to borrow some of her clothes for special occasions. That generosity helped me make a good impression when I was interviewed to join my sorority, Alpha Kappa Alpha, as I borrowed her dress and shoes for the occasion.

However, despite having what I thought of as all the advantages, my roommate did not have the confidence that I associated with the "beautiful people." I thought she had a golden life. However, she allowed herself to be bullied and abused by her boyfriend. I could not believe that a person with these advantages would allow someone else to demean her. Other lessons learned—"All that glitters is not gold. Beauty is only skin deep."

The dormitory that I lived in was reserved for scholarship students—those who were in the top percentile of their high school classes. Thus, I was surrounded by students who were topnotch. At the end of each seminar, we talked about our classes and the grades we received in various "difficult" courses. I learned from this experience that I could compete with students that I considered to be very smart. Because I could compete, that fact gave me the confidence to join various on-campus organizations, and even to run for office.

Although I was not successful in my run for office, I learned a valuable lesson from this defeat. Even if you do not win, the world does not come to an end, and you need to continue to work toward your goals. This lesson came in handy when I applied to both the Second District Court of Appeal and the Florida Supreme Court. I had to apply twice for both courts because I was not the successful applicant the first time around.

Even though I was a Zoology major at Howard, I became interested in a possible new career area. During the late 1960s and early 1970s, our country was in the midst of the civil rights movement and the war in Vietnam. There were legal matters associated with these issues. Because of my concern in these areas, I became interested in attending law school.

I was a scholarship student and could not afford to change my major or extend my time in undergraduate school. I learned, however, that you did not need to have a particular major for law school, so I continued down my scientific path. After graduation, I took entrance examinations for both medical school and law school. My final decision is obvious. This was another lesson learned, which became advice that I give to young people: Don't be discouraged if you finish college and still must make decisions about the direction of your life.

While making my decision between law school and medical school, I worked for two years before I started law school. I worked at an insurance company, where I first encountered the four-day work week and flexible work hours. In fact, the company allowed me to move from an account representative position to the computer operations area of the company to work an evening shift while I was in law school. I had gotten a scholarship that covered my tuition, but I worked to pay for room and board. My father was not able to help me; I had a brother and a sister in undergraduate school and any money he had was used to help them. He did give me a down payment for a car, because I needed transportation to and from school, work, and home. With his limited resources, my father did what he could to help all of us along the paths we had chosen.

This change of job assignment also gave me an opportunity to study while at work. As a computer operator, I was responsible for running various computer jobs on a mainframe (no individual computers in those days). Often a job would run for hours without much attention from the operator. Under those circumstances, I could do my assignments without waiting until I got home, which was generally after 11:00 pm. I sometimes worked with a gentleman on the 3:00 to 11:00 shift who would tell me to go home and study because he could cover the shift for both of us, yet another angel. The company's decision to allow me this latitude was the beginning of my personal assistance and mentorships from law school to the present.

Law school was my first nonsegregated learning experience. It was clear to me after only a few days on campus that there were professors and students who were not pleased to see people who looked like me. Despite the treatment Black students received from some, not all, I learned to survive and often thrive. One of the people who helped keep me going physically was a lady who worked at a local pizza restaurant. I would come in and order a one topping pizza, but because she knew I was a struggling law student, she put multiple toppings on my pizza. Those pizzas became a meal for several days.

I found unofficial inspiration and mentorship from people who I am not sure knew that they were part of my reasons to keep going. Three of the people associated with the law school who come to mind were my constitutional law professor, a lady who worked in the office of student affairs, and the lawyer who supervised the school's Neighborhood Legal Services Clinic.

While I was not the most talkative student in my classes, I did participate to some extent. I really enjoyed my constitutional law class, so much so, that I also took advanced constitutional law, which was not a required course. My professor was an interesting person aside from his interactive and fun class discussions. He was adamantly opposed to the war in Vietnam and had filed several law-suits in protest of that war. He made constitutional law come alive and made it applicable to our daily lives. After several responses to questions that I asked during class, he began calling me "the voice of reason." I cannot adequately explain what a boost this was to my mental well-being. I truly began to believe that I could compete at this level, in this integrated environment, in a predominantly white profession.

I began law school having never met or seen in person any lawyer or judge. I really did not understand what to expect from law school or how to navigate the nuances of what courses and professors to take, or extracurricular activities in which I should become involved. So, when I had a question, I went to the office of student affairs and talked with Mrs. Garcia. In the early 1970s, she understood the diffi-culties that the Black students were experiencing. As a result, she was always there to explain and give advice about classes and teachers. She was instrumental in having me appointed as a student member to the committee that reviewed admission applications. Mrs. Garcia was an angel (mentor) in disguise!

During the summer after my second year in law school and during my final seminar, I worked in the legal clinic that was a part of the law school. The attorney/professor who supervised the clinic was a dynamo who understood the problems faced by people who could not afford the services of a private attorney. She taught us to appreciate and understand these challenges. She allowed us, under her supervi-sion of course, to handle cases from intake to trial. Her mentorship gave me/us the confidence to talk to clients, opposing counsel, and judges. What an incredible opportunity to gain first-hand experience in how to practice law! What an opportunity to actually practice law! I felt like I was becoming the lawyer I wanted to be.

For me, the end of law school brought a certain amount of uncertainty. I was not sure what I really wanted to do or how to assist the people who needed my services. I finally decided to work with the new agency in DC that was going to administer the city's newly enacted rent control law.

My future husband, the late Fred L. Buckine, and I were law students together. As one of my long-lasting mentors, he steered me to this agency. We were law school colleagues, and he was the assistant director of the agency. He explained to me the significance of the rent control office, how it was designed to help people, and the role I would play in this important area—affordable housing.

Thus, my first job out of law school was as a hearing officer, hearing cases involving requests for rent increases by landlords and petitions by the tenants for rent decreases based often on the landlord's failure to keep the premises in a habitable condition. I enjoyed that opportunity to contribute to the community by holding both the landlords and the tenants to their contractual obligations.

A couple of years after finishing law school and beginning my first job, I got married. My husband's father was deceased, and his mother lived alone in Florida. She was not in good health, so my husband and I decided to move to Florida to be near her.

Prior to moving to Florida, we had our older daughter. My father, who lived with us, became my daughter's caregiver at his insistence. I wanted to hire a person to care for her because my father, who had worked hard all his life, was now retired. I wanted him to enjoy life and do whatever he wanted to do by way of relaxation after a job well done. He informed me that he wanted to take care of my baby because he missed out on so much when my siblings and I were growing up because he worked as many hours as he could. He moved to Florida with us, and he took care of both of my children until his death when they were ages nine and six. Solomon Quince (affectionately called Dear) was the first angel/mentor in my life. He died in 1986, at the age of seventy. I will always regret that he did not live to see me invested as a judge.

Our intention was to return to DC at some point in the future. My husband had taken the Florida Bar exam after law school, but I had taken the Virginia Bar exam. Therefore, when we moved to Florida, I had to sit for the Florida exam before I could practice law there. Florida did not and does not have a waiver or reciprocity provision.

I practiced general civil law for a short period of time, but after giving birth to my second child, I decided I wanted a regular nine to five job so I could spend more time with the children. Both Fred and I were in private practice at this point, but after a move from Bradenton to Tampa, Fred worked at the State Attorney's Office, and I began my thirteen-and-a-half-year tenure with the Florida Attorney General's Office.

It is interesting to note that prior to my position with the Attorney General's Office, I had only been involved with preparing and arguing one appeal. That appeal was while I was in private practice in Virginia. A friend and I represented a young man who was convicted of armed robbery. The appeal of that case was to the Virginia Supreme Court. This was my first appearance before a supreme court, and I was unusually nervous. But my partner in this appeal process, Ida Outlaw, was there and we kept each other grounded and helped each other prepare and present the case despite our trepidations. Although the appeal was not successful, we had represented the defendant at the trial level where we had convinced the trial judge to give the defendant the low end of the sentencing range.

Together, Ida and I worked on several cases; we were mentors to each other. Joe Cocker had it right when he made famous Lennon and McCartney's song, I get by "With a Little Help from My Friends." This experience gave me the confidence to apply for an appellate position with the Attorney General's Office.

In the Attorney General's Office, I learned appellate law and constitutional law. I argued cases in the Second District Court of Appeal, the Florida Supreme Court, the Federal District Court and the Fifth and Eleventh Circuit Courts of Appeal. Although I did not have an opportunity to argue a case at the United States Supreme Court, I filed several briefs in that court.

It is also in this position that I made some lifelong friends and had many mentors who have continued to support me to this day.

Unfortunately, there are many people in our profession who believe one is less than a true lawyer if he or she is a "government lawyer." Nothing can be further from the truth! It has been my experience, as one who has devoted the bulk of her legal career to public service/government work, that brilliant, competent, hardworking lawyers can be found throughout the profession, including in the government sector. I found many of them in the attorney general's office.

The thirteen and a half years I spent with the Florida Attorney General's Office were some of the best years of my life both professionally and personally. The Florida Attorney General's Office was headquartered in Tallahassee, but there were multiple offices around the state, one in each of the five areas where there was a District Court of Appeal (Tallahassee, the Tampa area, Miami, West Palm Beach, and Daytona Beach). The office that I was assigned to was in Tampa.

When I began my tenure, there were only seven attorneys in the Tampa Bureau Criminal Division; today there are thirty. In Florida, defendants have an appeal of right from the circuit courts to the appellate courts, and they freely exercise that right. One can imagine that attorneys are faced with new and varied issues each day. There were several seasoned attorneys, especially in the Tallahassee office, that we called when we needed advice on how to proceed, but we generally learned from and relied on each other.

There is no greater learning experience than conferring with colleagues on how to handle a particular case. That is the kind of collegial relationship we developed at the Attorney General's Office. My friend, Robert Krauss, was one of the persons who served as both a mentor and mentee. He was a colleague who gave sage advice on the handling of multiple issues. But he and others in the office were more than colleagues. We developed a relationship that was more than friendship, we became a family that not only included attorneys but also several support staff persons. We were a family that played together and were there for each other. Several of us spent a lot of our leisure time together. We planned opportunities to be together, sporting events, dinners, and activities at each other's homes. We spent some holidays together, and we celebrated our personal special days together. The relationships did not change even after I became the Tampa Bureau Chief.

These colleagues encouraged me to apply for both the judgeship on the Second District Court of Appeal as well as on the Florida

Supreme Court. It was a bittersweet day when I left the Attorney General's Office to take my place on the Second District. The love, encouragement, and continued friendship of my family at the Attorney General's Office helped sustain me during difficult times when others thought I did not belong on the court and let me know it. In a room full of lawyers and judges, when I was with my judge colleagues, I was sometimes asked if I worked for one of the white male judges, assumptions made and expressed.

This was not a new experience for me to be placed in the position of having to explain who I was. In one of my first appearances as a lawyer, I approached the bench as my client's case was called. The judge, in a resounding voice, asked me if I was the defendant. Mind you, I was dressed like all the other lawyers in the courtroom, and I looked, at least by my dress, like a lawyer. I swallowed my tongue and my pride and proceeded to explain my position as the defendant's attorney. I won that case! It was not the last time I was reminded that I was not the "usual" attorney people were accustomed to seeing in the courtroom.

My relationship with my colleagues at the Attorney General's Office of necessity changed somewhat when I was appointed to the Second District Court of Appeal, as this was the court where we had argued the bulk of our cases. Although I did not handle criminal cases for at least the first six months of my time on the Second District, I eventually was on panels when attorneys from the Attorney General's Office were representing the State.

Thus began the period of my life where I saw my A.G. family only at public functions, and they were always invited to public occasions such as investitures, inductions, and bar association speeches. I had also developed a great relationship with the Attorney General, Robert Butterworth, and other members of his staff in Tallahassee, and administered his oath of office after he was reelected in 1998. I missed my more private times with them, but I knew that we would resume our personal relationship once my time on the bench was concluded. To this day, these colleagues, friends, mentors, family are still in my life, we still share activities and spend time together, even in retirement. Today we call ourselves the "A.G. Alums."

Although my relationships on the District Court were in no way similar to what I had enjoyed at the Attorney General's Office,

I nonetheless found mentors and friends on that court. Even though I was now a judge, I was intimidated to be working with, as a colleague, judges that I had appeared before as counsel for the state. But a couple of them, the late Judge Herboth Ryder and the late Judge Monterey "Buddy" Campbell, took me under their wings and got me through my years on the court. Their mentorship was invaluable! Not only did they give me advice and help me understand some of the issues that arose in various cases, but they also acknowledged when I made valid points that they had not considered. This type of give and take helped me to grow as a judge. Both encouraged me to apply for a position on the Florida Supreme Court and believed I could handle the work and be successful there.

After being appointed to the Florida Supreme Court by Governor Lawton and then Governor-Elect Jeb Bush, my leave-taking from the District Court was hard, but not as heart wrenching as leaving the Attorney General's Office. I learned a lot from the judges on the Second District; although our relationships never progressed to the point where I considered them family, they were wonderful colleagues and friends. They were, of course, invited to my investiture at the Supreme Court, and some of them attended.

My experiences on the District Court prepared me for the formidable case load that awaited me at the Supreme Court. You can imagine the number of cases we were assigned on a court with seven members and, for the most part, all decisions made by the entire court. At the District Court level, the cases were almost always decided by three-judge panels. During the time I was on both the District Court and the Supreme Court, Florida was the fourth most populous state in the United States, thus the caseloads in both courts were tremendous. During my final couple of years on the Supreme Court, Florida became the third most populous state.

Over the years, I learned a valuable lesson concerning mentoring and friendship. Not only was it good to receive help, but it was also good and a part of our responsibility to be a mentor and friend to others. Thus, at the Attorney General's Office, at the District Court, and at the Supreme Court, I tried to be a friend and mentor to attorneys that I encountered, especially younger attorneys.

None of us enter the profession knowing exactly what to do under all circumstances. If we are left to our own devices, we are going to make mistakes. Those of us who have practiced for a while should and must help steer others along the path to a successful practice and, hopefully, fewer mistakes.

Additionally, we can and must help young people who are not necessarily a part of the legal profession. Throughout my career, I have tried to mentor and encourage young people to look beyond their immediate circumstances to the possibilities that lie ahead. I have shared some version of this story of my origins and my legal career, including my path to the Florida Supreme Court with students from the elementary, junior high, high school, college, and graduate school levels.

All too often I still encounter students who are the first generation in their families with high school and college diplomas. As a part of my mentoring and encouragement efforts, I invited children from my church in Tampa to come to Tallahassee for my investiture as a justice on the Supreme Court. The church chartered a bus, and I had the marshal of our court, Wilson Barnes, reserve a section of the court for these children.

It was a joy to see their faces and know that they were witnessing history as I was the first African American female to be appointed and serve on the Florida Supreme Court. If even one child was inspired by the event, then I feel that I had "helped somebody." Hopefully, that was not the only time when a person was inspired by what I had achieved from very humble beginnings—beginnings that were much like many in that audience.

My appointment to the Supreme Court did not end my desire and attempts to encourage people to dream dreams and work toward those dreams. The Florida Supreme Court is headquartered in Florida's capital, Tallahassee. Therefore, my husband and I moved from Tampa to Tallahassee, leaving our legal and social family in Tampa. By then, we were empty nesters as both of our children were in college; Peggy (who also went to law school), was at Florida Agricultural and Mechanical University in Tallahassee and Laura (who went into accounting), was at the University of Central Florida in Orlando.

In making such a move, we had to create a new community. I purposefully attended community and bar functions so I could meet people. A source of support was my membership in Alpha Kappa Alpha Sorority, Incorporated. There was and is a graduate chapter of the sorority in Tallahassee (there are two graduate chapters there now), so I transferred my membership from the Tampa chapter to the Tallahassee chapter. The beauty of being in a sorority is the immediate sense of home when you move from one city to another.

One of the first persons I met in Tallahassee who was a part of the legal profession was June McKinney; I met her at a Tallahassee Women Lawyers meeting. She was working at the Attorney General's Office in Tallahassee (as of this writing, she is an Administrative Law Judge with an outstanding record of judicial excellence and demeanor), and we bonded over the fact that we had the A.G.'s office and Howard University in common. From that time to now, we developed a symbiotic relationship that benefited both of us.

Mentoring and friendship are two-way streets. That has certainly been the case with me and June. We are both mentor and mentee to each other. We have helped each other through every situation life has to offer, including graduations, investitures, family illnesses, and deaths. When I have been in distress, whether personally or professionally, she has been there to give much-needed advice, and I have been there for her in stressful situations. Although she is almost young enough to be my daughter, angels come in all shapes and ages.

In addition to June, Alpha Kappa Alpha Sorority and the Links, Incorporated became my social units. It was and is difficult to develop friendships when you are a judge or a justice. At least, I found that to be true. People seem to assume that because you hold a particular position you are not open to pursuing relationships outside of your position. As a result, these groups and individuals formed my network in Tallahassee.

My network also included members of the Supreme Court. Justice Leander Shaw was an African American male on the court at the time I was appointed. During my first weeks on the court, he talked with me about the inner workings of the court; he had been on the court for more than fifteen years and had served as Chief Justice. His advice and counsel helped me to navigate these new waters. The only other female on the court, Justice Barbara Pariente, also was available to explore ideas and viewpoints. When we are open and receptive, we can find mentors at all stages of our lives.

I retired from the Florida Supreme Court on January 7, 2019, after serving on the court for twenty years. In Florida, judges had to retire at age seventy. Although a constitutional amendment was passed by the electorate in November of 2018 that raised the retirement age to seventy-five, it was not applicable to those of us who retired at the same time the amendment became effective.

Fifteen days after I retired, I embarked on a 113-day cruise around the world. It was a marvelous trip! I visited twenty-three countries and made some new friends along the way. My friend Bob Krauss and his wife, Kathy, encouraged me to take this journey, and I will be forever grateful to them for making me commit to this type of travel.

I went on a second lengthy cruise (seventy-five days) in January 2020, which circumnavigated South America and Antarctica. I got back to the United States on March 20, 2020, just when everything was going on lockdown because of the coronavirus. I hope to go on more excursions of this nature in the not-too-distant future. In the meantime, retirement has taught me two other important lessons.

I cannot just sit at home reading, cooking, cleaning, and watching television. I need to be engaged in my community; public service and mentoring know no age limit. Thus, I became engaged in the political process by being a poll watcher and by making donations to worthy candidates. I also coauthored a couple of op ed pieces about the importance of voting, and on the reasons the Florida "anti-protest" bill that the legislature was considering and passed was antithetical to the First Amendment.

In addition, I began to realize that most voters have little knowledge about some of the issues they are asked to decide when they cast their ballots. Florida has an initiative process whereby amendments can be made to the Florida Constitution.

On the November 2020 ballot, there were six proposed amendments. Because some of them had grave consequences that were not readily apparent, I analyzed the amendments and did presentations throughout the State to various groups concerning same of the ramifications of either a yes or no vote. The initiatives ranged from what was termed "open primaries," to a gradual increase in the minimum wage, to making constitutional changes proposed by citizens more difficult to pass. Of these three, only the minimum wage increase received the required 60 percent affirmative vote for passage.

This led me to get involved in our state's sixty-day legislative session, by analyzing some proposed statutes and/or amendments to existing statutes. Because of the presentations on the proposed constitutional amendments, some of the same groups and organizations asked me to discuss proposed legislation.

We can and must find ways to help our communities by using whatever gifts we have been given. We must also use these gifts to help the next generation understand the value of the village. Public service and mentoring are life-long actions. Mentoring need not be a one-on-one process; we can mentor many people at the same time. I believe this is the essence of a free and democratic society.

The persons mentioned herein, and others, have mentored and guided me through the years. Often, we are in the right place at the right time to encounter those who can help when we need it most. Life's journey is never taken alone. We must embrace the angels, mentors, and friends that we find along the way.

Thank you to the angels, mentors, and friends that have been in my life. As you have helped me, I hope that I, too, have helped someone along the way.

BIO

Peggy Quince

Retired Justice Peggy A. Quince was the 79th Justice of the Florida Supreme Court; she served on that court from 1999 to 2019. From 2008 to 2010 she served as the Chief Justice of the Florida Supreme Court, the first African American female to lead a branch of Florida government.

As Chief Justice she concentrated her time and energy on steering the Florida court system through the Great Recession, on matters concerning the funding of the Florida court system, on the mortgage foreclosure crisis, on diversity, on children aging out of foster care, and on issues involving human trafficking. She carried those issues forward to the Judicial Council of the National Bar Association when she served as Chair of the Judicial Council from July 2008 to June 2009.

Justice Quince has been a longtime public servant beginning with her position as a Hearing Officer in Washington, DC with the Rental Accommodations Office. In this position she administered the city's new Rent Control Law, holding hearings and writing decisions concerning issues involved with requests for rent increases by property owners and rent decreases by tenants. After moving to Florida, she began a thirteen-and-a-half-year tenure with the Florida Attorney General's Office, where she prepared and argued appeals before the Second District Court of Appeals, the Florida Supreme Court, the federal district and appellate courts, and the United States Supreme Court.

In 1993, she was appointed by the late Governor Lawton Chiles to the Second District Court of Appeal. Justice Quince served on the Second District until 1998 when she was jointly appointed by the late Governor Lawton Chiles and then Governor-Elect Jeb Bush to the Florida Supreme Court.

Since her retirement in January 2019, Justice Quince has tried to travel the world and serve her community. She presently serves on several boards and commissions that have a direct impact on the administration of justice, organizations such as the Florida Bar Foundation, which awards grants to legal services organizations representing the underserved in our communities. She serves on an Independent Review Panel that reviews and evaluates petitions involving allegations of wrongful convictions. Justice Quince has also voluntarily evaluated proposed amendments to Florida's Constitution and bills proposed by the legislature and presented discussions of these issues on webinars throughout the State and continues to speak to various legal and civic groups on legal issues and their impact on our communities.

Justice Quince has received numerous awards and honors, including the National Bar Association Judicial Council's William H. Hastie Award, the American Bar Association's Margaret Brent Women Lawyers of Achievement Award, and the Lifetime Achievement Award from the Government Lawyers Section of the Florida Bar.

I Had Never Considered This Step

17

Fernande R. V. Duffly

*O*utspoken *children can try any parent's patience, but when that loquaciousness is nurtured, confidence blooms. And when voice meets inspiration, careers can blossom.*

For Justice Duffly, that early, nurtured voice proved critical in responding to the sexist experiences and predatory behaviors that she experienced in the workplace—experiences that so many young women have faced and continue to encounter.

Justice Duffly shares how she channeled her life experiences into her work as a judge, deciding cases with compassion, combined with a rigorous respect for the rule of law.

Lauren Stiller Rikleen, Editor

How does a Chinese Dutch immigrant from Indonesia, who spoke no English on landing in Portland, Oregon, a few weeks shy of her seventh birthday, decide to become a lawyer, and eventually a member of the Massachusetts Supreme Judicial Court?

I grew up a confident, outspoken child who believed I could do and be anything. For this I credit my parents and both my grandmothers: my Dutch Oma and my Chinese Oma, who came to live with us in the United States after we immigrated there in 1956.

My parents met in Indonesia, where my Dutch father had gone after working with the Dutch underground during WWII, planning to leave Europe behind. He met my Chinese mother there, in a ballroom dancing class taught by my grandmother, who had never worked before, but now was eking out a living after her husband died in a Dutch airstrike that had gone awry. (She also learned how to make her own clothing patterns and to sew, later copying from magazines designer clothing she sewed for me.) My parents fell in love and married, planning to remain and raise a family in Indonesia, but soon after my birth an anti-Chinese regime change caused them to flee overnight to the Netherlands.

My first, enduring memories begin in Holland, where I spent most weekends with my Dutch grandmother after my brother and sister were born. My father was the oldest of seven children and everyone except my Dutch Opa doted on me. In my earliest memory of my gentle, loving Oma, she is standing up to him. Even to my three- or four-year-old eyes, this was memorable—she was bathing me in the big porcelain tub and he came in, stood in the doorway, angry that "his hot water" was being used up. My Oma, using a calm but fierce voice, looked up at him and said, "the baby needs a bath," then resumed washing me. He stood there a moment looking at her before leaving without a word.

I learned later that he physically abused her, and she had more than once run away, but having no place to go, eventually returned home. Much later, as a judge visiting the International Court in The Hague, I visited shelters for battered women, including one in Amsterdam, a one-hour train ride from my Oma's home.

I knew no lawyers growing up. My dad worked in a factory until he eventually became successful selling life insurance; my mom stayed home to care for my sister and three brothers, until she ran the exotic fish and pet shop that they started in our garage and told stories to children at the local library.

I talked a lot as a child—which got me noticed in school, and sometimes in trouble—and people often commented that I should become a lawyer, though I never met a lawyer until I volunteered at Legal Services in the 70s. This, and an article in the *New York Times* about famed civil rights lawyer Leonard Boudin, sparked my interest. Could I turn the one attribute I knew I had into a voice for change?

I was opposed to the war and started to speak up in small groups, ignoring the roar in my ears. I belonged to a woman's group, where my interests were supported. I made a bet with myself that if my LSATs were high enough, I would apply to Stanford and Harvard Law Schools. I challenged Harvard's deferral and asked for an interview. The interviewer wanted to know if I expected special consideration as a minority. I said no but believed that my experiences made me a stronger person and, therefore, a strong candidate.

On arriving at Harvard Law School in the fall of 1974, I joined new female law students at a meeting of the Women's Law Association and learned that "Ladies Day" (the one day in which female students, who were otherwise ignored, were selected to answer questions in class posed in the Socratic method) had only recently been banished after pressure from the women who preceded us. That did not, however, stop the practice of one professor who continued to pick a woman from each new class (including ours) to become his live-in partner.

There were still few women students, no tenured professors, and a sole associate dean. She became an ally who funded our small group of women to travel to colleges throughout the United States, meeting with women and students of color to encourage them to apply and offering to mentor them on acceptance. We believed we could access the power of a Harvard Law School degree and use it to challenge the status quo.

In the year before graduating from Harvard Law School, I read law firm descriptions for signs women might be welcome as summer associates. I interviewed with those that passed muster but in one interview with a top firm, the male interviewer, commenting on my pregnant state, said, "You think you'll come back after the baby is born, but once you have that baby you won't be able to leave it." I didn't receive an offer.

The firm that hired me never mentioned my pregnancy. After accepting that firm's offer to become an associate (and later partner), I learned that this silence had been a consciously arrived at decision.

Still, the atmosphere at the firm was not uniformly welcoming to women—after only a few days, one partner suggested we should have dinner without my husband; another walked by my desk, pointed his cigar at me and then at his office, and said, "You, in there, 15 minutes." To the first invitation, I offered to bring my husband; to the second, I typed a memo and suggested different times when I might be available. I later learned that he, and other partners, were having affairs with their secretaries. I never attended a firm holiday party after observing, during the first, the behavior of male lawyers with female employees.

When I was again pregnant, I researched the leave policies of other firms, and discussed it with a lawyer in town who also was pregnant. I created a draft for my firm that offered generous leave to new parents without impact on partnership decisions. Without this policy, having our third child and being a partner in the firm would not have been possible (though it was still a major challenge).

When I believed my compensation was lower than that of my male partners, I advocated for changes to the client credit allocation system but failed to effect change. I might have left the firm but for the partners I worked directly with, including Sam Adams, a former partner who retired as a judge from the Massachusetts Superior Court to return to a leadership role in the firm.

Sam had loved being a judge and thought I would, too. With this encouragement, I applied to the Probate and Family Court where I then often appeared. I had never considered this step, and doubt I would have done so if he had not suggested it to me and told me he believed that I was a good candidate for the job.

Before there was a formal vetting process, those appointed weren't always good judges. In one case, a judge who was angry that he hadn't been able to get counsel to settle a case sat with his back to us throughout the trial, reading a newspaper. In another, a judge entered a final judgment with a remedy that was not supported by the evidence and the opposing side had not requested; he told me he would change it only if I agreed not to appeal his decision.

Some didn't treat women very well. During one motion hearing, the judge directed a comment to the primarily male group of lawyers waiting to appear regarding my personal appearance and suggested they might like to go out with me. Others responded inappropriately to female attorneys and clients. I was scheduled for a bench trial and after opening arguments, the male judge said to opposing counsel that I could have assured for myself a positive outcome had I worn the dress I had on at a bar association dinner we all recently attended. Opposing counsel feigned deafness; the court stenographer—who was assigned solely to that judge—did not record the comment. Another judge entered an order against my client that granted custody of the parties' children to the husband, who had not even requested it; the judge informed me he would change it only if my client agreed not to move out of state to marry her fiancée.

I began to think that I might be able to make a positive contribution to a court that deserved better. Ultimately, with Sam's support, I applied for an opening but was initially unsuccessful. I learned that some (male) lawyers had opposed me for being too aggressive. I didn't change my approach, which I considered appropriate advocacy for my client, but did become more involved with bar organizations and attended bar events where I could meet with lawyers informally and in a relaxed atmosphere so they could get to know me as a person, not just opposing counsel. Several lawyers who had not supported me did so when I next applied.

On the Probate and Family Court, I began the practice of providing written decisions so attorneys and clients would understand the basis for my orders. I think because of this, some lawyers began to ask if I would consider applying to the Appeals Court. Until then I hadn't, and realized that, until someone else suggested it, I may never have applied to either court. I began to appear on panels that sought to inform lawyers about what being a judge was like, and took that opportunity to encourage them to apply, specifically acknowledging that they might feel reluctant to do so until someone else suggested it and could offer guidance—and that this is what I was doing for them.

When I was selected as a candidate for the Supreme Judicial Court, I received a huge amount of negative press generated by a fathers' rights group that often appeared to oppose judges. I was fortunate to be able to gain the support of a father who'd had three different cases pending in three Family Courts in the Commonwealth that I consolidated in order to achieve a better overall result for all parties and the children. Under separate orders, the total child support obligation exceeded the father's pay as a bus driver, and he fell behind despite working overtime. It was clear he felt an obligation to support his children but wasn't earning enough to meet all three orders; he also wanted visits with each child but wasn't sure how to achieve that.

I consolidated the cases and ordered all three mothers and the father to appear in my court so I could hear their concerns and work with them to arrive at an order that addressed their needs. By bringing them together, I hoped everyone would recognize the challenges of the separate orders and be willing to consider options that would work for everyone. Such an agreement was ultimately achieved.

My time on the Appeals Court and Supreme Judicial Court was the most rewarding of any job in the law that I have held, in part because the men and women who were my colleagues were truly collegial and we supported each other's efforts to achieve the best possible decisions. The presence of women and men, gay and lesbian judges, and judges of color contributes to better decision making, greater understanding of minority experiences and points of view, and the high regard in which I believe our opinions are held.

BIO

Justice Fernande (Nan) R. V. Duffly

Justice Fernande (Nan) R. V. Duffly served as an Associate Justice of the Supreme Judicial Court of the Commonwealth of Massachusetts until her retirement in July 2016. Prior to her appointment to the Supreme Judicial Court in 2011, Justice Duffly served for eight years as Associate Justice of the Massachusetts Probate and Family Court, and for eleven years as Associate Justice of the Massachusetts Appeals Court.

She is a member and past President of the National Association of Women Judges (NAWJ), and served as NAWJ's delegate to the American Bar Association's House of Delegates and as liaison to the ABA's Commission on Women in the Profession. As a member of the ABA, Justice Duffly served as a Commissioner on the Commission on Women and on the Hispanic Legal Rights Commission and was active in the Minority Caucus. She currently serves as an elected member of the ABA Council of the Section of Civil Rights and Social Justice. She is a founding member of the Asian American Lawyers Association of Massachusetts and has served as a member of the Steering Committee of Lawyers Defending American Democracy.

Justice Duffly currently teaches Civil Procedure at Northeastern University School of Law.

Throughout her career as a lawyer and a judge, Justice Duffly sought to promote equal access to justice and a diverse legal profession. Justice Duffly became the first female litigation partner and the first partner of color at Warner & Stackpole (now K&L Gates). As an attorney, Justice Duffly served on numerous boards and committees that sought to promote equal access to justice, including the Boston Bar Association's committees on pro se litigation and attorney volunteerism; the Volunteer Lawyers Project; Lawyer's Committee for Civil Rights Under Law; the Probate and Family Court's committee on pro se access to the courts; and the Supreme Judicial Court's Standing Committee on substance abuse.

The first Asian American woman appointed to any court of the Commonwealth in its history, Justice Duffly has mentored judges, lawyers, and law students, and has worked to increase collaboration among judges, legislators, educators, and practitioners to increase diversity in the profession. A frequent speaker and lecturer, she has advocated for increasing the number of women on state and federal courts in the United States, as well as on courts of other countries.

BIO

The Joy of Serendipity and Risk

18

M. Margaret McKeown

*J*udge McKeown's description of her three-year confirmation saga following her nomination to the Ninth
Circuit Court of Appeals provides a rare insight into
the politics of the judicial nomination process. Ironically, her experience surviving an avalanche while
mountain climbing in Tibet years earlier reinforced
qualities she would need in abundance as she navigated the Senate confirmation process.

Her avalanche metaphor served as an appropriate
backdrop to a flawed process—and one that historically has treated women differently than men. Lawyers
engaged in ensuring an independent judiciary will find
her story not simply a historic artifact, but a description of a system in need of repair.

Lauren Stiller Rikleen, Editor

It was a bluebird day, sunny with a clear sky after days of heavy snowfall. Time to get climbing. The day began with an uneventful ascent to bury a cache of food. On our way back down, somewhere around 21,000 feet, I heard a teammate yell the dreaded word: "avalanche." Looking up at a wall of ice and snow barreling toward us, I feared the worst. It was the fall of 1981, and I was the only female member of the first United States expedition to Mount Shishapangma in Tibet. China had agreed to allow two American teams into the country that year—one to Mount Everest and one to Mount Shishapangma (also called Xixabangma). Rising 26,335 feet above sea level, the latter peak is the fourteenth highest in the world.

For me, joining the expedition was serendipity. A climber had dropped out at the last minute and by chance I was free. Having just finished a White House Fellowship, I had a window of time before I returned to Perkins Coie's Seattle office as the first female partner.

I was a solid climber, but I had never scaled peaks in the Himalayas or been part of an expedition. I saw the expedition as an adventure of a lifetime and a chance to see Tibet. My goal was to support the team. I was realistic about my skills, though I knew I had the endurance and stamina to be a good team member. With less than a month to prepare, I donned my double leather climbing boots each morning as I walked around the White House grounds and after work as I tromped up and down the C&O Canal.

It was quite a jump from endurance training at sea level in Washington, DC, to the practice hikes at 12,000 feet, a drive over a 16,000-foot mountain pass, and finally our base camp at 14,000 feet. From there we slowly moved across the Tibetan plateau, ferrying our supplies to ever-higher elevations. As we approached the mountain, the scenery was spectacular, with giant seracs (glacial columns) rising as a gateway to Mount Shishapangma.

The day of the avalanche, I was on a rope team with a fellow climber from Seattle and our porter, a Tibetan man named Wang Du. We were a compatible team and made steady progress, never expecting the near disaster in store.

Of course, I had seen spectacular avalanches in movies, watched snowstorm extravaganzas in my native state of Wyoming, and witnessed small snowslides during my cross-country skiing days. But nothing prepared me, even my avalanche training, for the reality of this massive event. The sound and fury of the avalanche was like nothing

I had experienced—a river of cascading snow, sheets of ice, and frozen rocks thundered down the mountain toward our vulnerable team.

I felt the force of the freezing mix envelop my body. Then everything went dark. In those moments of terror, my mind went wild with possibilities—broken bones, lost limbs, even death and who would tell my family. Time stood still. I knew I could not succumb to panic, or all would be lost.

I pushed horrific images of my team's demise out of my mind and focused on the singular goal of escape. Thinking back to avalanche training, I knew we needed oxygen. Eventually, miraculously, our group of three managed to maintain "air holes" with our ice axes. Tethered together by our rope and trying to keep above the force of the deluge, we slowed—and then stopped—our downward slide.

Sharing that moment of humanity was humbling and spiritual. Our other teammates, separated from us by several thousand feet and by the tremendous upheaval of snow, trudged up the mountain to our rescue. When we finally, joyfully reunited, we headed back to our tents.

I slept for hours and awoke to a lively discussion of plans to start climbing again. Some teammates argued that the avalanche was a fluke. The burning question for them was when to start the next ascent. My answer was never.

Intuition and common sense told me it was time to stop. As we headed to base camp, I was able to reflect with a clear head—my goal was to make it safely down the mountain and out of Tibet, find my way back to Beijing, and then Hong Kong, have a long-awaited chocolate milkshake, and go shopping, which I did. And so, the team split up; the several members who forged ahead were unable to summit because of weather and avalanche conditions.

I have long had a plaque on my desk that reads, "Remember, when you are out on a limb, the world is at your feet." Before the expedition, I simply didn't know how far out on a limb I would be. It is impossible to avoid being shaped by a near-death experience. Surviving the avalanche taught me critical lessons about the importance of preparedness, of remaining calm and focused, and of having a great team to lean on when the going gets tough.

I did not expect that fifteen years later, I would find myself thinking back to the lessons of the avalanche—this time in the context of my nomination and confirmation to the federal bench. When

I learned I would be nominated, I suspected the process—like that day on Mt. Shishapangma—would test my stamina, my endurance, and my resolve. But I never imagined that surviving the nomination process could be more daunting than an avalanche.

As serendipity brought me to the climb, serendipity brought me to the bench. Although a seat had opened on the Ninth Circuit for a nominee from the Pacific Northwest, no new judge had been appointed for more than a decade. In early 1995, I was enjoying my law practice—a nice mix of commercial and intellectual property litigation and pro bono work—when a federal judge in Washington approached me to ask if I was interested in the seat because, unbeknownst to me, my name had been floating about. I dutifully listened, wrote down a few notes on a restaurant napkin, then tucked it in my purse and forgot about it.

As it turns out, I would need those napkin notes sooner than expected. There was a push to move forward quickly on my nomination, which is ironic in light of what happened next. When the White House called to tell me that I was President Clinton's intended nominee, I was humbled and honored. The aides told me to begin transitioning out of my practice since I was likely to be confirmed within a few months. They could not have been more wrong. My confirmation took nearly three years.

Under the U.S. Constitution, the President "shall nominate, and by and with the Advice and Consent of the Senate, shall appoint" federal judges. So, although judges enjoy independence from the executive and congressional branches once confirmed, the appointment process is political. Indeed, Senator Al Simpson of Wyoming told me early on, "politics is a contact sport." How right he was. For the next thirty-two months, I remained in limbo, trying to keep my law practice intact while remaining nimble enough to responsibly transition away.

Before I was formally nominated, the White House asked me to meet with Senator Orrin Hatch, Chair of the powerful Senate Judiciary Committee. The meeting was cordial, and Chairman Hatch was well prepared, questioning me on case after case, down to the footnotes in the briefs. As a lifetime Girl Scout and a troop leader at the time, I decided to bring him some Girl Scout cookies on the theory that, while I knew that demonstrating my legal chops would be key, a human touch never hurts. The White House was shocked when

I handed over the cookies, but the next day Senator Hatch called the White House and said my nomination was "good to go." I was nominated in 1996.

I learned from Senator Hatch that personal relationships were important to him and others in the Senate. For several years before law school, I worked for Senator Clifford P. Hansen from Wyoming, who took the time to personally call Senator Hatch before our meeting. Senator Hansen later told me that I was the only thing he and President Clinton agreed on. Senator Simpson supported me, along with Senator Hatch. Despite having bipartisan backing from a number of corners, my nomination was labeled "controversial."

In the months that followed, I was caught in the clash between Congress and President Clinton. Some senators opposed my nomination because of my work on the first federal Gender Bias Task Force (despite Justice Sandra Day O'Connor's endorsement of our report). Others howled about my role as lead counsel in pro bono litigation to fend off an anti-gay initiative in Washington state. Conservative groups even labeled me a "wolf in sheep's clothing": a secret activist hiding behind my corporate commercial practice.

The fight over my nomination played out during the biggest political quake of the time—the investigation and eventual impeachment of President Clinton after his relationship with Monica Lewinsky. The scandal ground regular Senate business—such as confirming judges—to a halt.

As the months passed, accusations and anonymous attacks on my work on behalf of women and the LGBTQ community flew in the press. I told my mother to quit reading USA Today, which chronicled attacks from interest groups and senators alike. The attacks and the waiting took a toll on me and on my family.

I continued to wait, even as President Clinton ran for and eventually won reelection. As a matter of course, my nomination "died" when the congressional term ended. President Clinton's second term began, and I was nominated all over again in 1997.

Each month, as I imagined that the roadblocks were eroding, something else would pop up. The most memorable event was when the White House called me on a Friday night and told me to be in Washington the following Tuesday to meet with more senators. I politely told them that I was in a three-week jury trial in federal court and could not leave because of ethical duties to my client. They insisted it was critical—trial or no trial—so with the grace of the judge and opposing counsel, I flew to Washington only to have the meetings cancelled.

I was stunned. Senator Patty Murray of Washington State, who had been a steadfast supporter throughout the process, worked her magic and managed to get the meetings reinstated. I saw three senators and their staffs and was on the evening flight out of Washington and back in court in Seattle the next day.

As my nomination lingered, I saw other nominations—both judicial and executive branch—being withdrawn. There were times when I considered whether to withdraw to be able to focus completely on my law practice at Perkins Coie, the firm that had supported me so generously since I was a young associate.

But I was concerned that if I withdrew or if the White House dropped my nomination, there would be whispers that a lapse in ethics or some other scandal drove my withdrawal. As lawyers, reputation and ethics are the backbone of our careers. I did not want to be the poster child for a failed nomination. So, I harked back to the wisdom of the country crooner Kenny Rogers and his old song, *The Gambler*:

> You've got to know when to hold 'em
> Know when to fold 'em
> Know when to walk away
> And know when to run

Unlike on my expedition, when I knew it was time to "fold 'em" and "walk away" from that mountain in Tibet, this time I chose to "hold 'em" and face the mountain. I insisted to the White House that I wanted an up-or-down vote.

Studies published in *Judicature* examining judicial nominations during this period confirmed that female nominees were delayed at a greater rate than male nominees. Long delays for Court of Appeals nominees were becoming de rigueur. Before my hearing, there had been a period of eighteen months in which no hearings were held for Court of Appeals nominees.

At long last, my hearing was scheduled for February 1998. I was elated and anxious about the cascade of questions I was sure to face.

I got to work preparing for the avalanche, drafting and practicing responses to scores of potential hearing questions.

Happily, my village was there to support me as they had been throughout the process—family members, law school classmates, White House Fellows, colleagues from my firm, co-counsel and opposing counsel from many cases, the Girl Scouts, neighbors, and friends from across the country. Two Republican congressmen, my former law partner, Representative Rick White of Washington State, along with Representative Tom Campbell of California, whom I knew as a fellow White House Fellow and from my days as counsel in antitrust lawsuits, offered testimony in support of my nomination.

Just as my rope team was critical to my survival on the climb, these teammates and cheerleaders were essential to my success that day. Although navigating confirmation to the bench might appear to be a solo endeavor, I knew deep down that I would never have stayed the course without "the team" supporting me at every step of the journey.

The hearing began amicably, with Senator Murray and Senator Slade Gorton, a Republican from Washington State, supporting my nomination. Senator Murray noted that I had survived "the political and judicial battles," and Senator Patrick Leahy, a seasoned Vermont Democrat, observed that "this delay is the result of a process that has become a little bit crazy." I couldn't have agreed more.

Then the hearing took a contentious turn. Senator Hatch lobbed the first questions, asking whether I believed that "it is a violation of the U.S. Constitution for a state to pass a law prohibiting the placement of a child in a home where homosexual activities are present when neither guardian in the home is the biological parent of the child?"

And the questioning proceeded from there: "Do you believe that it is constitutional for a United States district or appellate court judge to interfere with a legislative or democratic process such as a citizen initiative?" "Do you believe that the Constitution protects partial-birth abortion?" "Do you believe the death penalty violates the Constitution?"

And on and on about my view on the constitutionality of the V-chip, on guns, on whether the Boy Scouts have a right to restrict gay leaders, and whether my lawsuit opposing the Washington State anti-gay initiative should have been blocked by the Republican Guarantee Clause of the Constitution. The Democratic senators protested the nature of the questions, but Senator Hatch counseled something to the effect that what goes around comes around. The two-hour session came to a close.

But the ordeal was not over. Just days later, I began receiving faxes containing scores of questions from the Senate Judiciary Committee demanding answers in less than forty-eight hours. And so it went: "What role did you play in writing, reviewing, or editing the Gender Bias Report?" "Do you believe judicial activism exists?" "Do you agree with the A.C.L.U. that the Boy Scouts' ban on homosexuals constitutes unlawful discrimination?" "Are there any views or positions espoused by the A.C.L.U. with which you disagree?" "What is your view on state efforts, such as, but not limited to, parental notification laws, to restrict the right to abortion?" And finally, some easy ones: "Which current Supreme Court Justice do you most admire?" (Justice O'Connor.) "What is the worst Supreme Court decision?" (*Plessy v. Ferguson.*)

At last, in March 1998, after nearly three years in the process, the Senate took a roll-call vote on my nomination. The day of the vote, my sister and I were hiking in Bryce Canyon National Park and our motel did not have C-Span. Senator Murray's office kindly held a phone to the television. After a few nay votes at the beginning, the vote was anticlimactic: I was confirmed 80 to 11. Senator Hatch graciously called to congratulate me.

My confirmation saga was not easy, though others endured much worse. In surviving the avalanche of the process, I learned a number of lessons. To begin, Senator Simpson called it right—this was a political process, and much as it felt like it was about me, I was simply a chess piece in a larger game.

The attacks on my pro bono work advocating for the civil rights of women and LGBTQ individuals were not unexpected, but I wouldn't have done anything differently. Those projects were some of the most fascinating, meaningful endeavors of my career, including one case that took me to the U.S. Supreme Court.

One cannot curate a federal judicial nomination, and even if doing so were possible, timing and serendipity play a large role. I experienced a far more interesting and textured life by seeking a meaningful law practice instead of one geared toward securing a judicial nomination. I am most proud that throughout it all, I kept my values intact.

As on my climb, I thought more than once of that plaque on my desk: "Remember, when you are out on a limb, the world is at your feet." And what a world it has been and what an honor to serve on the U.S. Court of Appeals for the Ninth Circuit.

BIO

M. Margaret McKeown

Judge McKeown was appointed to the United States Court of Appeals for the Ninth Circuit in 1998. Before her appointment, she was the first female partner at Perkins Coie in Seattle and Washington, DC, and served as a White House Fellow.

Judge McKeown chairs the Ninth Circuit Workplace Environment Committee and is a member of the National Workplace Conduct Working Group and the U.S. Judicial Conference Committee on Judicial Conduct and Disability. She has served as chair of the ABA Commission on the 19th Amendment, president of the Federal Judges Association, and chair of the U.S. Judicial Conference Codes of Conduct Committee.

She is on the Council of the American Law Institute, the Judicial Advisory Board of the American Society of International Law, and the editorial board of *Litigation Magazine*. Judge McKeown is immediate past chair of the ABA Rule of Law Initiative and a current special advisor. She is also a member of the American Academy of Arts and Sciences.

Among her many awards, Judge McKeown has received the ABA Margaret Brent Women Lawyers of Achievement Award, the ABA John Marshall Award, and the Girl Scouts Cool Woman Award.

Judge McKeown is the author of *Citizen Justice: The Environmental Legacy of William O. Douglas—Public Advocate and Conservation Champion* (2022). She has lectured throughout the world on international law, human rights law, intellectual property, litigation, ethics, judicial administration, and constitutional law and has participated in numerous rule-of-law initiatives with judges and lawyers.

Judge McKeown graduated from Georgetown University Law Center and holds an honorary doctorate from Georgetown University.

Lessons from a Blessed Journey

19

Ann Claire Williams[1]

Inspirational careers are forged by challenge, strength, courage, and legacy. Of these qualities, it is the legacy that is most remembered.

Former Judge Ann Claire Williams describes her tireless efforts to ensure that every ladder that she has climbed remains extended and supported for those who follow. When she saw a need to provide access and support to those who lacked opportunities, she created structures and programs to address those needs.

Her valuable life lessons are universally applicable. Her examples demonstrate that some of the hardest challenges we face can also be the foundation for the grit and resilience upon which a successful career is built and support for subsequent generations is fostered.

Lauren Stiller Rikleen, Editor

---

[1] The views and opinions set forth herein are the personal views or opinions of the author; they do not necessarily reflect views or opinions of the law firm with which she is associated.

I was raised in Detroit, Michigan, by two loving parents who told my two sisters and me that, because we were Black, we would have to work twice as hard to achieve whatever we wanted in life.

My parents both grew up in the segregated South, and their families moved north for better opportunities. Even though they had college degrees from historically Black colleges, they were not able to get jobs for which they were well qualified for many years.

My father, Joshua, drove a bus for twenty years before he was able to retire, return to school for another degree in Education, and become a teacher. He enrolled at Wayne State University while I was studying there, and I was overjoyed to be in class with him. My mother, Dorothy, had to teach in a home for delinquent children for twelve years and worked for five years as a substitute teacher in the Detroit public schools before the Detroit public schools allowed Black people to have full-time teaching positions.

My parents were angry and frustrated by the discrimination they faced all of their lives, but they refused to be defeated and participated in the civil rights movement. They held on to the American dream and worked so hard to achieve it.

Their examples taught me that no matter what roadblocks I faced, if I believed in myself and worked very hard, I could succeed. They always encouraged me to dream big dreams and made me believe my dreams could come true. While growing up, the thought of being a lawyer never even crossed my mind; I didn't know any lawyers or judges. And my legal career has not been a straight or easy path, but I feel so fortunate and blessed for what I have been able to achieve.

I stand on the shoulders of my parents and so many others who reached out and lifted me up during my journey. Because of the help and blessings I received, I feel an obligation to give back, making the path easier for others. In that spirit, I am sharing some of the life lessons I have learned along the way.

I.   WORK HARD BECAUSE YOU DON'T KNOW WHO IS WATCHING

When I was in my second year of law school at Notre Dame, Luther Swygert, Chief Judge of the U.S. Court of Appeals for the Seventh Circuit and a Notre Dame Law School graduate, contacted my Dean,

David Link, to ask for a recommendation of a well-qualified Black woman who could serve as his law clerk. I had two classes with Dean Link, and he also attended hearings that I conducted on police misconduct for the Black Cultural Center in South Bend, Indiana. Dean Link, along with Professor Howard Glickstein, who I worked for at the Notre Dame Center for Civil Rights, recommended me for the position. Our law librarian, Kathleen Farmann, the only woman on the law faculty, helped with my resume and preparation for my clerkship interview.

Because Judge Swygert had three candidates he wanted to hire and only two open positions, he recommended me to his colleague, Judge Robert Sprecher, who hired me. I was one of the first two Black women law clerks on the Seventh Circuit and it was an incredible experience. In addition to clerking for Judge Sprecher, I was also able to assist the Seventh Circuit Staff Attorney's office by drafting orders and working with panels of appellate judges on cases that did not have oral arguments. In that way, I got to know many of the other appellate judges who later became my colleagues. Judge Sprecher became a lifelong mentor, and the clerkship was a pivotal opportunity that opened many doors.

II.   IF YOU DON'T GET WHAT YOU WANT WHEN YOU WANT IT, KEEP ON PUSHING

After clerking for Judge Sprecher, I applied to the U.S. Attorney's Office, Northern District of Illinois, with the encouragement and support of now-Judge Marianne Jackson, the first Black woman assigned to the Criminal Division. I was hoping to be assigned to CRAD, the Criminal Receiving and Appellate Division, where I would handle search and arrest warrants, try simple cases, and handle appeals.

At the time, CRAD, which was the typical starting place for a criminal prosecutor, was overwhelmingly White and male. I was not assigned there. Three other White female attorneys, one Black male attorney, and I were assigned to the Civil Rights and Public Protection division instead. While I was very disappointed, I knew I needed to get my foot in the door. I soon realized that there was one silver lining to the assignment: Ilana Diamond Rovner was my supervisor. She was very supportive and became a sponsor throughout my career, as well as a very dear friend. And several years later our career paths crossed again when we both became judges on the District Court. After she became the first woman on the Court of Appeals for the Seventh Circuit, I also followed in her footsteps. I still remember that historic day when Judge Rovner, Judge Diane Wood, and I sat on the first all-female panel.

After working in the Civil Rights division, I recognized that I wasn't getting the experience I needed, so I asked the CRAD Chief if I could transfer. He said no. So, I went to the CRAD Deputy Chief and said that my colleagues and I would like to take on some appeals. The Deputy Chief made those assignments, and we all got experience briefing cases and arguing before the Seventh Circuit. I also enlisted the Deputy Chief to ask the CRAD Chief to assign us duty days so we could get investigative and trial experience, and he agreed. After about a year, I got transferred to CRAD and ultimately became Deputy Chief of that division.

The CRAD experience demonstrated the importance of saying yes, being strategic, speaking up for myself, and continuing to push to reach my goals. My philosophy has always been that when a door is closed, you find a way to open it, or you move to a new door.

III. SAY YES TO OPPORTUNITIES, EVEN IF THEY ARE NOT PART OF YOUR PLAN

When I was CRAD Deputy Chief and on maternity leave with my first child, I learned that the CRAD Chief was moving to a different position and that someone else had been selected to replace him. Because I thought I had earned the promotion, I immediately went to the U.S. Attorney, Dan Webb, and asked why I hadn't been selected. He advised me that he had something else in mind for me—Chief of the Organized Crime Drug Enforcement Task Force. I did not want that position because I had already worked in the drug unit. He explained that I would oversee major drug investigations in a five-state region, report to the main Justice Department in Washington, DC, and work with the U.S. Attorneys and all the federal agencies in the region. The next day I said yes.

There were only twelve regional drug task force chiefs nationwide, so the job gave me my first national exposure. When my name came up for a District Court position, I was politically independent, as my previous positions prohibited involvement in politics. So, it was a real benefit to report to D. Lowell Jensen, U.S. Associate Attorney General, who later became a U.S. District Court Judge. It also was helpful to have worked with five well-respected U.S. Attorneys, four of whom also became federal judges. For example, U.S. Attorney Sarah Evans Barker, who later became a U.S. District Court Judge, had previously worked for Illinois Senator Charles Percy, who recommended me to President Reagan.

At the time, I was not aware of the influence of the people I was working with, but saying yes to the drug task force position opened the door to the District Court. With the strong support of the Cook County Bar Association, I was renominated when my first nomination lapsed during the Senate recess.

Saying yes to other opportunities was also critical to my appointment to the U.S. Court of Appeals for the Seventh Circuit. When I first became a U.S. District Court Judge for the Northern District of Illinois, I joined the Federal Judges Association (FJA), which currently has a membership of over 1,100 district and appellate judges.

Every four years the FJA holds a quadrennial conference in Washington, DC. In 1993, Senior District Court Judge Hubert Will, a mentor of mine, who helped found the FJA, asked me if I was going to the quadrennial conference. I told him no because of my heavy workload. Judge Will insisted that I attend the FJA board meeting and explained there would be a White House reception during the conference, so I said yes.

To my surprise, he nominated me to be the Treasurer of the FJA and eventually I became the President-Elect and President of the FJA. I was the first judge of color to serve as an officer and I worked with federal judges throughout the country. My involvement in the FJA quadrennial conferences led to my introductions of Presidents George W. Bush and Barack Obama at our White House receptions, which were highlights of my career.

I also met many federal judges when I was appointed to become the first woman of color to chair a judicial conference committee—the Court Administration and Case Management Committee (CACM). When the previous CACM chair, Fifth Circuit Court of Appeals Judge Robert (Bob) Parker, told me he wanted to recommend that the Chief Justice of the Supreme Court appoint me to succeed him as chair, I was stunned and a bit hesitant. It was not something I had ever considered. But I decided that if Bob saw me as the right candidate for chair, I should have confidence that I was ready for the position. I knew as a woman of color it would be a historic appointment, so I took a leap of faith and told Bob yes. I am so glad I did. As CACM chair, I worked on significant issues such as courtroom sharing, electronic filing, cameras in the courtroom, and alternative dispute resolution. I also appeared before the Senate and House Judiciary Committees and I was invited to teach new district court judges for seven years at the Federal Judicial Center.

When I was being considered for the Court of Appeals, I received tremendous support from many federal judges throughout the country. All these experiences taught me how important it is to just say yes to opportunities, even when you cannot see where the yes will take you.

IV. LET PEOPLE UNDERESTIMATE YOU AT THEIR OWN PERIL

When I was in the U.S. Attorney's Office, I had moments when I knew I was being underestimated because I was a woman, or Black, or young. I remember during one trial, a defense attorney objected to my redirect examination of a witness, claiming that the defense had not been given a witness statement before trial. I kept meticulous records of information I turned over to the defense and was able to quickly show that the statement had been turned over. In that moment, he and the other eleven defense counsel realized that I was a very good trial lawyer, and they stopped making frivolous objections.

I had a similar experience when I was being vetted for the District Court by attorneys from seven different bar associations, including a meeting with twenty-five lawyers from the Chicago Bar Association. One CBA lawyer asked, "Well, Miss Williams, if you get this, you will be thirty-five, the youngest judge, and you will be Black and you'll be a woman, how will you handle it?" I said, "Well, I've been Black and a woman all my life, and I've been able to handle that so far, and as to age, that will change."

I did not let that question throw me. I knew that if I was appointed to the bench, regardless of my race, sex, or age, I had the ability and determination to be a good judge and the work ethic to learn whatever I did not know. At that point, I had tried twenty-five cases, which was far more than many of the judges already on the District Court. Although all my trials and appeals were criminal, I also had experience with civil cases, both from my clerkship and through many years of teaching trial advocacy at Northwestern Law School and with the National Institute for Trial Advocacy (NITA). Of course, I had never been a judge and knew I had a lot to learn, but I knew I had to take the leap and take advantage of that incredible opportunity.

V. RECOGNIZE THE POWER OF ONE AND YOUR ABILITY TO CREATE CHANGE WORKING WITH OTHERS

When I was studying for the bar exam, I heard about a bar preparation class that was being taught to Black law school graduates by Professor Ronald Kennedy at Northwestern Law School. I tried to join the class but was told that I could not because it was only for Northwestern Law School graduates. I passed the bar exam the first time, but I knew that the passage rate for Black law school graduates was lower than for other law school graduates.

When I was working in the Civil Rights and Public Protection Unit of the U.S. Attorney's Office, I learned that Al Moran, another Black prosecutor, was a Northwestern graduate. I asked him if Professor Kennedy was still offering the bar exam preparation class only to Northwestern graduates, and Al said yes. He introduced me to Professor Kennedy, and I asked him to extend the course to non-Northwestern graduates. He said no. I then asked if he would show a group of us how to teach the class so that we could offer it to non-Northwestern law school graduates. He agreed and in 1977, when the non-Northwestern graduates passed at the same rate as the Northwestern graduates, we created Minority Legal Education Resources, Inc. (MLER). MLER is a not-for-profit organization with classes taught by volunteer lawyers.

From the beginning, the course was offered to any law school graduate, regardless of race, ethnicity, or law school attended. When MLER started, I had been a practicing lawyer for only two years. I taught each MLER bar review class twice a year for over thirty years. In its forty-plus-year history, MLER has helped thousands of lawyers pass the Illinois bar exam at rates equal to the overall pass rate. The creation of MLER shows that one person, joining with others, has the power to make a difference.

In my second year on the District Court, a group of Black women attorneys felt there were issues unique to us, and we wanted to create a group to address those common interests and concerns. I shall never forget when in 1986 my husband, David, and I were invited to the black-tie dinner and reception at the Supreme Court in Washington, DC, for more than forty newly appointed district court judges. All the judges and their spouses were in a receiving line to meet the Justices of the Supreme Court. Judges wore name tags identifying their districts. When David and I stepped forward to meet the then Chief Justice, he reached over me to shake David's hand saying, "Congratulations, Judge." David responded, "No Chief, my wife is the judge in our family." I agreed, "That's right, I'm the judge in the family," and the Chief immediately apologized. Although we handled the slight with humor, in that moment I was reminded again that no matter how much I could achieve, I would always be seen first as a Black woman.

That experience was not unusual and was something that Black women lawyers have always had to grapple with and continue to grapple with. How to best handle those situations is an example of the conversations that we could share in an affinity group. So, we started the Black Women Lawyers Association (BWLA), which just celebrated its thirty-fifth anniversary. By creating a safe and supportive environment professionally and personally, BWLA allows its members to blossom and develop leadership skills that serve them well in their careers and in the larger legal community.

After cofounding MLER and BWLA, I worked with U.S. Bankruptcy Judge Jack Schmetterer, who was President of the Chicago Federal Bar Association, to start Just the Beginning—A Pipeline Organization (JTB-APO) with a multiracial group of judges and lawyers, including iconic groundbreaking judges Constance Baker Motley, Leon Higginbotham, Nathaniel Jones, Damon Keith, George Leighton, and James "Skiz" Watson. We first gathered in 1992 to celebrate the integration of the federal judiciary and the legacy of Chicago Judge James Benton Parsons, the first judge of color appointed to any U.S. District Court. Since that time, JTB-APO has expanded its mission to offer educational and career-oriented programs related to law to students of color, first-generation students, and other underrepresented groups, from middle school through law school, with the goal of increasing the diversity of the bench and bar. For example, this year, in partnership with the Judicial Conference of the United States, 160 JTB law student scholars are serving as summer interns with federal appellate, district, bankruptcy, and magistrate judges across the country.

When I was on the District Court, I also learned of the public interest fellowship program created by Skadden, Arps, Slate, Meagher & Flom. Skadden funded two-year fellowships for recent law school graduates to work for public interest organizations. When a long-running antitrust case called *In Re Folding Carton Antitrust Litigation* settled and was assigned to me, I had to determine how the settlement money remaining in the cy pres reserve fund would be spent. I ordered that the money, which ultimately ended up being $3.2 million, be used to fund fellowships for lawyers to work in public interest service organizations. I selected the National Association for Public Interest Law (NAPIL), now Equal Justice Works, as the recipient. The program pays for the Fellows' salaries for two years and also provides funding to help repay student loans. I am proud to be called "the Mother of Equal Justice Works" which, over the years, has helped sponsor more than 2,500 Fellows nationwide, with 85 percent remaining in the public interest sector.

MLER, BWLA, JTB-APO, and Equal Justice Works are all organizations that address and help overcome barriers for people of color and others from underrepresented groups, with the goal of making the motto engraved on the U.S. Supreme Court building, "Equal Justice Under Law," real for all people.

VI. FOLLOW YOUR PASSION AND OPPORTUNITIES WILL EMERGE

Before I went to law school, and while getting my Masters' Degree in Guidance and Counseling, I worked full-time as an elementary school music and homeroom teacher in the inner-city schools of

Detroit. I did not grow up thinking I was going to be a lawyer or a judge. I saw Perry Mason on television and read about the amazing Justice Thurgood Marshall and Judge Constance Baker Motley, but being a lawyer was not on my radar screen. When I was growing up, women were typically encouraged to become teachers, social workers, nurses, and secretaries—not lawyers. While no one told me I could not be a lawyer, no one told me that I could be a lawyer. I applied to law school only because a friend of mine, with whom I was competitive, said he was going to law school.

I didn't have a clue about what law school required and rolled into campus the day before classes began. That night, my classmate Willie Lipscomb, who later became a judge, asked me if I had done the reading for the first day of class. I asked, "What reading?" He explained that we had been assigned cases to read for class the next day. He had been in a pre-law prep course during the summer and was already familiar with legal terminology and procedures, but he had to explain it to me. My initial law school experience is the reason I am so committed to exposing students of color, first-generation students, and students from other underrepresented groups to the legal profession and how they can pursue legal careers.

Once I became a lawyer, I still had a passion for teaching and have continued to train law students, lawyers, and judges throughout my legal career. I have also had a continuing deep interest in Africa. As a descendant of enslaved people, I knew my ancestors came from the African continent. In addition to being the place of my ancestors, Africa was the place my mother, who was an avid traveler, always wanted to visit. By the time I started traveling there, my mother's health prevented her from going with me. So, each time I go to Africa, I am honoring my mother.

I took my first trip to Africa to meet with members of the Ghanaian judiciary in 2001 when I was President of the FJA. For the next two years, I went back to Ghana with other judges to conduct trainings. Through NITA, I participated in trial and appellate advocacy training for prosecutors for the International Criminal Tribunal for Rwanda (ICTR) in Arusha, Tanzania, and the International Criminal Tribunal for the former Yugoslavia (ICTY) at The Hague. That led me to work with Lawyers Without Borders, to collaborate with and teach judges, magistrates, prosecutors, defense attorneys, public interest attorneys, and civil lawyers in nine African countries.

Those collaborations have kept me returning to Africa because, in every program I do, I see the light in the eyes of the people we train. Despite the many difficulties the judges and attorneys face, the desire to create a stronger justice system burns bright. Because I have been so blessed in my career, I want to give back to people who work so hard to make equal justice real in their countries, no matter the challenge.

One of the law firms that worked with Lawyers Without Borders and NITA and was regularly involved in these African exchanges, was Jones Day. When I decided to retire from the bench, Jones Day Managing Partner Stephen Brogan offered me my current position to create and lead the firm's Pro Bono Rule of Law Africa Initiative. I never imagined that I would have this opportunity when I left the judiciary, so I said yes.

Stepping down from the bench has led to other opportunities, including my appointment as Chair of the American Bar Association's Standing Committee on the Federal Judiciary, which provides evaluations to the Senate Judiciary Committee for every district, appellate, and Supreme Court Presidential nominee. In this capacity, I testified on behalf of the Standing Committee during the confirmation hearing for now Justice Ketanji Brown Jackson and presented our peer-reviewed, nonpartisan rating of Well Qualified.

VII. CONCLUSION

Reflecting on my career, I am so grateful for all the lessons I learned during the course of my career: work hard because you don't know who is watching; if you don't get what you want when you want it, keep on pushing; say yes to opportunities, even if they are not part of your plan; let people underestimate you at their own peril; recognize the power of one and your ability to create change by working with others; and follow your passion and opportunities will emerge. Most of all, my parents taught me to dare to dream big dreams and work hard to achieve those dreams, and instilled in me a responsibility to give back. They both insisted that I never let the black robe get in the way of my humanity.

I am so grateful to the many other people from all walks of life who have lifted me up throughout my career. In addition to the support of my parents, the unwavering support of my devoted husband David, children Jonathan and Claire, and numerous judges and attorneys has allowed me to say yes to so many experiences that have exceeded even my biggest dreams. I am grateful to have been so blessed and will continue to dedicate my life to equal justice for all.

BIO

Judge Ann Claire Williams (Ret.)

Judge Ann Claire Williams (Ret.), a trail-blazer and leader, created and leads the Pro Bono Rule of Law Africa Initiative for Jones Day. Devoted to promoting the effective delivery of justice worldwide, particularly in Africa, she has partnered with judiciaries, attorneys, nongovernmental organizations, and the U.S. Departments of Justice and State to lead training programs in Ghana, Indonesia, Kenya, Liberia, Namibia, Nigeria, Rwanda, Tanzania, Uganda, and Zambia. She also has taught at the International Criminal Tribunals for Rwanda and the former Yugoslavia.

President Ronald Reagan nominated her in 1985 to the U.S. District Court, Northern District of Illinois, making her the first woman of color to serve on a district court in the three-state Seventh Circuit. In 1999, President William Clinton's nomination made her the first judge of color to sit on the U.S. Court of Appeals for the Seventh Circuit and the third Black woman to serve on any federal circuit court. She brings her vast experience on the bench to serve as a resource for Jones Day's leading trial and appellate practices.

Judge Williams has served on many judicial committees and, as treasurer and president of the Federal Judges Association, was the first person of color to become an officer. Committed to public interest work, she helped found Just the Beginning—A Pipeline Organization, the Black Women Lawyers' Association of Chicago, Minority Legal Education Resources, and the Public Interest Fellowship Program for Equal Justice Works. She serves on the boards of the Carnegie Corporation of New York, University of Notre Dame, the NAACP Legal Defense and Education Fund, iCivics, Board of Counselors for Equal Justice Works, Weinstein International Foundation, National Institute for Trial Advocacy (NITA), and Museum of Science & Industry Chicago. She also chairs the American Bar Association's Standing Committee on the Federal Judiciary through August 2023 and chairs the Advisory Board of the International Law Institute-South African Centre for Excellence.

She is a recipient of numerous awards and honors, including the Edward J. Devitt Distinguished Service to Justice Award, the American Bar Association Margaret Brent Women Lawyers of Achievement Award from the Commission on Women in the Profession, the National Bar Association's Gertrude E. Rush Award, the National Association of Women Lawyers' Arabella Babb Mansfield Award, the Association of Corporate Counsel Chicago Chapter's Thurgood Marshall Award, *Chicago Lawyer* "Person of the Year," and *Newsweek Daily Beast*'s "150 Fearless Women in the World."

BIO

The Spark of Manifest Injustice

20

Bernice B. Donald

*J*udge Donald offers a richly detailed gift to readers *that allows us to see how drive, strength, and compassion helped her move past the barriers erected by our country's history of racial prejudice and reach the highest levels of the legal profession. She built on her own experiences with racism by constantly striving to shape a more inclusive profession.*

Judge Donald's life should drive all of us to see the link between the protection of the rule of law and the honest retelling of our history within our school systems and beyond. Her example should also challenge us to commit to building workplaces that are rigorous in rooting out systemic bias—both consciously and unconsciously expressed.

Lauren Stiller Rikleen, Editor

In 1957, I began my education at six years old in a two-room school-house, in Olive Branch, Mississippi. As I sat down at my desk, I noticed that my schoolbooks were falling apart. There was no running water in the school, and we were directed to use the outhouse for a toilet. I didn't know that this was an abnormal learning environment for students until a few weeks into the school year.

Every year, the all-Black Union school closed its doors so that my classmates and I could work the fields for the next two months. Every morning I watched the buses chauffeur white students to their schools as we harvested the crops. One day I remember asking my mother, "Why can't we go to school too?"

Three years earlier, the Supreme Court had decided *Brown v. Board of Education*.[1] This case declared school segregation unconstitutional.[2] In reaching this decision, the Court noted that education is a "principal instrument in awakening the child to cultural values, in preparing him for later professional training, and in helping him to adjust normally to his environment."[3]

But the education that we received was far from equal to the education received by our white counterparts. Our facilities remained decrepit and our resources remained limited. Indoor plumbing was not even built into the school until 1959, when Mississippi built a *Plessy* compliant school for Blacks. Eight years after *Brown*, threats to limit the state of Mississippi's federal funding forced Mississippi's white schools to open its doors to Black students. For my classmates and I, a separate, unequal, and disparate educational experience followed us long after this landmark case was decided.

In high school, during my sophomore year, the school district finally offered the "choice" program. This program allowed Black students to choose whether they wanted to attend white schools in the district. When one of my friends asked me if I would attend Olive Branch High School with her, an all-white high school, I agreed. I don't know if I knew how monumental that decision was for me at the time. In retrospect, however, when I made that decision, I visualized myself putting away the tools that I used to harvest the crops and getting back on the bus to go to school.

[1.] 347 U.S. 483 (1954).
[2.] *Id.* at 495.
[3.] *Id.* at 493.

During high school, I worked in some white people's homes. I frequented the same shopping centers as them, washed dishes for them, cleaned office buildings for them, and attended classes with their children. But I was never considered one of their peers. So, I was really worried and scared that being one of the first Black students to integrate the school would impact my life in a significant way—for better or worse.

As I walked through the doors of the high school, the atmosphere was very hostile. They called me ugly names and refused to treat me as one of their peers. The school even canceled prom and various social events for fear of "race mixing."

But I knew early on that I was not there to make friends. I was there for access to the school's wealth of resources. I was a dark-skinned Black girl with a speech impediment, from a poor family, just seeking to make a life for myself by pursuing passions that would make my mother proud. So, that is exactly what I did. I spent hundreds of hours studying their cutting-edge textbooks; I utilized their state-of-the-art science labs; I explored their well-stocked libraries; and I met frequently with their speech therapists to eradicate my impediments.

Even when teachers were dismissive and spoke condescendingly, I fought for my education. I sat in the front row of one class by myself until the day that I graduated and received my diploma.

My high school experience became the reality of a discussion in *Brown* when the Court referenced how opponents of equal protection laws were against the "letter and spirit . . . wish[ing] them to have the most limited effect."[4]

By the end of high school, I had received several scholarships for my academic achievement. But because of the high school's racist policies, my guidance counselor never informed me that I had received scholarship offers that would provide the necessary resources for me to attend a college.

Here I was, a student in a place of opportunity, yet my own teachers and administrators built an infrastructure in favor of my ruin.

It is fair to say that high school gave me the greatest gift—adversity. The challenges I faced gave me the resolve to rectify my speech impediments, expand my worldview through reading books

---

[4.] *Id.* at 489.

in the library, and study assiduously, which ultimately led to me becoming the first Black student to be admitted into the Honor Society at Olive Branch High School.

My exposure to the manifest injustice in the education system was the spark that piqued my curiosity for change.

I.   THIS LITTLE LIGHT OF MINE

I grew up in a strong family from Desoto County, Mississippi, one of ten siblings. I was the sixth child of the ten and would think of myself as the "beginning of the second half" instead of one of the middle children. My father was a self-taught mechanic, and my mother was a domestic worker. I loved my father for the fundamental values that he instilled in me, such as courage, self-confidence, generosity, risk-taking, and a zest for life. But in pivotal moments of my life where I questioned my purpose or direction, recollections of my mother's voice and teachings emerged vividly in my mind.

"Bernice, you are as good as anyone else," she said, "But you are no better than anyone else." From a very young age, I have felt God's presence leading me into purpose. As a child, I would sit in the front row of my church pew, listening to God's teachings. I had so many questions involving why society treated people who looked like me the way that they did. But hearing the word gave me strength to confront my reality and find peace in the storm. At that time, it was not common to question the status quo. And often, I didn't question it. But there was something inside of me that burned to give a voice to the shadows.

Fast-forwarding to the summer of 1971, I received my first job. Two years prior, I enrolled in college at Memphis State University (now University of Memphis) after applying for several grants and loans to support myself through school.

During my sophomore year, my financial responsibilities became weighty, so I applied and accepted a job at the Bell Telephone Company. Accepting this job was one of the pinnacles of my life. I loved my time at the telephone company and always thought that I would work there for the rest of my career.

When I applied to law school in 1974, I knew that I would one day graduate and become a lawyer in their legal department. Working in the company's legal department was my biggest goal throughout law school and I could not wait for that dream to manifest in my life. So, when I graduated from the University of Memphis Cecil C. Humphreys Law School in 1979, I finally applied for the position. I sent in my newly minted resume and cover letter. And after several weeks of no response, I decided to call.

"Hi Bernice, he is not available to answer your call," the hiring director's receptionist answered.

"He's wrapped up in meetings," she said again two weeks later.

"Sorry, Bernice. He's not here."

After a few weeks of no response, I decided to visit the hiring director's office while I was in Birmingham for a work conference.

Standing at the closet door in my hotel room, I pulled out my freshly pressed blue suit that I recently picked up from the dry cleaners. I put the suit on and at that moment I felt invincible. Today was the day that I was going to chase after my dreams. Sure, I was taking a leap of faith. But I knew that when the hiring director met me in person, that my application would come alive and he would see a dedicated and exceptional young lawyer who was committed to the telephone company. So, I went for it.

When I entered the lobby of the telephone company, I called the hiring director once again. But this time he answered.

"Hi, this is Bernice. I wanted to know if you had time to discuss my application in person?" I said.

"Hi Bernice. I have been meaning to give you a call. I wish that I could meet with you but I have a meeting in about two hours," he said.

"Oh, that's fine! I am actually in the lobby of your building right now if you have a few minutes to chat with me," I said.

There was a long silence on the phone followed by a grunt. "Fine. Come up," he said. I took the elevator up to his floor. As the elevator doors opened, I saw him standing outside of his door. The hiring director greeted me and ushered me into his office.

"Hi, thank you for taking the time to meet with me," I said. "I have worked for this company for eight years and I love it. When I went to law school, I dreamed of working in the legal department," I went on.

"Bernice. You are never going to work in this company's legal department. We hire lawyers from the country's ivy league law schools. You, on the other hand, went to a law school that was not very good . . . and you were a night student. I'm sorry, but you just don't fit the company's mold," he said.

Holding back tears from the reality that I would never have the chance to pursue my dream, I found the strength to utter the words: "Thank you. May I be excused?" When he responded "yes," I quickly walked out of his office. Before I could reach the receptionist's desk, teardrops flooded my eyes. So, I did what I always did when something like this happened; I called my mom.

Through tears and stuttering breaths, I explained to my mother the conversation that I had with the director. "Mom," I paused, "What am I going to do?" There was a long silence in between my question and her answer. Anxiously waiting for her comforting response, I repeated myself. "What . . . am . . . I . . . going to do?" I said, desperately waiting for answers. When she finally responded, she said something that would change my life fundamentally. She said, "Bernice, did you plan on working for the telephone company for the rest of your life?" "Well, uh . . . yes, I did," I said.

Following my response, she affirmatively and unequivocally told me: "There is some good in everyone. Go back to the telephone company. There is value in all honest work. You give a full day's work for a full day's pay—anything less is stealing. You cannot control what people think or say about you, but you are responsible for the reputation that you create and you must hold yourself accountable for how you respond to people. So, yes, you fell down, but don't take a nap, get up. You are the only person responsible for your dreams."

After hanging up the phone, I sat quietly in my hotel room for a while. I looked around the room as a glare of light came in through the window. That is when I came to the conclusion that there are other people like me. There are people who were raised in a big family, people who were raised poor, people who graduated from "not very good" law schools, and most importantly, people who used all of the characteristics that made them who they are to shine a light on the profound contributions that people have made to this country from the shadows of mainstream and ivy leagues. This moment in my life is what made me recognize that I had a desire to carry the light with me, too, and spread the voices of those people.

II. KINDLING THE COAL

A few months after being turned down from the telephone company, my professional curiosity knew no bounds. I took a leap of faith and started my own legal practice. I later obtained a position, close to pro bono, with nonprofit and public interest organizations, defending indigent and low-income clients at the Memphis Area Legal Services.

Shortly after beginning work with the public interest organization, my supervisor left to become the County Public Defender. When he asked me if I would join his office as Assistant Public Defender, I quickly said yes. I enjoyed my job. But working with indigent clients accused of crimes proved challenging because it exposed me to the disparities that existed within the criminal justice system.

My experience working at the County Public Defender's office is what led me to run for judge of the General Sessions Criminal Court at the age of thirty. In the state of Tennessee, no Black woman had ever held the position of judge at that time. But I wanted to be in a position of power so I could ensure that others were treated with respect by those in power. I saw too often how people, including myself, were not always treated with respect, and it was simply unacceptable.

My confidence in myself, however, did not change the world's views on what a judge in the state of Tennessee looked like. I quickly learned that battling the image that a judge is white and male would be an uphill climb.

During my campaign for judge, I sought to place an advertisement at a local radio station. As I sat in the radio station, one of the receptionists was heard to say:

"Where is Bernice Donald! If she isn't here in ten minutes, we are leaving!" I stood up from my chair in the lobby and answered, "I am Bernice Donald. I am here, I have been here."

"You're Bernice Donald? You don't look like a judge," she said.

"What does a judge look like?" I responded.

While I was taken aback by the entire exchange, I did not take offense to her comment. In the state court's 185-plus-year history, almost all of the judges to date had been male and white. With that history, I knew that winning this election was greater than me and the good that I wanted to bring to the bench in Shelby County. There was a desperate need for diversity and a demand for progress.

I won my first election in 1982, making me the first female African American judge in Tennessee history. Little did I know, however, that the pressures of shoveling the pathway through bushes of bias and scrutiny would be so great.

III. FUELING THE FLAME

In 1982, I had a desire to help as many people as I could and add my perspective to the ongoing conversations in legal academia. My passion to explore the history and development of legal frameworks is why I sought a position as Adjunct Professor at the University of Memphis Law School. I loved to study the law, so I thought that maybe teaching would be a long-term career goal.

However, six years after being elected to my first judgeship, I was appointed as the nation's first female African American bankruptcy judge. Seven years later, President Bill Clinton nominated me to serve as a District Court Judge in the Western District of Tennessee, making me the first female African American to hold that position.

Being the "first" was not an easy task. Often, my voice and perspective on certain issues was the lone violin playing a new song in a room full of veteran audience members whose ears were trained to hear another sound. It was difficult consistently finding effective ways to pitch the message that diversity is always a good idea. Although I was the first, I encouraged my colleagues to understand that I was not an anomaly in an otherwise unqualified pool.

The racial and gender makeup of the population in law schools, large law firms, and the judiciary still do not reflect the country or the communities they serve. This issue is ever prevalent in today's society, where only 5 percent of lawyers are Black.[5] This number is consistent across almost all spectrums of the profession, including the percentage of minority hires, partners, and judges. But it gets worse when discussing compensation; the numbers drop to a minuscule 1 percent

---

[5.] Commission on Racial and Ethnic Diversity in the Profession, *2020 ABA Model Diversity Survey*, AMERICAN BAR ASSOCIATION, 11–16.

of minorities who are represented in the top 10 percent of earners in the field.[6]

While the issue of diversity in the profession is not a new conversation, it is a critical one. And now is the time to examine the numbers and ask the question: is the pipeline to law school, partnership at a large firm, and judgeships broken for minorities? I testified to the United States House of Representatives that I think it is.

The Court has long emphasized that legal education "cannot be effective in isolation from the individuals and institutions with which the law interacts."[7] Moreover, in 2003, the Supreme Court held that diversity in public institutions was a compelling interest.[8] The Court stated that "ensuring that public institutions are open and available to all segments of American society, including people of all races and ethnicities, represents a paramount government objective."[9] The Court further noted that, "[n]owhere is the importance of such openness more acute than in the context of higher education."[10]

But in 2021, the ABA reported that only 8 percent of the incoming law student class were Black students.[11] Similarly, only 5 percent of the incoming law student class were Hispanic students.[12] Together, only 13 percent of the incoming law student class were Black and Hispanic students.[13] This is a problem considering that the total population of Black and Hispanic Americans combined is 33 percent.[14]

[6.] *Id.* at 16.

[7.] *Id.*; *see* Sweat v. Painter, 339 U.S. 629, 634 (1950).

[8.] *See* Grutter v. Bollinger, 539 U.S. 306, 331-333 (2003).

[9.] *Id.*

[10.] *Id.* at 332.

[11.] American Bar Association, *70 Years after 'Sweatt,' How Much Progress Have African American Law Students Made?*, available at https://www.americanbar.org/news/abanews/aba-news-archives/2020/02/70-years-after-sweatt--how-much-progress-have-african-american-l/.

[12.] *Id.*

[13.] *Id.*

[14.] Nicholas Jones, Rachel Marks, Roberto Ramirez, & Merarys Rios-Vargas, *2020 Census Illuminates Racial and Ethnic Composition of the Country*, U.S. Census Bureau, available at https://www.census.gov/library/stories/2021/08/improved-race-ethnicity-measures-reveal-united-states-population-much-more-multiracial.html#:~:text=In%20 2020%2C%20the%20percentage%20of,33.8%20million%20people)%20in%202020.

Large law firms are no different from law schools with regard to diversity. "Progress in law firm diversity is still proceeding slowly."[15] In 2020, the ABA reported that, while 26.5 percent of all associates are lawyers of color, only 10.2 percent of all partners in law firms are lawyers of color.[16]

In 2021, the ABA reported that "the federal judiciary is [also still] overwhelmingly dominated by judges who are white and male, and that has changed very little" over the past few years.[17] Only 9.8 percent of federal judges are Black, and 6.3 percent are Hispanic.[18] But 79.7 percent of federal judges are white.[19]

"The legal profession [as a whole] has been very slow to diversify by race and ethnicity over the past decade."[20] In 2011, 11.7 percent of the profession were lawyers of color.[21] Ten years later, lawyers of color represented only 14.7 percent of the profession.[22] This change represents a 3 percent increase over the decade, which is simply unacceptable.

Justice Ruth Bader Ginsburg once stated in an interview with the *U.S. News & World Report* that "women belong in all places where decisions are being made. It shouldn't be that women are the exception."[23] Justice Ginsburg was referring to the "real, although not entirely obvious, consequences" of the gender imbalance on the Supreme Court and how those consequences could be influenced by bias.[24] This concept is true for racial and ethnic biases as well.

As long as lawyers of color are underrepresented in the profession, they too are not in "places where decisions are being made." They are not in rooms to proffer their diverse perspectives on education,

---

15. *Id.* at 14.

16. *Id.*

17. *Id.* at 68.

18. *Id.*

19. *Id.*

20. *Id.* at 13.

21. *Id.*

22. *Id.*

23. Mary Kate Karey, *Ruth Bader Ginsburg's Experience Shows the Supreme Court Needs More Women*, US NEWS (May 20, 2009), available at https://www.usnews.com/opinion/blogs/mary-kate-cary/2009/05/20/ruth-bader-ginsburgs-experience-shows-the-supreme-court-needs-more-women.

24. *Id.*

strategic business decisions, criminal justice, judicial decision making, and more. The room where it happens should have a seat at the table for stakeholders from all walks of life to weigh in on decisions that will impact their communities. And the slow increase of 3 percent every decade should be considered a threat to that kind of inclusivity.

IV. BLAZING THE TRAIL

In 2010, President Barack Obama nominated me to serve as judge of the United States Court of Appeals for the Sixth Circuit. In 2011, I was confirmed by the Senate to serve in that position, once again making me the first female African American to serve on the court. After serving as judge for several years on the District Court, my love and passion for studying the law made me optimistic about my new position.

Throughout my years as judge, I have been involved in various organizations that do extraordinary work within the legal profession. I have actively served in numerous positions within the American Bar Association and the National Bar Association. The American Bar Association made me the organization's first female African American officer when the 400,000+ member organization elected me to serve as Secretary. I also served on the ABA's Board of Governors for six years and their House of Delegates for twelve years. In addition, I chaired several sections of the ABA, including the Criminal Justice Section, the National Conference of Special Court Judges, and the Commission of Opportunities for Minorities in the Legal Profession.

As further detailed in my bio, I have been the recipient of numerous awards and recognition, including, within the ABA, the Spirit of Excellence Award, which is the organization's highest honor recognizing contributions and achievements of lawyers of color, and the Margaret Brent Women Lawyers of Achievement Award, the highest honor in the ABA for women lawyers. I have recently become the first person competitively selected by the National Judicial College to receive the Justice Sandra Day O'Connor Award.

For every organization that I have been involved in and every award that I have received, I consider it a privilege to bring my voice to the table. I sought to offer a new perspective on diversity and inclusion through my years of experience on the bench. I have seen the law develop in a way that falls short of providing adequate remedies to some people; but I have also seen some of the most brilliant legal scholars challenge the law's shortcomings and offer a new framework for the courts to apply.

One of the shortcomings that I feel the law does not adequately grapple with is the effect that implicit bias may have on judicial procedures and outcomes. When I was first elected to the General Sessions Criminal Court in 1982, the first accused to ever appear before me was a white male. When he entered the courtroom, there were two Black minute clerks, surrounding the courtroom were four Black Sheriff's deputies, and a Black prosecutor. The defendant approached the bench with fear and trepidation. He requested a thirty-day continuance, which I granted. When the defendant returned to the courtroom thirty days later, he had hired a Black lawyer to represent him. The young man was likely concerned about his ability to receive justice in a courtroom without any diversity. When I realized this, I took immediate action to create a diverse courtroom.

I often share that story because everyone wants justice irrespective of their race, ethnicity, social status, or backgrounds. The essence of the concept "achieving justice" is to provide an environment where all parties are heard, shown dignity and respect, and decisions surrounding the case are made impartially.

Justice Sandra Day O'Connor is often credited for the quote: "a wise old man and a wise old woman will reach the same conclusion in deciding cases." And this statement is often true. But it is just as true that life's perspectives and experiences color the way that the wise old man and wise old woman will reach those conclusions.

Reducing bias in the courtroom is incredibly important to me. Throughout my years on the bench, I have traveled the country discussing how implicit bias can influence the outcomes of cases.

V.   CARRYING THE TORCH

Over the years, I have been referred to as a trailblazer in the legal profession. I do not think of myself or the pursuit of my passions as a trailblazing mission, however. Every organization that I have served in, every case that I have decided, every law clerk that I have hired, and every day that I have served on the bench has been a collection of decisions that have helped challenge and shape my service.

When I think of a trailblazer, the words that come to my mind are "direct," "resilience," and "pioneer."

A few weeks ago, one of my past law clerks sent me a note that one of my opinions was quoted in a recent law review article. The article analyzed my dissenting opinion in a case involving the Restaurant Revitalization Fund. The article states that my dissent in this case "underscored the majority's failure to acknowledge the history of systemic discrimination in the United States"[25] and that some people "reject the notion of systemic racism altogether." When I read this article, it made me think about the power of communicating clearly and directly in oral and written form.

I strive to make my communications in my opinions direct so I can develop trust and a relationship with the reader. A judicial opinion is nothing more than a detailed explanation of how a judge reaches a conclusion in a given case. But too often, opinions exclude elements of full transparency and are overinclusive of vague, yet narrowly targeted language. In the *Vitolo* case, I felt I had to dissent because if I did not, the opinion would ignore the practical consequences that our decision could be exacerbating the country's history of systemic racism, discrimination, and oppression. The opinions that we write should let readers know that we, too, are people who are making decisions not detached from reality.

A trailblazer is also someone who is resilient in the face of many challenges. When I travel to conferences or lectures, many introducers recognize that I have received over 100 awards for my service on the bench. Sweet lawyers, professors, and law students will congratulate me and highlight my success in the field. But what people do not see, however, is how many times I have failed and been told no. "No, it's

---

[25.] Goldburn Maynard Jr., *Biden's Gambit: Advancing Racial Equity While Relying on a Race-Neutral Tax Code*, YALE L. J. F. (Nov. 28, 2021), https://www.yalelawjournal.org /forum/bidens-gambit-advancing-racial-equity; *See* Vitolo v. Guzman, 999 F.3d 353, 366 (6th Cir. 2021) ("The majority's reasoning suggests we live in a world in which centuries of intentional discrimination and oppression of racial minorities have been eradicated. The majority's reasoning suggests we live in a world in which the COVID-19 pandemic did not exacerbate the disparities enabled by those centuries of discrimination.").

not your time"; "no, the world isn't ready for a female African American judge"; no because I went to a "not so good law school." I have failed more times than I have succeeded.

Yet, every time that I was told no, my mother's voice whispered, "when you fall, don't take a nap. Get up." And the older that I get, the more that I realize that we cannot afford to take a nap. Change doesn't happen overnight, and it is not for the weak of heart. Real change takes decades of spirited leaders who are willing to fail more than they succeed for the mere opportunity to push the needle forward. There is no quitting time when the work is so great.

A pioneer is one who creates a path that leads to the discovery of new territory. While some believe that pioneers intentionally carve out their path, the truth is that they are traveling in a direction hoping that there is something on the other side of the journey. Some refer to them as trailblazers, while others refer to them as explorers.

While the journey has not yet come to an end for me, I am still exploring new talent in the profession, still exploring nuances of legal frameworks, still traveling to discuss the importance of finding new solutions to old problems, and still believing that the small contributions that I have made to this profession will impact those who come behind me in a significant way. I was the first to hold many positions on the bench, and I am still the only one on some courts after four decades of service. But I will not quit.

As the country continues to travel the dark path for the search of justice and equality, it is our duty to carry the torch of truth to light the way for those who will come behind us. Like a relay race, leaders in this profession are desperately awaiting the next generation of changemakers so we can pass the torch.

BIO

Bernice B. Donald

The Honorable Bernice B. Donald was nominated to the United States Court of Appeals for the Sixth Circuit by President Barack Hussein Obama on December 1, 2010, and renominated in January 2011. She was confirmed 96–2 by the Senate on September 6, 2011, becoming the first African American woman to serve as a judge on the U.S. Sixth Circuit Court of Appeals.

Prior to joining the Court of Appeals, Judge Donald was appointed in 1995 by President William Jefferson Clinton to serve on the U.S. District Court for the Western District of Tennessee, where she was the

first African American woman to serve on that court. Judge Donald served as Judge of the U.S. Bankruptcy Court for the Western District of Tennessee from June 1988 to January 1996. She was the first African American woman in the history of the United States to serve as a bankruptcy judge. In 1982, she was elected to the General Sessions Criminal Court, becoming the first African American woman to serve as a judge in the history of the State of Tennessee.

Judge Donald received her law degree from the University of Memphis Cecil C. Humphreys School of Law, where she later served as a member of the Alumni, Law Alumni, and University Foundation Boards of Directors, and as an adjunct faculty member. She received an LLM from Duke University School of Law and an honorary Doctors in Law from Suffolk University. She frequently serves as faculty for the National Judicial College and the Federal Judicial Center (FJC) and served as a member of the FJC's Board of Directors from 2003 through 2007. Judge Donald currently serves on the Board of Directors for the Appellate Judges Education Institute and is a member of the prestigious American Law Institute. For the past several years, Judge Donald has served as faculty for the National Trial Advocacy program at the University of Virginia. In 2021, Judge Donald delivered the Justice Stevens Lecture at the University of Colorado School of Law. On October 22, 2018, Judge Donald delivered the distinguished James Madison Lecture at the New York University School of Law. She has served as a Jurist in Residence at the Universities of Cincinnati, Washington, American, and Georgia Schools of Law. In 2021, Judge Donald delivered the Justice Stevens Lecture at

Colorado University School of Law. Judge Donald has lectured at numerous law schools, including the University of Tennessee, Vanderbilt, University of Memphis, Yale, Fordham, Berkeley, Northwestern, Harvard, Regents, and University of Illinois. In February 2022, she lectured at Boston University School of Law. She is a frequent lecturer on implicit bias and diversity, equity, and inclusion; is a chapter author in the book *Enhancing Justice: Reducing Bias* (ABA 2018) and a coeditor of the upcoming book *Extending Justice: Strategies to Increase Inclusion and Reduce Bias*, to be published by Carolina Academic Press.

In 1996, Chief Justice William H. Rehnquist appointed Judge Donald to the Judicial Conference Advisory Committee on Bankruptcy Rules, where she served for six years. In 2011, Chief Justice John G. Roberts appointed her to an indefinite term on the Judicial Branch Committee of the Judicial Conference of the United States. On October 1, 2019, Chief Justice Roberts again appointed Judge Donald to serve on the Advisory Committee on Bankruptcy Rules, where she also serves as Liaison to the Advisory Committee on Appellate Rules.

An internationally recognized legal scholar, Judge Donald has lectured and trained judges around the world for many years. Judge Donald has served as faculty for numerous international programs, including in Armenia, Cambodia, Bosnia, Botswana, Brazil, Egypt, Kazakhstan, Kenya, Kyrgyzstan, Mexico, Morocco, Myanmar, Namibia, Pakistan, the Philippines, Romania, Russia, Rwanda, Senegal, South Africa, Tanzania, Thailand, Turkey, Uganda, and Vietnam. In 2003, Judge Donald led a People to People delegation to Johannesburg and Cape Town, South Africa, and traveled to Zimbabwe to monitor the trial of a judge accused of judicial misconduct.

Judge Donald is an active and dedicated member of both the American Bar Association and the National Bar Association. In the American Bar Association, she was the first African American female officer when she was elected to serve as Secretary of the 400,000+-member professional organization. Judge Donald held numerous leadership positions in the ABA, including two three-year terms on the Board of Governors, and more than 12 years total in the House of Delegates.

She chaired the National Conference of Special Court Judges, the Criminal Justice Section, the Commission of Opportunities for Minorities in the Legal Profession and initiated the highest ABA Award recognizing contributions and achievements of lawyers of color—the Spirit of Excellence Award, given during each Midyear Meeting. She received the Spirit of Excellence Award in 2011.

She currently serves as the Chair of the National Bar Association's Judicial Council Education Committee and has received the Judicial Council's President and Chair Awards, along with other special service awards.

Judge Donald has served as President of the National Association of Women Judges and the Association of Women Attorneys.

In June 2005, Judge Donald cofounded 4-Life, a skills training and enrichment program for students ages six to fifteen, designed to teach children to become positive, productive citizens. In 2020, she was elected to serve as a member of the National Academy of Science, Engineering, and Medicine's working group on Racial Disparities in the Criminal Justice System.

Judge Donald has been the recipient of over 100 awards for professional, civic, and community activities, including the Distinguished Alumni Award from the University of Memphis, the Martin Luther King Community Service Award, and the Benjamin Hooks Award presented in 2002 by the Memphis Bar Foundation. In 2013, Judge Donald was elected to the Board of Directors of the American Judicature Society, and in August 2013, she was featured in the *Federal Lawyer Magazine*. During the 2013 annual meeting of the National Bar Association, Judge Donald received the William H. Hastie Award. The Hastie Award is the Judicial Council's highest award and is presented to recognize excellence in legal and judicial scholarship and demonstrated commitment to justice under the law. In 2013, Judge Donald also received the Difference Makers Award from the Solo, Small Firm & General Practice Division of the ABA, and the Pioneer Award from her fellow classmates at East Side High. Judge Donald received the Justice William Brennan Award by the University of Virginia in January 2014, and the Pickering Award from the Senior Lawyers Division of the ABA in August 2014. In 2017, Judge Donald received the prestigious Margaret Brent Women Lawyers of Achievement Award from the ABA Commission on Women in the Profession. Most recently, Judge Donald received the 2019 University of Memphis Pillar of Excellence Award, designed to recognize attorneys who have made significant contributions to the practice of law in their civic and professional lives.

In 2020, the American Bar Association Labor and Employment Law Section successfully petitioned the ABA Board of Governors to create the Judge Bernice B. Donald Diversity, Equity and Inclusion Award. Judge Donald was the inaugural recipient.

Also in 2020, the ABA Tort Trial and Insurance Section presented Judge Donald with the Lifetime Liberty Achievement Award. The ABA Antitrust Section inducted her into the Hall of Feminism in 2021; she also received the National Bar Association's Lifetime Achievement Award, and the Be the Dream Award from Mayor Jim Strickland, City of Memphis, in 2021. On February 28, 2022, the Tennessee General Assembly honored her for a lifetime of dedicated service.

The Battlefield While on the Battlefield

21

Linda Strite Murnane

Judge Murnane began her military service at a time when women were not welcomed into the ranks of those who seek to protect our country. The hurdles she overcame and the injustices she endured were a shameful part of the armed forces' disgraceful history of bias.

Women who serve in the military owe a debt of gratitude to Judge Murnane for her persistence and courage in the face of outright hostility. Her steadfast determination to succeed has helped open doors for others who, hopefully, will never again have to endure such inhumane treatment in order to serve their country with devotion and distinction.

Lauren Stiller Rikleen, Editor

> The qualities that are most important in all military jobs, things like integrity, moral courage and determination, have nothing to do with gender.[1]

These words etched in the glass ceiling at the Women in Military Service for America Memorial served as inspiration for those of us who chose to be members of the United States military.

For twenty-nine and one-half years, I had the privilege of serving as a member of the United States Air Force. When I enlisted in the Air Force in 1974 as an airman basic, with three years of college but without a bachelor's degree, I was required as part of the enlistment process to sign a document declaring that I had no children and acknowledging that if I became pregnant, I would be discharged from the military.

The document also stated that if I falsely completed the document, that is, if I had children but did not disclose it, I would be subject to disciplinary action, including criminal charges for fraudulent enlistment. Male counterparts enlisting at the same time I entered the service were not required to make such a declaration, of course, and if they became a parent, there was no obligation for them to separate from military service.

This overt gender-based inequality was not new in the military. Women in the military were traditionally paid less than their male counterparts prior to the 1973 decision by the United States Supreme Court in *Frontiero v Richardson*, 411 U.S. 677 (1973). Sharon Frontiero, the plaintiff in the case, was a lieutenant in the United States Air Force who applied for housing and medical benefits for her husband, Joseph. She claimed her husband as a "military dependent."

At that time, male members serving in the military who were married were entitled to apply for housing, medical benefits, and to receive additional pay by providing a copy of their marriage license. Female members of the military were not afforded the same benefits, and had to prove that their husbands relied on them for at least one-half of their total support before receiving the same benefits for the civilian spouses.

The Supreme Court decision applied a strict scrutiny test in deciding that the military policy was unconstitutional.

[1.] Brigadier General Rhonda Cornum, former prisoner of war and U.S. Army Surgeon.

It was against this historically gender-based discriminatory background that my military career began.

At the time I was making the decision to embark upon a military career, I knew I wanted to become a lawyer and hoped that I might one day become a military judge. In assessing the obstacles, I would have to face based upon the work environment I was entering, I was, in essence, facing a reproductive choice as well as a career choice. That was a particularly challenging decision given that at the time of my initial enlistment I was only twenty-two.

The military policy relating to separation of women upon becoming pregnant changed when a group of women, led by Ruth Bader Ginsburg and others who were at the American Civil Liberties Union, took up the cause of women and maternity in cases like those of Tommie Sue Smith and Susan Struck, leading to a change that allowed women to have children and remain in the military provided they could establish a plan that ensured care for those children in case of remote or unaccompanied assignments.

For women who chose the path I chose, therefore, there was no such thing as being offered a job for less pay than your male counterpart because the U.S. Supreme Court held that the past practice of mandating less pay than your male counterpart was unconstitutional in its 1973 decision. However, that did not result in a level playing field for women pursuing a legal career in the armed forces as the discretionary decisions about where one would get assigned and in what legal roles one would be used would routinely result in a dramatic variation in the possibility of promotion.

Promotions in the military included the requirement to submit an "official photo," which had to be included in one's promotion file. This was a photo in uniform and one spent hours ensuring that every detail of the military uniform was precise, including the requirement that women have a "mature hair style" in accordance with military dress and appearance regulations. While the official military photo requirement was applied to both men and women, the hair regulations applied to women were quite specific, including not being able to have a hairstyle that allowed one's hair to touch the bottom of the collar of the service dress jacket.

Since I had enlisted in the military without having completed a bachelor's degree, before my transfer to the judge advocate general department or corps, I had to first complete my final undergraduate year and my law degree. I also had to compete for and be selected for service as a commissioned officer.

Immediately after completing the enlisted basic training, I was assigned as a journalist or "public affairs specialist" at Langley Air Force Base, Virginia. I did not attend any technical training school but rather reported to my first assignment after six weeks of learning about how to march in drill formations, and about the most critical of military teamwork skills. I arrived at Langley Air Force Base in January 1975. At the time the United States was pulling out of Vietnam, and the military had planned to airlift Vietnamese who had been helpful to the U.S. military bringing them to refugee reception centers located on various military installations around the United States.

By April 1975, I volunteered to deploy to one of the Vietnamese reception centers, writing news stories and photojournalism pieces in support of Operation Homecoming/New Arrivals. I don't recall seeing any military women at the tent city at which I was assigned other than perhaps some nurses or medics. I was certainly the only female public affairs specialist, living in a tent and showering in a make-shift field latrine facility.

My news pieces earned national wire service recognition, so when I returned from my deployment, I felt the time was right to ask my supervisor if he might consider allowing me to participate in a program called "Operation Bootstrap" through which I could complete my last nine months to obtain my bachelor's degree. He supported that request and off I went in August of 1975 to finish my BA in political science at the branch campus of the College of William & Mary.

The next obstacle was to apply for and be selected for a commission as a second lieutenant. As the military was then in a draw-down mode due to the withdrawal from Vietnam, the commissioning programs were really only interested in candidates who had degrees in computer science, math, and engineering. Folks with "soft core" degrees like mine were not in high demand.

The military was transitioning, however, from the days of the military draft and selective service obligations for men over eighteen to an all-volunteer force. The Vietnam War had been intensely unpopular, and the military was not meeting its volunteer recruiting quotas. As a result, they instituted a 12 percent quota for women candidates for officer training school. It was through that 12 percent quota that I got selected and became one of 12 women in a commissioning class of 112 persons.

After obtaining my commission as a second lieutenant, I applied for the Air Force's Funded Legal Education Program, which would have allowed me to attend law school full-time at the Air Force's expense. My first application was unsuccessful, and I had the unique opportunity to meet with one of the general officers who sat on the board that selected the successful candidates and to ask him how I might improve my application for the next opportunity.

The general explained to me that what my application lacked was a showing of "commitment." I recall asking him how the board defined "commitment," telling him that I had started out as an airman basic, deployed to the Vietnamese refugee reception camp right out of basic training, gotten my undergraduate degree with honors, and gone to Officer Training School and gotten my commission, all within two years.

He candidly replied that if I had attended the United States Air Force Academy for my undergraduate degree, the board would know I was "committed." I told him, "Sir, with all due respect, women weren't eligible to attend the Air Force Academy when I was attending undergraduate school." He replied, "Well, there is that."

Undaunted, I enrolled in the night law program at Loyola Law School in New Orleans, Louisiana, which involved working full-time as a second lieutenant at Keesler Air Force Base in Biloxi, Mississippi, and commuting 200 miles each night, four nights a week, to complete my first semester of law school. I then reapplied for the Funded Legal Education Program. Apparently, the combination of my passing grades, my career achievements, and the 800 miles a week on the road demonstrated the commitment that was lacking in my earlier application, as I was notified that I had been selected for one of the seven slots in the entire Air Force to attend law school full time.

The next challenge, however, came when I learned the same day that I was pregnant with my first child. When I enlisted in the Air Force in 1974, women were required to separate from the service as soon as they became pregnant. By the time I was selected to attend the Funded Legal Education Program, women were allowed to apply to remain in the service provided they could adequately describe how their child would be cared for in case they had to deploy. Since women had been required to separate when pregnant, when I was selected to attend the full-time law program shortly after the policy changed, the Air Force and the Department of Defense hadn't had the opportunity to consider how to handle a pregnant woman attending a funded law program.

Lest the reader think that surely this isn't an issue anymore in the military, Congress is debating the Cadet Act of 2021, which would change a 100-year policy that cadets attending military service academies may not have children or be married.[2]

It was as the result of this unique challenge that I had the benefit of ten days of maternity leave with my first child, born while I was attending law school under the Funded Legal Education Program. I had only five days of maternity leave with my second child, born also while I was attending law school under the Funded Legal Education Program, since she was born at the start of the five-day spring break.

When people speak to me about time taken for "self-care," I think back on the birth of my two daughters, both surgical deliveries, and being back in class ten days after delivery of each child and have to smile about "self-care." In the end, I finished my law degree program in two and one-half years, having won the American Jurisprudence Award for Academic Excellence in Constitutional Law in the semester in which my first child was born and having been selected as one of the first six Urban Morgan Fellows in International Human Rights in the semester in which my second child was born.

In May 1981, I was transferred within the Air Force to become a military attorney or judge advocate. I was then a captain. Promotions to the most senior grades in the military required a type of increased responsibility in duties that would sometimes be particularly difficult for women. Assignments were made out of a central career management office.

It was not uncommon, particularly in the earlier years in my legal career, for those women who were effective litigators to have the legendary "too aggressive" label applied if they tried to rely upon the same tools and devices as their male counterparts to negotiate positive outcomes for clients. Senior commanders are assigned a staff

---

[2] https://www.congress.gov/bill/117th-congress/senate-bill/2376?s=1&r=38.

judge advocate who serves as the senior legal advisor on legal aspects of all operational, personnel, and military good order and discipline.

The challenges I faced while trying to be a parent to two children, particularly with a spouse who was unwell, were at times overwhelming. At my first assignment as a judge advocate, my daughter who was born with hearing and vision challenges was hospitalized for a good part of the first year of her life. At one point, she was in pediatric intensive care diagnosed with septicemia. Her father, my husband, was an inpatient on the orthopedic ward having undergone one of the six spinal cord surgeries he had to address an L-5 S-1 spinal compression. My nearly three-year-old was at home with me, and I had childcare arrangements for her that allowed me to manage the long hours at the office while also visiting my infant and my husband at the hospital.

I distinctly recall a conversation with my staff judge advocate— the senior legal officer in my office—when I was in this circumstance. He called me in and told me that he planned to send me to a base in Alabama to attend a six-week training course. My home base was in California.

I told him that this was a uniquely bad time for me to be away with my daughter in pediatric intensive care and my husband an inpatient at the hospital. His response was, "You can be a mother or a lawyer. I need your answer by 4:30 today."

With my family entirely dependent on my military status for health care, I made the incredibly difficult decision to go to Alabama for the training course. I left my three-year-old with friends from my faith community, and my husband and daughter in the hospital.

When I returned from the six-week training course, my infant daughter had been moved to a civilian hospital about an hour drive from the base. She was to undergo surgery. My husband was not well enough to be at the hospital with her although he was now home. I went to the same boss, and asked if I could take three days of leave to be with my daughter while she had her surgery. He said he'd see when the date of the surgery was closer.

He waited until about two weeks before the surgery date, and called me into his office to tell me that he had decided to give two of my male peers the same days I had requested leave as "days off." I candidly don't know what "days off" are in the military. Either you are on leave or you are on duty. He said the two peers had arranged to have sod laid at their homes that day and that I would have to sit second chair on my first court-martial case those days.

As a result of that decision, I prepared and conducted direct and cross-examination in a fully litigated trial the three days my daughter was in the hospital for her surgery. After my trial, I drove the hour to the hospital she was in, rocked and held her, slept at the hospital, showered at the hospital, and drove back for trial until I could bring her home.

In order to advance to more senior military grades, women had to be assigned to positions as deputy staff judge advocates and staff judge advocates. With nearly all senior commanders being men, and many committed to seeing women fail as members of the military, finding a commander willing to accept a female senior legal advisor was often very challenging.

It was a common phrase in the military among the few women who were working to achieve more senior grades that "in order to be thought of as half as good, a woman had to work twice as hard." "Fortunately," the sisterhood shared among themselves only, "that isn't difficult."

There were intentional obstacles placed in the way of women's progress as members of the military. Maternity leave for a woman after delivery of a child was ordinarily set at six weeks, at which time the woman was expected to be back within the military's stringent weight and fitness standards. More than one woman found that within one year of having had a child, they had to decide whether to accept a remote assignment that would require them to be separated from their infant for up to one year.

In looking for support at least in the late 1970s and early 1980s, you couldn't find senior women who had remained in service to advise and guide you through the process. The only woman judge I met in my first years as a military lawyer was a woman who was best known for her great fondness of Manhattans, and her somewhat significant reputation for being inebriated at many official events.

Today, the news headlines routinely report startling numbers relating to sexual assaults and rapes of military members by service members. As I entered the Air Force and during nearly all of my military service, there was little attention paid to concerns of women regarding sexual harassment or sexual assault.

At one time, as a captain in my first assignment as a judge advocate (lawyer) I suggested that, instead of sending two male armed agents from the Air Force Office of Special Investigations to respond to a woman's complaint of rape or sexual assault, it might be better to send at least one woman on the initial response team. I had the audacity to propose that there be special training and a sex offense response team organized. My effort to do that was supported by a female MSW social worker assigned to the military hospital, and it came after a very difficult rape trial which resulted in a conviction but what I felt was a disproportionately lenient sentence. I was told that it was "not politically expedient" to be talking about setting up a sexual assault response team and my suggestion was dismissed.

The experiences in that first legal office, however, led quickly to a series of much better assignments, most often with supportive supervisors who truly were dedicated to helping me succeed. Those who recognized my talent and gave me opportunities to serve as lead prosecutor or defense counsel in the most significant cases helped me to land upon the decision to pursue an assignment as a military judge.

Getting those better assignments came when I reached a breaking point, and asked to be admitted to the hospital. I had become suicidal. The experience I had dealing with the impossible situation at that first assignment, however, later served me well as I came to fully understand the difference between premeditation, and overt act. Thankfully, while I may have premeditated resolving my situation through means at my disposal, I never engaged in an overt act, saving me from committing a serious crime.

Assignment as a military judge, particularly for those who had families, posed another set of unique challenges. Military judges at that time were assigned to a circuit and would routinely be on the road presiding at courts-martial or administrative hearings in a regional area that might take you on the road 200 or more days a year. When you consider that military members earn 30 days of annual leave, that there are some paid holidays, and when you deduct 104 days that fall on the weekends, you spent very little time at home. Not many women were in the judge advocate general's departments when I arrived as a judge advocate in 1981 after obtaining my commission and my law degree. There were very, very few women who went on to serve as military judges.

At the time I was initially appointed as a military judge in 1994, there was, I believe, one other woman about to rotate to a new non-judge military assignment and one additional woman coming to the bench. We were a very small minority. Having said that, the military judiciary is small by comparison to other benches, with about twenty-two to twenty-six judges having been the norm when I was serving.

It came as no significant surprise to me once I was assigned as a military judge that it seemed I had a disproportionately high number of cases assigned to my docket that dealt with sexual assault, rape, domestic violence, child sexual abuse, and child pornography. This wasn't a concern to me as I felt I was able to afford each and every person in my courtroom, regardless of their role, a fair and impartial opportunity to achieve justice.

Unlike many of my civilian sisters who have shared stories with me about their experiences, particularly early in their careers on the bench, I was, for the most part, treated with the appropriate decorum and respect for the role of the judge by the litigants who appeared before me. I can say with certainty that no counsel in my courtroom and no military supervisor during my time on the bench ever referred to me as "honey," "darling," or "sweetheart." I did hear that I had a couple of nicknames that were used in referring to me, including "Judge Iron Pants" and "Midnight Murnane."

However, the treatment by my peer military judges was a different story. As a military judge, and serving in the grade of lieutenant colonel, I recall sitting in my office. I was now a trial judge and in my fourth year on the bench. I was the only woman on the trial bench in my circuit in Washington, DC. One day, sitting in my office, I heard the four male judges laughing in the office next door. I poked my head around the corner and said, "Am I invited to the fun?" One of the judges—again a peer—said that they were all laughing because an advance sheet had just been published which contained decisions involving women judges currently on the bench, and said, "sort of like the Playboy edition of the Military Justice Reporter." And then, as if that wasn't bad enough, he turned the advance sheet sideways, and said, "The centerfold isn't all that great."

By this time, I had plenty of tools in my tool belt on how to handle situations like this one, and I made a lighthearted remark like, "I may not be offended but Judge X (a more senior and quite well-respected judge) might be and she would punch your lights out if she heard you say that," or something like that.

Later that day, a female lieutenant colonel who was a circuit defense counsel in the office who had overheard what happened that day came to my office and said, "Colonel, you have to do something about this." And I did.

I went to the Chief Trial Judge's Office and reported the event, asking him to see if I could handle it myself, but I wanted him to know about it. I left a note in my Circuit Chief Judge's box that said something like, "I'm either all the way in or all the way out. I did not appreciate what happened in the office today and I would like to speak with you about it."

When I returned from the Chief Trial Judge's Office, my Chief Circuit Judge asked to speak with me. The first thing he asked was "Who else did you tell?" I told him it was none of his business who else I told, and that if he was worried about who else I told, I guess he knew that something had happened that should not have happened in the office, and I asked him what he was going to do about it.

I was reasonably certain that I had sealed my fate at that point and would not likely be promoted to colonel, but that really didn't matter to me. I did what I needed to do. I went to the female defense counsel and told her I had handled it and that I didn't think that would ever happen again.

The next day, one by one, each of my colleagues who were judges engaged in the conduct the day before came into my office to apologize. And of course, I couldn't resist lecturing them a bit on sexual harassment and gender equality in the workplace.

When the next assignment forecast came out, I had been selected to colonel, and also was selected to become the Chief Circuit Military Judge for Europe. I don't know precisely why or how that happened, but I can tell you that the Chief Trial Judge of the Air Force to whom I related the events in the Circuit was an ally and a person who was committed to ensuring equal opportunity in the service.

And so it came to be that between 2000 and 2003 I was fortunate to have what I think is the best job in the global universe, as I was honored to serve as the Chief Circuit Military Judge for the European Circuit. The jurisdiction for which I and my Deputy Chief Judge had responsibility included all U.S. Air Force installations in

Europe, Southwest Asia, and Northern Africa. I had responsibility for a travel budget that exceeded one-quarter of a million dollars, and my deputy and I had to ensure the timely trials with just the two of us throughout our theater of operations. Following the attacks on the World Trade Towers in New York on 9/11, we picked up responsibility for those bases at which U.S. airmen were serving in support of Operations Iraqi and Enduring Freedom.

As a result of that occurrence, I had the opportunity to deploy five times to preside at trials of U.S. airmen charged with criminal offenses in Oman, Qatar, and Saudi Arabia. I was also asked to participate on the first U.S. Military Assistance Mission to Rwanda after the sanction period following the genocide.

Unique challenges come when one deploys as a judge to preside at a trial in the combat zone, and in particular being "the first" to do so in those operations was also unique. There wasn't another woman to ask for advice on how to address such things as being in Saudi Arabia where women were otherwise not permitted to drive and how one might best navigate that issue while being in the country to preside as a judge at a trial.

As for support from other women in the effort to advance my military career, I suspect I joined the military too early in the evolutionary process to benefit much from having "sisters" I could turn to for advice. I recall having looked at dramatically lower statistics for promotions of women judge advocates from the grade of lieutenant colonel to colonel. I had raised this concern with senior leaders in the Air Force throughout my career—all of them men, of course.

In 2003, while serving as a colonel and a Chief Circuit Military Judge, a woman was nominated to be a brigadier general in the judge advocate general corps. I recall congratulating her, and since she was a peer while pending her confirmation, I said to her, "I am so glad you are going to be a brigadier general. Perhaps you could do something about the disparity in promotion opportunities for women in the JAG corps." Her response startled me, as she said, "I don't think of myself as a woman. That's how I got where I am."

In truth, my engagement with organizations like the National Association of Women Judges, the International Association of Women Judges, the American Judges Association, and the American Bar Association's Judicial Division and International Law Section often provided me with better sounding boards than any experience within the unique military environment.

In retrospect, I think I am grateful I didn't know some of the things I would face, as I might not have had the courage at the age of twenty-two to consider embarking on what became a grand adventure and a fantastic, rewarding, and fulfilling legal career as a member of the U.S. military. I developed a strong set of skills in addressing sexual harassment and inappropriate behaviors by professionals, regardless of the gender, which served me well both in my military service but also, importantly, in the very challenging and unique opportunities I had following my military career.

When I left the bench, and retired from the military in 2004, there were many more women judges, and shortly after I retired, my service branch, the Air Force, appointed its first female Chief Judge, Colonel Dawn Eflein.

The words of Major Rhonda Cornum with which I began this essay are truly the key to success in the military. However, in my view, having those core qualities common to military professionalism of integrity, moral courage, and determination are essential to success, and those qualities have nothing to do with gender.

BIO

Linda Strite Murnane

Colonel (USAF, Ret.) Linda Strite Murnane served 29.5 years on active duty, enlisting in 1974 as an airman basic, the lowest enlisted grade, and retiring as a colonel (O-6) in the position of Chief Circuit Military Judge for the Eastern Circuit in Washington, DC.

Colonel Murnane obtained her undergraduate and law degrees while on active duty, the former from the Christopher Newport branch campus of the College of William & Mary in 1976 and the latter from the University of Cincinnati College of Law in March 1981. She presided over the first trials conducted in the combat zones during Operations Iraqi and Enduring Freedom, and served on the first U.S. Military Assistance Team in Rwanda following the genocide.

Following her retirement from the Air Force, she served as the Executive Director of the Kentucky Commission on Human Rights and served at the International Criminal Tribunal for the former Yugoslavia and at the Special Tribunal for Lebanon for eight years. She has received the American Bar Association's Margaret Brent Women Lawyers of Achievement Award, and Mayre Rasmussen Award, as well as the Ohio State Bar Association's Nettie Cronise Lutes Award for advancing the cause of women in the law.

Her leadership positions within the American Bar Association include the role of Chair of the Judicial Division and its National Conference of Specialized Court Judges (NCSCJ). She was appointed by the ABA President to chair the Standing Committee on Armed Forces Law for two years. She is a past cochair of the ABA International Law Section's International Human Rights Committee and serves as a delegate to the ABA House of Delegates representing the NCSCJ. She is an active member of the International and National Associations of Women Judges and of the Federal Bar Association, and chairs the Ohio State Bar Association's Military and Veterans Affairs Committee.

Linda is married to Lt. Col. (USAF, Ret.) Kevin Murnane, and they have two daughters, Christina Veillon and Rachel Lyn Manuel, and three grandchildren.

She served as "Of Counsel" with the Cusack Law Office, LLC, in Beavercreek, Ohio. She was recently confirmed to be an Associate Justice on the High Court of the Republic of the Marshall Islands.

BIO

Do Not Let Fear Win Over Change

22

Angela M. Bradstreet

"*W*e *must never doubt our ability to do what we want to do.*"

Adherence to those words helped Angela Bradstreet advocate for herself as a lawyer and a lesbian in the 1980s. It also helped her respond to homophobia and sexism by using her voice to advocate for change.

She followed her professional passions and succeeded as a lawyer, a judge, and an activist, dedicated to using the power of the legal profession to improve people's lives and remove systemic barriers to success.

Judge Bradstreet's examples demonstrate why silence can be a weapon for the perpetrators of harassment or bias, and shows us that speaking up is the only effective way to bring about change. She also reinforces the need for us all to protect our own fragile democracy.

Lauren Stiller Rikleen, Editor

I was twenty-two and life was good. I had landed a coveted position as an associate at a prestigious law firm in my hometown of London where I was born and raised. Then, in a few seconds, my whole life was turned upside down when my parents discovered my sexual orientation and all hell broke loose.

After a terrible scene, I tried to lead a double life but the stress was unbearable. At the age of twenty-four, I left England for the United States with nothing more than a backpack, no place to live, and without knowing a soul. I had managed to land a fellowship at Berkeley Law School's LLM program and got a part-time job at a family law firm to fund the balance of my frugal living expenses. As difficult as it was to leave my native country and all those dear to me, I knew that was my only choice if I wanted to live an authentic life.

Being a woman lawyer and a lesbian in the early 1980s was not for the faint of heart, even in California. I was the third woman to join a terrific midsize law firm in San Francisco. Unfortunately, the two women who were senior to me did very little to help me.

In fact, the only woman partner at the time appeared to feel threatened by my presence at the firm and did nothing to help me negotiate the politics that exist in any workplace. It saddened me that she acted as if there were no room for more women in the firm's partnership ranks. Perhaps that experience is, at least in part, why I think it is so important to mentor, or as I prefer to say, *womentor*, other women following us and why this book project is so wonderful.

I desperately needed a womentor upon joining the firm, since I was assigned to the most powerful rainmaker in the firm who had never worked with a woman associate before. Encouragement was not, shall we say, his strong point. He seemed to thrive on criticizing—in a loud and angry tone—virtually every assignment I did, to the point that I would often return to my dingy studio apartment late at night in tears.

I saw, however, that he was a brilliant lawyer and that I was learning from the best. So, I decided to fight back and wrote him a long note (before email!) detailing how he was mistreating me and stating that such behavior was neither warranted nor acceptable. It worked! Within a few months I had changed things around to the point that he selected me to second chair several high-exposure and lengthy trials. He became my most fervent supporter and we remain fast friends almost forty years later.

That experience taught me that speaking out and insisting on being treated with respect results in respect from others. Sometimes it is hard for us to stand up for ourselves. We may see it as being risky because it potentially creates conflict. Dr. Deborah Tannen has written extensively on how men are often socialized to be more comfortable with conflict than women.

I know that each time I have spoken out, both for myself and others, I have been respected for it. For example, I took the initiative when I felt I should be considered for partnership. Word had filtered down to me that some partners were inclined to postpone the decision for another year. I wrote an analytical memorandum to the managing partner explaining my rationale for why I deserved to be a partner without delay and spoke to a couple of key partners to obtain their support. The partnership voted me in soon after that.

I also found that my requests that the firm credit my various bar association activities toward billable hour requirements and my requests that the firm sponsor various community events were successful when made in a thoughtful manner. Over the years, my presidency of California Women Lawyers, the Queen's Bench Bar Association (San Francisco's local women lawyers' groups), and the San Francisco Bar Association took up literally hundreds of hours. When I pointed out to my partners the benefits to them from a client relations perspective, and when a few clients thanked them for my involvement, both the emotional and financial support from my partners grew in leaps and bounds!

People skills are also critical to a successful and fulfilling career. I have seen many lawyers who may be excellent legal writers but have no idea how to connect with a judge or jury or with their peers. Throughout my career, I have forged collaborative relationships with colleagues and clients, many of which remain today.

Those relationships resulted in my nomination as managing partner of the firm (then about seventy-five attorneys in size). There was a catch, however. It was suggested that I be the "personnel" managing partner and that a male be the "financial" managing partner. Of course, no such arrangement had ever existed before. After I had suitably calmed myself, I responded that the proposal was neither workable nor acceptable to me. And—voilá!—I went on to serve two terms as one of the first female and LGBT managing partners in the Bay Area.

We must never doubt our ability to do whatever we want to do.

The truth is that I did not have a clue about profit margins or net profits per partner before I started the job but I sure as hell learned about all of it! I recall a woman lawyer seeking my counsel when she had been asked to be managing partner by her firm. She was convinced that she was not ready, despite having served five years on the management committee. I counseled her that of course she was ready and that we have enough external glass ceilings without creating our own internal ones!

Such internal glass ceilings can include being afraid to ask for what we want. Early on, I had a difficult time asking for business. I feared rejection, so it was easier not to ask in the first place.

But I came to realize that asking for business is not personal—it's business! And no one gives you business unless you make the ask. We often expend countless hours and energy developing relationships, but have great difficulty actually asking for the business and then wonder why it is not forthcoming. I tried to do it in ways that I felt comfortable with and that were consistent with my personality.

It was not an accident that most of my book of business came from women in-house counsel who valued diversity and desired to spread their business to women and minorities. I adopted different approaches depending on the personality of the potential client.

I vividly remember summoning the courage to ask a close friend who was the President and CEO of a bank for business years after we became friends. She had often mentioned using another law firm's services. I was reluctant to ask her for her business, because I was worried that would negatively impact our friendship. I have never heard any man express the same concern! I began to realize that she was waiting for me to ask her, so the next time she mentioned the other law firm, I inquired, "Why aren't you using my services?" She immediately responded, "You are right." I proceeded to represent her bank until I stopped practicing law.

Other potential clients were less direct and preferred a more subtle approach, but in all cases, the common denominator of success was making the ask.

Honing a specialty is also important. My interest lay in employment law. But how could I sell myself as an employment litigator when I had spent the first five years at the law firm in the commercial and products liability litigation department and the firm did not have an employment practice? I decided to write a couple of articles, take some courses, and then hold myself out as an employment litigator. It worked and I soon built up a seven-figure book of business.

In my entire career I have never experienced a male lawyer tell me he was not an expert in whatever area he practiced, yet numerous women have come to me expressing doubts about the adequacy of their expertise. I counsel them that, whether in the courtroom or interacting with clients or peers, we must convey confidence in our abilities; perception becomes the reality in the minds of others.

Jurors have told me that if they perceive that an attorney is unsure or hesitant, that has led them to question the strength of her client's case. I have encountered women fixating on a question they forgot to ask at trial or in a deposition, rather than the wealth of information they obtained. And many have expressed feelings of personal failure if they were unsuccessful at a hearing or a trial when the result had nothing to do with their competence and everything to do with the merits. I reminded them what I continue to remind myself— that internal glass ceilings impede us (after all we have plenty of external ones to face!) and we must be vigilant in recognizing them and breaking them down.

Throughout my career I have experienced my fair share of homophobia and sexism in the profession. I will never forget having to listen to homophobic comments made by a client at a dinner when I was a young associate and I remain mad at myself to this day for not speaking up at the time.

But I did just that a few years later at a San Francisco Bar Association board meeting, during a discussion of the issue of gay marriage. When the opposition speaker decided to analogize gays to Nazis, I politely pointed out to him the reason I had come to this great country, that he was talking about me, and that I had never thought I would have to listen to such hate language. After an endless silence he apologized.

To this day, I still mentor young attorneys who are in the closet and unsure about coming out. An acquaintance asked me if I would meet with his daughter who was interested in a legal career. The dynamics of the meeting changed when the daughter shyly asked me about the "social scene" in San Francisco, and it became a tearful discussion about how she could come out to her parents. There is no right time to come out. It is different for everyone.

It is, however, important to state that I do not know anyone who is truly happy and has peace of mind, and who is still in the closet. It took me several years to come out after I came to this country. Once I did, it was a huge relief. While I never fully reconciled with my parents, my mother did meet and get to know my wife before my mother died. She told me how much she liked her, which I think was my mother's way of apologizing.

Gender discrimination in the legal profession tends to be more subtle nowadays, but remains problematic. I know I am not the only judge to be asked if I am the court reporter or the only judge to be interrupted or lectured to. And I know of very few women lawyers who have not been subjected to demeaning sexist remarks at some point in their careers.

How we all deal with these situations will vary according to our personalities—but we must call them out and no one should get a pass. I handled one particularly sexist male attorney who constantly interrupted me in depositions with sexist comments by presenting him with his very own "women lawyers for justice" pin from the local women lawyers group; the entire group of all-male attorneys broke out into applause and laughter. I had chosen to make the point with humor and it was effective as he immediately ceased his inappropriate behavior and proudly wore the pin to every appearance in the case from that time on!

An example that I still find painful to recall involved highly inappropriate behavior that constituted sexual harassment by a male judge when I was a junior associate. He capitalized on the disparity of power by asking me to play tennis with him. After the game, it was quickly apparent that he had planned and reserved a table for dinner at a restaurant.

It was the most uncomfortable dinner I have ever had that included being subjected to several inappropriate sexual remarks and attempted touching. At one point someone waved at him, and he then said to me, "How do you like being out on a date with a celebrity?"

With a knot in my stomach, I responded that we were not on a date. I was too afraid of retaliation to report it and had no idea who to even report it to. Thank goodness, we now have written policies and other mechanisms that encourage reporting of such behavior and prohibit retaliation. The same judge was formally investigated years later and I finally reported my experience.

The glass ceiling is also very much intact despite large cracks that have been made. As President of California Women Lawyers in 1992 and President of the San Francisco Bar Association in 2005, I focused on the external glass ceiling women lawyers face and created the No Glass Ceiling Initiative. Brilliantly chaired by fellow Brentee Mary Cranston, one of the first women managing partners of a national law firm, we created a blue-ribbon committee that included male and female general counsel of Fortune 500 companies and former San Francisco District Attorney and now honorable Vice President of the United States, Kamala Harris.

We set specific percentage goals and challenged law firms and the public sector to commit to placing far more women into positions of power, including on management and compensation committees, as well as increasing the number of women managing partners and general counsel. The Initiative received national acclaim and a survey three years later showed that significant progress had been made. Over 100 Bay Area firms endorsed the initiative and numerous city and women's bar associations adopted and distributed it nationwide.

But we still have a long way to go. For example, disparities in equity partner compensation continue to exist. I learned that the hard way when, early on as an equity partner, I felt undervalued compared with my male counterparts who did not have my book of business nor were involved in community activities. I realized that speaking out about my own expectations ahead of time was key, especially when this seemed to be the norm among the male partners. It can be hard to talk about ones' own worth but none of my male partners seemed to have a problem doing so!

I have often counseled other women about the importance of pointing out all the ways they have added value, which may include bar association and community activities that add enormously to their firm's reputation and standing.

My involvement in bar association activities promoting the advancement of women and equality has been a passion and a joy. I encourage the readers to find their passion and to give back in some way. It is deeply rewarding.

In 1995, I led a delegation to the World Wide NGO Forum on Women, near Beijing, where we presented workshops on sexual harassment and LGBT issues, exchanging experiences and ideas with women from all over the world. I gained a whole new perspective on the problems women in other countries in the world face. For example, I will never forget how women from Pakistan described the horror of being raped on tea plantations as a regular occurrence. A professor in law from Japan expressed delight with our sexual harassment policy guidelines, telling us she had never seen any before. Women from Third World countries spoke about the need for water as their most important priority.

There were also frightening aspects of attending this Conference in China that reinforced how we must never take our constitutional form of government and the rule of law for granted. Upon entry into China, our sexual harassment and LGBT materials were confiscated by customs! One night I returned to my hotel room and found papers and other items strewn all over the room—it had been ransacked. The feelings of vulnerability and invasion of privacy were terrifying. I swore there and then never to forget all the freedoms our laws and Constitution give us.

The next day I stood for hours in torrential rain with twenty thousand other women. But it was worth it. It was a privilege to be there to witness first-hand our beloved Hillary Clinton declare to the world that, "Women's rights are human rights, and human rights are women's rights." Standing right next to me in the crowd was Jane Fonda!

Testifying at Justice Ruth Bader Ginsburg's confirmation hearing was another highlight. I was invited to speak by California's first woman senior Senator Dianne Feinstein, who was one of the first women to be appointed to the Senate Judiciary Committee along with Carol Moseley Braun. I spoke in my capacity as then President of California Women Lawyers and focused on Justice Ginsburg's brilliant advocacy of women's equality when she was a lawyer at the ACLU and her advocacy of reproductive rights. When a small group of anti-choice women lawyers issued various statements to the media criticizing my remarks on choice, I was told that interest in membership of California Women Lawyers spiked!

During my Presidency of the San Francisco Bar Association in 2001–2002, we challenged the propriety of judges being members of Boy Scout troops that excluded gays and lesbians. When I received death threats nationwide and was told by a national radio host that he wouldn't want his children around me, I admit to momentarily losing the joy, but never the hope. As a result of our action, the California Supreme Court amended the commentary guidelines to the Canons of Ethics.

I am proud that the San Francisco Superior Court was the first trial court in the nation to adopt a resolution prohibiting membership of a judicial officer in any nonreligious organization that excluded gays and lesbians. Other trial courts and bar associations throughout California followed suit. Over a decade later, the California Supreme Court changed the Canons of Ethics to make such membership a violation of the Judicial Canons of Ethics.

Whatever your passion is, be sure to follow it! Which brings me to the rewards of public service. I spent twenty-five years at the same law firm, and I had a wonderful legal career there. Everyone assumed I was going to continue working there until retirement. But change is healthy (as well as scary). I had grown tired of the billable hour and found myself searching for a meaningful way to give back. In my opinion, there is no better way to do that than public service.

I was not ready to seek a judgeship at the time, and in 2007, I had the privilege of being appointed State Labor Commissioner by Governor Schwarzenegger. I had previously sought and had been interviewed by the Governor for a different position. While I came close, another highly qualified candidate was chosen. I share this because how we deal with disappointment can affect our career development. I was able to see that the decision was not personal and that it actually resulted in a much better "fit" for me as Labor Commissioner.

I will never forget visiting the garment factories in Los Angeles to enforce California's minimum wage laws and seeing first-hand the injustices of the underground economy. I vividly recall the terrified eyes of Matilda A. and her relief and happiness when I assured her that I was not from immigration and that I was there to protect her rights to be paid in full for the fourteen hours of work that she performed each day. In that moment I knew that public service was how I wanted to end my career and the past eleven years that I have served as a judge has felt like eleven minutes!

Women judges, including women of color and lesbian and transgender women, bring perspectives to the bench that are often unique. For example, we spearheaded the availability of lactation rooms at our Court and many of us have standing rules encouraging diverse and less experienced attorneys to be given more responsibility in trials and other hearings.

We also should not be afraid to display the empathy that we often feel that can help put litigants at ease. At a child molestation trial I presided over (the appeal process has been exhausted), I had the ten-year-old girl who was the victim sit close to me when she attended the sentencing so I could talk directly to her and tell her that a unanimous jury believed her.

A kind word to a new colleague or an inexperienced trial attorney conducting her first trial can help immeasurably to put her at ease. We have all been in her shoes before and it is incumbent on us to pave the way and help those who follow us.

In looking back over the past forty years since I first came to this great country, I realize how important it is not to let fear win over change. My best personal decisions involved making fundamental life changes that have been critical to my well-being. It took me too long to start asking for what I wanted, but with hard work, I finally overcame my own internal glass ceilings.

Some of my most treasured memories are working with other women to promote the advancement of women in the profession. And I learned that holding dear to our own moral compass and being true to ourselves are the only paths to a fulfilling career and a happy life.

BIO

Angela M. Bradstreet

Hon. Angela M. Bradstreet (Ret.) joined ADR Services, Inc. as a mediator in 2022 after twelve years as a Judge of the Superior Court for the County of San Francisco. Judge Bradstreet spearheaded the Court's highly successful judicial settlements program and presided over civil trials and settlements for the last six years of her judicial career. Recognized for her extraordinary ability to settle difficult cases, Judge Bradstreet was regularly entrusted to handle many of the Court's largest, most complex, and emotionally charged matters. In addition to her settlement work, she presided over numerous jury and court trials. In 2017, Judge Bradstreet was honored by the San Francisco Trial Lawyers as Judge of the Year.

Prior to her appointment to the bench, Judge Bradstreet served as the California Labor Commissioner for over three years, enforcing California's minimum wage and hours laws. Before that, she worked in private practice for twenty-five years at a major local law firm, and served as the firm's first woman firm-wide managing partner and one of the first LGBTQ managing partners in the Bay Area. Her litigation and trial practice focused on the areas of commercial and employment litigation. Judge Bradstreet was selected as one of the Top 75 Women Litigators in California in 2005.

Widely recognized as a pioneer for the advancement of women and LGBTQ equality in the legal profession and in the judiciary, Judge Bradstreet is a former President of the Bar Association of San Francisco, California Women Lawyers, and the Queen's Bench Bar Association. She is a recipient of the California State Bar's Diversity Award, the Minority Bar Coalition's Unity Award, the Anti-Defamation League's Jurisprudence Award, the Barristers Club Judges Award, the International Action Network for Gender Equity & Law Award, and the Lifetime Achievement Award from Queen's Bench Bar Association. She is also the recipient of the Margaret Brent Women Lawyers of Achievement Award, the highest award given by the American Bar Association's Commission on Women in the Profession, in recognition of accomplishments of women lawyers in the nation who have excelled in their field and been leaders in advancing women in the legal profession.

Judge Bradstreet has a Bachelor in Law degree from the University of Bristol, England, a Masters in Law from the University of California, Berkeley School of Law, and an honorary doctorate degree in law from Golden Gate University.

BIO

Overlooked, Underestimated, and Interrupted

23

Tani Cantil-Sakauye

*J*ustice Cantil-Sakauye began her career before the explosion of research on unconscious bias that underlies much of our diversity, equity, and inclusion conversations today. But she intuitively recognized and addressed the "innocently ignorant," along with those who expressed their bias and misogyny more directly.

Justice Cantil-Sakauye offers strategies from her own work experience for "dealing" with both conscious and unconscious bias. Her essay reinforces what others take for granted, for example, that early career internships are opportunities of privilege and not universally available to those with less economic means. Yet she shows us that all types of jobs can offer real-world learning experiences that can apply to any career path.

Lauren Stiller Rikleen, Editor

As a young, petite Filipina, I did not look like the typical American lawyer when I graduated from law school in 1984. So, perhaps I should have been pessimistic about my job prospects. After all, I attended law school during the deep recession of 1981–82, when unemployment hit an all-time high of 11 percent. Expectations for many third years were low, but pessimism is not a posture I'm familiar with.

The fact that I had gone to law school at all was not something anyone expected, including me. My grandparents—and, briefly, my parents—were farmworkers, and no one in my family expected the children of my generation to go to college, let alone law school.

The idea of opportunity was a vague concept I heard about but did not understand. No one spoke to me about college when I was a student in my Sacramento public high school. Counselors didn't tell me to apply for college; I stumbled my way toward it.

After high school, I went to a local community college because that's where my friends were going. I joined the debating team on a lark, and as someone who first learned to debate three older siblings, it was a natural fit. My debating instructor was my first academic mentor and he encouraged me to think about a career. I often overheard the white men I defeated in those debates talk about going to law school and I thought, heck, if they can do it, *I* can do it too. My mentor agreed and told me, "You can be anything you want."

In law school, many of my classmates secured internships during summer breaks. I wanted to do something different—and needed to make money—so I got a job as a blackjack dealer in a South Lake Tahoe casino. Part of me envied classmates who secured impressive internships. They were making connections and getting a head start in their careers while I flipped cards to inebriated patrons.

I didn't realize it at the time, but my days at the card tables would help me become a better lawyer. After all, in dealing cards all day to intentional risk takers, I revealed very little of myself and had a ringside position to observe all the different personalities, mostly male, bluster, brag, and pontificate while they competed to win at cards. I learned that people bluff in all sorts of situations. I watched people jockey for position and pretend to be drunk while counting cards. With card counters, I knew they would have another pretend-drunk friend in the back waiting for a signal to come and drop in a huge stack of mixed chips at the last minute.

These experiences—and the environment of a 1980s casino where the then-male and female gender stereotypes were on full display—created a rich learning experience for a minority female budding lawyer. Interacting with all the different personalities and proclivities expanded my twenty-two-year-old world and gave me a bounty of human experiences to ponder.

My experience as a blackjack dealer later helped me manage witnesses, prepare witnesses, pick better juries, understand power plays, and discern the difference between fibbers and fabulists. Having watched gamblers, I saw how a fib about your cards led to exaggerated wins when later told to other players around the table. Dealing blackjack in a casino prepared me for the strategies, tactics, and theories of trial. Things were never again what they seemed or as they were told to me; I learned to look deeper and longer.

After I took the bar exam and awaited the results, I stayed in Sacramento and worked as a cocktail waitress at a new dance club. I lasted about five weeks: I could not tolerate the pinches, pats, and mind-numbing prattle. Fortunately, I passed the bar. Unfortunately, I had no leads and no connections. But my strategy was simple: apply everywhere, be resilient, and interpret each "no" as "find another way."

I interviewed for a job in the San Francisco public defender's office. I was turned down and later I was told that the interviewer said I looked like I couldn't "hold my own."

At that time, the first studies about unconscious or implicit bias were still a decade or more away. Women, Asians, and my other friends of color didn't know the words for implicit or unconscious bias, but we didn't need to. We knew a bigot or a misogynist when we saw one. And bigots and misogynists were on a spectrum—from the buffoon to the jerk to the innocently ignorant. As an optimist, I assumed most of those on the spectrum were innocently ignorant and it was my job to educate them through perseverance and humor.

I was finally hired on a one-year trial basis at the Sacramento District Attorney's Office. I had a year to distinguish myself and was immediately given difficult cases. I worked every day and on weekends, and I discovered that the courtroom was my natural habitat. I loved it.

Yes, everyone in the court assumed I was a clerk; yes, jurors eyed me with curiosity and skepticism; yes, opposing lawyers were allowed to constantly interrupt me; yes, judges ignored what I had to say; yes, my male colleagues made sexist jokes and confused me with the one other Asian woman working in the office. And, yes, I was given a heavier caseload than men and those with more experience. When I asked my supervisor about this unequal workload, he said, "Opposing lawyers think you look beatable. That gives you an advantage."

My strategy that first year and thereafter was simple: Show up. Persevere. Be civil. Make friends with everyone, especially the clerks and bailiffs. Laugh at yourself. Be known. Don't hide in the shadows. Let others underestimate you at their peril.

My main weapon against bullies was humor. Riding on the elevator one day on the way to trial, the defense attorney looked me over and smirked: "Hey, Cantil, putting on a little weight?" I looked up at him and said, "Take care of those seven hairs left on top of your head, Mac. It looks like they're about to go the way the others went."

During one contentious trial in which I endured countless interruptions, from the male defense attorney with groundless or nuisance objections and from the male judge who for some reason believed I might need his aid as I cross-examined the witnesses, I noticed the defense attorney was wearing two different shoes. I said nothing. When he approached the jury box to deliver his final argument, I waved him over and whispered to him, "I just wanted to let you know that you're wearing two different shoes." And yes, my timing in part was to get into his head as he gave his closing argument, because splitting his attention and focus would serve me, and also as payback for all the meritless objections he made to break my focus and momentum when I was in mid-sentence questioning a witness.

I had to survive in their world to have any chance of succeeding, so I could then change that world for those who would come after me. In other words, I needed to be myself, reveal my personality, use my strengths, shore up my weaknesses, and strive as a prosecutor in trial so the next person who didn't fit the mold or look or sound like everyone else would give the legal establishment pause.

And that pause would be, to put optics, bias, and prejudice aside and say let's get to the work at hand and be fair, open, and accepting. Much later, when I became a trial judge, I used my experiences, both good and bad, to run a welcome, civil, respectful, and harmonious courtroom. Attorneys requested my court; others called it the Zen court. Because no matter the case, homicide, gang, sexual assault, multiple defendants, no matter the witness, the lifestyles and behaviors of attorneys, my courtroom was a place where justice was served.

Persevere. Endure. Laugh. Sometimes, when it's appropriate, say "enough is enough." During one trial, when a male judge ignored my objections, then acknowledged my male colleague who repeated what I already said, I asked to approach the bench. I said, "Judge, I understand that some men cannot hear a woman's pitch and since you seem not to be hearing anything I'm saying, I wanted to make sure you can actually hear me." He heard me after that.

After a year, I was offered a permanent position, although I would still be confused with the other Asian in the office. I joked with her that I never corrected that misrepresentation when they thought it was me who handled her winning case.

Oh yes, besides perseverance, civility, and humor, I counted on friendships and solidarity with other women lawyers and attorneys of color. That's how I got involved in ethnic and minority bar associations. By supporting each other, we grew, got better, and paved a path of opportunity for the next generation, just as my parents and grandparents had done for me.

BIO

Chief Justice Tani G. Cantil-Sakauye

After almost twelve years in office, Chief Justice Tani G. Cantil-Sakauye has emerged as one of the country's leading advocates for equal access to justice, civic education, and reform of court funding models and procedures that unfairly impact the poor.

When she was sworn into office in January 2011 as the twenty-eighth Chief Justice of California, she was the first person of color and the second woman to serve as the state's Chief Justice.

In recent years, Chief Justice Cantil-Sakauye has raised awareness of the unfair financial impact of fines, fees, and the bail system on the poor. She is a leading national advocate calling for bail system reform by addressing concerns about fairness and public safety.

As leader of California's judicial branch and chair of the Judicial Council, Chief Justice Cantil-Sakauye has led the judicial branch out of the state's worst fiscal crisis since the Great Depression. She has improved the branch's efficiency, accountability, and transparency in how it conducts business, sets policy, and discloses information.

When she became Chief Justice, she opened meetings of the Judicial Council and its advisory bodies that were once closed to the public and has made public comment more accessible. Judicial Council meetings are now webcast, as are state Supreme Court oral arguments. She initiated a review and oversaw changes in court rules that will improve how judicial branch entities prevent and address harassment, discrimination, retaliation, and inappropriate workplace conduct. During the COVID-19 pandemic, she pushed for remote court operations and issued hundreds of emergency orders so that courts continue to operate safely. She also launched a program to make retired judges available to fast track the resolution of some criminal cases.

She has been recognized for her early work on domestic violence issues, support for minority bar associations, and for advancing the role of women and minorities in the legal profession. The Chief Justice is a leader in revitalizing civic learning through her Power of Democracy initiative. She, along with other state leaders, fulfilled one of the initiative's goals in July 2016 when the state Board of Education unanimously approved an instructional framework that encourages civic learning. In 2019, she was honored with the Sandra Day O'Connor Award by the National Center for State Courts for her work inspiring, promoting, and improving civics education.

The Chief Justice has also convened leaders to address such issues as implicit bias, human trafficking, and truancy. All the Chief Justice's initiatives support her vision for a judicial branch that provides physical access through safe and secure courthouses, remote access through technology initiatives, and equal access to all Californians.

BIO

Moving Forward and Facing Back | 24

Anna Blackburne-Rigsby

*J*udge Blackburne-Rigsby speaks movingly of the
impact that her parents' own experiences had on her
life. Her mother grew up in the Jim Crow era of legalized segregation and discrimination. Her father was
the son of immigrant parents. Both parents imbued in
their daughter a commitment to service and justice.

Judge Blackburne-Rigsby's clear-eyed understanding of this country's painful history of segregation
and legal discrimination helped fuel her commitment
and dedication to ensuring a justice system that is
fully accessible to all.

It is a history that must never be ignored, forbid-
den from study, or forgotten.

Lauren Stiller Rikleen, Editor

I love this country and am proud of my service in the judicial branch of our democratic society, as the Chief Judge of the District of Columbia Court of Appeals. I have enjoyed my thirty-four-year career as a lawyer, and for twenty-six of those years, I have served as a judge. I believe that the law—and the rule of law—is tremendously important in a democracy. Our laws are, in many ways, a fundamental expression of our values—in noble and aspirational ways, but sometimes, as history has shown us, in deeply unjust ways.

As an African American woman, the grandchild of an immigrant, and the daughter of a parent who lived under the degrading laws of legal segregation based on race at one point in this country, I am inspired to work to ensure that the law is fair and impartial for all, and that there is access to justice for all.

I often turn to the words of someone I have long admired: Charles Hamilton Houston. He was one of the first Black students admitted to Harvard Law School in 1919, and he went on to become the dean of my alma mater, Howard University School of Law.

Houston was a Black man who became a lawyer at a time when laws legalizing discrimination based on race existed and were used to exclude and marginalize people like him. Yet, he saw enormous potential in the law's ability to strengthen our democracy—so much so that he became one of the key architects of the legal strategy to overturn those discriminatory laws. He believed that lawyers could use their legal education and training to be agents of social change, and use the law to unite and strengthen our country, rather than to divide people based on their racial differences.

Throughout my career as both a lawyer and a judge, I have been guided by my personal values, which I refer to as "My Three F's—Faith, Family, and Fortitude," while trying to ensure that all who come before the courts have access to justice and "equal justice under law."

I. FAITH

My faith and strong spiritual foundation have been vitally important in my life. My faith is the reason I seek to serve and to be of service to my family, my community, and my country. As we used to say in my family, service is the rent we pay for our time on earth.

One of my earliest lessons on the importance of service came from Dr. Martin Luther King, Jr. I remember my parents sharing their memories of participating in the historic 1963 March on Washington, where Dr. King gave his famous "I Have a Dream" speech. They talked of the hope and pride they felt as they marched with millions of Americans of all races in support of equality and racial justice.

Then, just five years later, I vividly recall sitting with my family in our living room, watching the news of Dr. King's death on the television. Even though I was a child, I understood what a dark and somber day it was, and I felt the shock and grief of Dr. King's assassination. But my parents reminded me of something Dr. King said in his speech at the March on Washington: "Out of the mountain of despair, a stone of hope." And I began to understand that I had a role to play in keeping Dr. King's hopeful vision of "equal justice under law" alive.

I have been guided by one of my favorite quotes of Dr. King's: "Life's most persistent and urgent question is: What are you doing for others?" In every decision I make, and at every crossroads I find myself, I aspire to serve, to do my best to ensure that our courts are fair and accessible to all, and to inspire hope in others.

II. FAMILY

My family is a source of strength and inspiration to me. Just their presence every day of my life is something I cherish and is one of my greatest gifts.

My mother grew up in North Carolina during the Jim Crow era of legalized segregation in the United States. She experienced racism and discrimination, which were manifested in laws that required that people be treated differently because of the color of their skin. These laws meant that my mother could not live in certain neighborhoods, shop in certain stores, or dine in certain restaurants because they were for "whites only," and she had to drink out of the "colored" water fountain. My mother vividly remembers standing in front of a shiny, porcelain fountain that said "whites only," and knowing that she had to use the other rusty, corroded fountain.

These laws dictated every aspect of my mother's life, and the lives of other African Americans, because they were born Black in

America. But my mother believed in the promise of our Constitution, and she has dedicated her life to the pursuit of justice.

My dad is the son of immigrants. My grandfather came to the United States from Jamaica with very few resources. He remembers having a difficult time finding work and being called all kinds of awful names just because he was born in a different country. But he worked hard and eventually started his own business. He owned a medallion taxicab business in New York City, and he passed on to my father the values of education, hard work, and using your resources to help others.

These values fueled my dad's thirty-eight-year career as a local elected official, and his persistent dedication to serving our community. As a first-generation American, my father took seriously his role in making sure that his constituents felt seen, heard, and welcome in the community.

Together, my mom and dad instilled in me and my sisters the importance of working to ensure equality for all people. From my mom's experiences, I learned that the law has enormous power to shape society. And from my dad, I learned the importance of listening to those around me and about my own ability to improve my community.

My husband is the most honorable, courageous, and noble man I know. I am so proud of his service to our country, both his thirty-three years of service as a United States Army Officer, retiring as a Colonel, and his service as a Judge on the Superior Court in the District of Columbia. He is the love of my life and my best friend. And we have a wonderful and supportive son, a recent college graduate, of whom we are very proud.

When I think about the ways in which I draw strength and inspiration from my family, I often think of the West African symbol of the mythical Sankofa bird. While in flight, the Sankofa both moves forward and gazes backward, all the while holding an egg in her mouth. The Sankofa symbolizes three important dimensions of individual and collective life: first, advancing toward the future; second, reflecting on and remembering the past; and third, the meeting of the past and the future, as the egg embodies the future generations that will benefit from the knowledge and wisdom of the past.

I hope that I can continue to honor these three dimensions of life by remembering the struggles and sacrifices of my ancestors, who made it possible for me to be where I am today, supporting those around me, and seeking ways to create a more just and equal future.

III. FORTITUDE

My path to the bench as an African American woman was paved with perseverance. I have known for as long as I can remember that I wanted to be a lawyer. I was inspired by lawyers involved in the civil rights movement, such as former Supreme Court Justice and Howard Law School alum, Thurgood Marshall, and many others. I wanted to follow in their footsteps to become a force for positive change, but I did not realize that my path would have unique challenges because of my gender and my race.

My mother decided to enroll in law school while I was in high school. During those years, I saw first-hand not only how much hard work and commitment law school required, but also how my mother had to balance raising a family, being a wife and mother, and being a law student. She went through law school with grace and grit, and after she graduated, she used her degree to serve in various community and civic organizations in addition to her professional obligations.

My mom's fortitude and commitment taught me that I could accomplish my goals as long as I was willing to work hard and stick with them no matter what and never give up. My dad has also always encouraged and supported my sisters and me in pursuing our professional and personal ambitions. His encouragement meant so much and made me believe that as a woman I could achieve my professional goals.

My parents showed me what it would take to follow my dreams. I stand on their shoulders, and the shoulders of generations of trailblazers who came before them.

I am often reminded of those trailblazers on difficult days at work. The courthouse where I work is a historic building in Washington, DC. It was a seat of government and served as a federal courthouse before it was our local courthouse, including during a time when the law was used to marginalize people based on their race.

Slavery existed in DC from the very beginning of the city's history. Black people in this city were bought and sold by slave dealers who exploited their labor for profit until the enactment of the District of Columbia Emancipation Act of 1862, which freed enslaved persons in DC. However, immediately following the passage of this law, a commission met in the very same building that is now our courthouse to determine how much money slave owners should be paid as compensation for their newly freed slaves, who were treated under the laws of that time as property or chattel, instead of as human beings.

On tough days, I reflect on how far our country has come since then, in many ways because of those who had the courage and willingness to make sure that the law works for all people and is fair to all people. Generations of leaders have worked to ensure that the words engraved above the entrance of the United States Supreme Court, "Equal Justice Under Law," are a reality for all who come before our courts. The fortitude of those leaders, on whose shoulders I stand, paved the way for opportunities that I have, including working in the historic courthouse building, serving as the Chief Judge of the District of Columbia Court of Appeals.

I am proud to be a judge because of the important role our courts have played throughout history in overturning discriminatory and unjust laws. Our courts—the judicial branch of our democracy—must continue to play this role in ensuring access to justice and fairness for all people. As a judge, I took an oath to uphold the tenets of justice for all, regardless of socioeconomic status, race, gender, religion, sexual orientation, or other identifying factors. I take seriously my responsibility to administer justice and work hard to ensure access to justice for all.

But as we still see in our courts, far too many people do not have access to justice because of persistent barriers in our legal system. In Washington, DC, the number of residents who face legal issues is far greater than those who are able to obtain legal services. A 2019 report by the DC Access to Justice Commission indicated that nearly 90 percent of tenants in landlord-tenant cases in DC appear in court without a lawyer. Those numbers are similarly high in domestic violence, child custody, and other family law cases, where about 90 percent of people are unrepresented.

This justice gap is due to a variety of factors, including the extremely high cost of legal services. Most people do not realize that the words "if you cannot afford a lawyer, one will be provided to you" only apply in criminal cases. But many people facing the loss of their homes, custody of their children, or even their personal safety do not have the legal representation they need because it is too expensive.

Improving access to justice for all members of the community requires courts to work hard and to be willing to adapt and change. It requires the openness and humility to listen to the needs of the people we serve and to be more accessible.

I am very proud of the work the District of Columbia courts have done to create a language access program, so no one is denied access to court services because they happen to speak a language other than English. I am also proud of our outreach initiatives and community engagement with underrepresented populations, as well as our efforts to recruit a diverse judicial workforce representative of the community in which we live.

Promoting racial equity has always been a priority for the District of Columbia courts. Nevertheless, recent events—especially George Floyd's death in 2020 and the protests for racial justice that followed—increased my concern that renewed efforts were needed to further improve racial equity in the courts. As a member of the Conference on Chief Justices, which is an organization made up of the Chief Justices of every state and territory's highest court, I helped launch the Blueprint for Racial Justice, which is a national initiative to take immediate and measurable steps toward improving racial justice, equity, and inclusion in the judicial system.

In alignment with this initiative, I used my roles as Chair of the DC Courts' Joint Committee on Judicial Administration to help launch an Advisory Committee on Racial Equity and implement a Racial Equity Initiative for the DC Courts. This work is not easy, but it is vitally important work for court systems to do in order to promote and maintain public trust and confidence in the judicial branch of our democracy. I am deeply committed to making sure our judicial system is, and continues to be, fair and accessible to all.

As I reflect on my career and life, I cannot think of better words than those of Mary Church Terrell, an African American woman who championed racial equity and women's suffrage in the late 1800s and early 1900s: "Lifting as we climb, onward and upward we go, struggling and striving, and hoping that the buds and blossoms of our desires will burst forth into glorious fruition ere long."

BIO

Anna Blackburne-Rigsby

The Honorable Anna Blackburne-Rigsby was appointed Chief Judge of the District of Columbia Court of Appeals in March 2017. Chief Judge Blackburne-Rigsby chairs the Joint Committee on Judicial Administration for the District of Columbia court system. She is a member and the President-Elect of the Conference of Chief Justices (CCJ) and chairs the CCJ Committee on Public Engagement Trust and Confidence.

Prior to being designated Chief Judge, Chief Judge Blackburne-Rigsby was nominated by President George W. Bush in August 2006 to serve as an Associate Judge of the District of Columbia Court of Appeals. Before that, she was nominated by President William Jefferson Clinton to serve as an Associate Judge of the Superior Court of the District of Columbia from 2000–2006, and she previously served as a Magistrate Judge on the Superior Court of the District of Columbia from 1995–2000.

Chief Judge Blackburne-Rigsby graduated from Duke University with a Bachelor of Arts degree in Political Science, and received the Duke University Presidential Leadership Award. Following graduation from Duke University, she was selected to be one of twelve Public Affairs Fellows of the Coro Foundation in San Francisco, California. She earned her law degree from Howard University School of Law, graduating in the top five percent of her class. While in law school, she served as the Lead Articles Editor of the Howard Law Journal and served as the Co-Captain for the Charles Hamilton Houston Moot Court Team.

Following law school, Chief Judge Blackburne-Rigsby was an associate at the law firm of Hogan Lovells US LLP (formerly Hogan & Hartson) in Washington, DC, where she litigated commercial, real estate, employment discrimination, and education matters before state and federal courts and administrative agencies. Chief Judge Blackburne-Rigsby later joined the District of Columbia Office of the Corporation Counsel (now District of Columbia Office of the Attorney General), where she served as Special Counsel to the Corporation Counsel, working as part of the senior management team. She then served as Deputy Corporation Counsel in charge of the Family Services Division, where she managed the Division's sixty-five attorneys and support staff, responsible for handling child abuse and neglect, child support enforcement, and domestic violence cases.

Chief Judge Blackburne-Rigsby has taught Trial Advocacy at Harvard Law School and Professional Responsibility as an Adjunct Professor at the David A. Clarke School of Law at the University of the District of Columbia. She has also taught Continuing Legal Education courses for the District of Columbia Bar and has trained judges from other countries in conjunction with the National Center for State Courts and the United States Department of State.

Chief Judge Blackburne-Rigsby has held offices in several judicial organizations. As an Associate Judge of the D.C. Court of Appeals, she chaired the District of Columbia Courts' Standing Committee on Fairness and Access, and she served on the District of Columbia's Access to Justice Commission. She serves on the Board of Directors for the National Consortium on Racial and Ethnic Fairness in the Courts and formerly served as the Consortium's President and Moderator. She is a former Chair of the Washington Bar Association's Judicial Council, a Past President of the National Association of Women Judges, and serves on the Board of Managerial Trustees for the International Association of Women Judges (Chair from 2010–2014). Through her many presentations at conferences throughout the world, Chief Judge Blackburne-Rigsby has sought to promote the rule of law and equal access to justice.

Chief Judge Blackburne-Rigsby has volunteered on the DC Rape Crisis Board; she is the former President of the Washington, DC, Chapter of Jack and Jill of America, Inc.; a member of the Washington, DC, Chapter of the Links, Inc.; and a lifelong member of the NAACP. She served as a Sunday school teacher at Shiloh Baptist Church and coached the girls' basketball team of St. Gabriel's Church.

In addition to receiving the 2020 American Bar Association's Margaret Brent Women Lawyers of Achievement Award, Chief Judge Blackburne-Rigsby has received numerous significant awards for her legal, judicial, and community service, including the Business and Professional Women's League's Sojourner Truth Award, the Women's Bar Association of the District of Columbia's 2014 Star of the Bar Award, the National Bar Association's Heman Sweatt Champion of Justice Award, the Greater Washington Area Women Lawyers Division's Charlotte E. Ray Award, and the National Association of Women Judges' Justice Vaino Spencer Leadership Award. In 2017, she was inducted into the Washington Bar Association Hall of Fame. In 2017, 2019, and 2021, she was honored as one of Washington, DC's Most Powerful Women by the *Washingtonian* magazine, among many others.

Born in the District of Columbia, Chief Judge Blackburne-Rigsby is married to Judge Robert R. Rigsby, Associate Judge of the Superior Court of the District of Columbia, former Corporation Counsel for the District of Columbia, Retired Military Judge, and Retired Colonel of the United States Army. They are the proud parents of one son, a recent college graduate.

BIO

Justice Ruth Bader Ginsburg: "A Richer System of Justice"

Deborah Jones Merritt

25

We *began this book with Marci Hamilton's reflections as a law clerk to Justice Sandra Day O'Connor. Her anecdotes about the Federalist Society "cabal" of clerks who hoped to influence the Justice's vote on cases involving reproductive rights have particular resonance today. At a time when surveys report that Americans' trust in the Supreme Court is dropping, her words about Justice O'Connor's steel-like strength demonstrate the importance of a Supreme Court that can be respected and trusted.*

We end this book with the chapter on Justice Ruth Bader Ginsburg, written by her former law clerk, Deborah Jones Merritt. Justice Ginsburg brought an incisive legal mind and a deep commitment to fairness and equality to her judicial role. The fact that she was confirmed by the Senate on a 96–3 vote is a testament to her extraordinary qualifications.

Professor Merritt shares examples of Justice Ginsburg's enormous contributions as a lawyer and a Supreme Court Justice, demonstrating the power of the law to help and change lives. It is fitting to conclude this book with her encouragement that, in these troubled times, courage and perseverance are the most important lessons we can learn from Justice Ginsburg's legacy—indeed, from every judge featured in these pages.

Lauren Stiller Rikleen, Editor

As she began her remarkable service on the Supreme Court of the United States, Justice Ruth Bader Ginsburg observed: "A system of justice will be the richer for diversity of background and experience" among its judges. "It will be poorer, in terms of appreciating what is at stake and the impact of its judgments, if all of its members are cast from the same mold."[1] Diverse backgrounds, Justice Ginsburg believed, generate differing perspectives. Those multiple perspectives, in turn, push the law to keep its promise of serving "*all* the people law exists (or should exist) to serve."[2]

---

[1] Statement of Ruth Bader Ginsburg upon her Investiture, reprinted in Ruth Bader Ginsburg, *The Progression of Women in the Law*, 53 VAL. U. L. REV. 951, 964 (2019).

[2] Ruth Bader Ginsburg, *Remembrance of Judge Myron H. Bright*, 102 MINN. L. REV. 1, 1 (2017). Justice Ginsburg frequently used this phrase in her speeches and writings. For other examples, see, *e.g.*, Ruth Bader Ginsburg & Robert A. Stein, *The Stein Lecture: A Conversation Between Justice Ruth Bader Ginsburg and Professor Robert A. Stein*, 99 MINN. L. REV. 1, 20 (2014); *Transcript of Interview of U.S. Supreme Court Associate Justice Ruth Bader Ginsburg, April 10, 2009*, 70 OHIO ST. L. J. 805 (2009) [hereinafter *Ohio State Transcript*].

Justice Ginsburg began her life as one of the many people that our laws did not fully serve. As a young woman, she faced blatant workplace discrimination—and our nation's laws offered her no remedy. As a Jew, she also suffered bias that no law redressed.[3] And all around her, she witnessed the discrimination and harassment endured by people of color. "We went into World War II with segregated troops," she often reminded audiences. "We were fighting a war against racism and yet our armed forces practiced racial discrimination."[4]

As a college student, the future Justice Ginsburg determined that law could address these inequities. "Law was a profession," she decided, "that enabled one to aid and repair tears in the community."[5] After receiving her law degree, Justice Ginsburg devoted her lifetime to repairing those tears—never losing faith that law could overcome prejudice and promote equity.

Much of that work focused on achieving gender equality. As an advocate, Justice Ginsburg was the first to persuade the Supreme Court that the Equal Protection Clause restricts the government's power to treat men and women differently. Her brief in *Reed v. Reed* prompted the Court to strike down a state statute that automatically preferred men over women when appointing the administrator of an estate.[6] This "arbitrary preference established in favor of males," the Court concluded, "cannot stand in the face of the Fourteenth Amendment's command that no State deny the equal protection of the laws to any person within its jurisdiction."[7]

That declaration represented a significant turning point in the law. It also produced a meaningful outcome for the plaintiff in the case, Sally Reed. Reed and her ex-husband had adopted a son, Richard, and then separated. Sally raised Richard while he was young, but her ex-husband obtained custody during Richard's teenage years. Richard,

---

[3.] "Those were my three strikes," Justice Ginsburg told one interviewer: When she graduated from law school, employers shied away from women, mothers, and Jews. Ruth Bader Ginsburg, *A Conversation with Associate Justice Ruth Bader Ginsburg*, 84 U. Colo. L. Rev. 909, 912 (2013) [hereinafter *Colorado Conversation*] (Annual John Paul Stevens Lecture). Few laws prohibited religious discrimination until Congress adopted the Civil Rights Act in 1964.

[4.] *Colorado Conversation, supra* note 3, at 924.

[5.] Ginsburg & Stein, *supra* note 2, at 20.

[6.] 404 U.S. 71 (1971).

[7.] *Id.* at 74.

unfortunately, became severely depressed while living with his father and killed himself. Richard's estate had no monetary value, but Sally yearned for the final connection to her deceased son that administering the estate would provide.[8] The Supreme Court's decision, secured through lawyer Ginsburg's advocacy, assured that the state could not deny Sally Reed that opportunity through an arbitrary preference for male administrators.

Two years later, advocate Ginsburg achieved another monumental victory: She convinced four Members of the Court to treat gender as a suspect class subject to the Court's highest level of constitutional scrutiny. The Court at that time had developed two standards to evaluate claims based on the Equal Protection Clause. It judged most claims under a lenient standard that upheld legislative classifications as long as they were rationally related to any legitimate governmental interest.[9] Classifications based on race, alienage, or national origin, on the other hand, had to meet a much tougher test. The Court deemed those classifications "inherently suspect" and subjected them to "strict judicial scrutiny."[10] The government could uphold those classifications only by demonstrating that they were "necessary" to obtain an "overriding" governmental interest.[11]

In *Frontiero v. Richardson*, then advocate Ginsburg urged the Court to apply this rigorous standard to a federal statute that made it easier for servicemen than servicewomen to claim spousal benefits.[12] Married men in the armed services could automatically claim housing and medical benefits for their wives, but a married woman had to prove her husband was financially dependent on her before obtaining those benefits. Four Justices agreed that this distinction between men and women serving their country was as "invidious" as a racial one—and should be subject to the same strict scrutiny.[13] Four other

---

[8] *See Colorado Conversation, supra* note 3, at 918 (recounting the facts underlying the *Reed* case).
[9] Frontiero v. Richardson, 411 U.S. 677, 683 (1973).
[10] *Id.* at 688.
[11] *Developments in the Law—Equal Protection*, 82 HARV. L. REV. 1065, 1090 (1969). In later years, this language evolved to require a "compelling governmental interest" achieved through "narrowly tailored means." *See, e.g.,* Fisher v. Univ. of Texas at Austin, 579 U.S. 365 (2016).
[12] 411 U.S. 677 (1973).
[13] *Id.* at 687–88.

Justices declined to adopt that level of scrutiny but agreed that the statute violated the Constitution's guarantee of equal protection.[14] Only Justice Rehnquist dissented from the decision.

Although the full Court did not designate gender a suspect class in *Frontiero*, the decision marked another key step in advancing women's constitutional equality. That opinion, along with the one in *Reed*, made clear that statutes distinguishing men and women deserved more than simple rational basis review. During the 1970s, the cases litigated by Justice Ginsburg established an intermediate level of scrutiny for gender-based classifications. Those classifications, the Court announced, must be "substantially related" to achievement of an "important governmental objective."[15]

After she joined the Court in 1993, Justice Ginsburg cemented that principle in our constitutional jurisprudence. Writing for the Court in *United States v. Virginia*, she confirmed that the Constitution requires an "exceedingly persuasive justification" for any state action based on a gender-based classification.[16] Applying that standard, the Court rejected the male-only admissions policy at the Virginia Military Institute, a prestigious college operated by the Commonwealth of Virginia. Chief Justice Rehnquist, notably, concurred in that judgment—a sign of how persuasive Justice Ginsburg's arguments had proven.[17]

These different levels of constitutional scrutiny may seem arcane, but they made a substantial difference in furthering the equality of

---

[14.] *Id.* at 691 (Stewart, J., concurring in the judgment); *id.* (Justice Powell, joined by Chief Justice Burger and Justice Blackmun, concurring in the judgment).

[15.] Craig v. Boren, 429 U.S. 190, 199 (1976). Justice Ginsburg did not represent the plaintiff in this case, but she authored an amicus brief that proposed the intermediate level of review to the Court.

[16.] 518 U.S. 515, 531 (1996).

[17.] *Id.* at 558. With typical modesty, Justice Ginsburg attributed the Chief Justice's changed views to his life experiences as much as to any legal arguments. Chief Justice Rehnquist, she often reminded audiences, had both daughters and granddaughters. Interacting with them, Justice Ginsburg surmised, "unconsciously opened his eyes" to the many challenges that women face. Ruth Bader Ginsburg & Linda Greenhouse, *A Conversation with Justice Ginsburg*, 122 YALE L. J. ONLINE 283, 295 (2013) (transcript adapted from the inaugural Gruber Distinguished Lecture in Women's Rights, which took the form of a dialogue between Justice Ginsburg and Ms. Greenhouse).

women. Under the rational basis standard that the Court applies to most statutory classifications, the Court will accept almost any governmental interest as legitimate. If Justice Ginsburg, acting as an advocate, had not persuaded the Court to apply a higher level of scrutiny to gender-based distinctions, administrative convenience and generalizations about gender differences could have supported statutory classifications like the ones in *Reed* and *Frontiero*. Justice Ginsburg's work, first as an advocate and then on the Court, made clear that "generalizations about 'the way women are,'" will not support rigid government distinctions between men and women.[18]

In addition to pursuing these constitutional victories, Justice Ginsburg applied her gender equity lens to statutory disputes. She famously dissented from the Court's 2007 decision in *Ledbetter v. Goodyear Tire & Rubber Co.*, where the majority held that a woman had waited too long to complain about gender discrimination in her pay.[19] Drawing upon her own experience as a female wage earner, Justice Ginsburg stressed the "realities of the workplace" that mask pay differentials and deter employees who are "trying to succeed in a nontraditional environment" from "making waves."[20] Given those facts, Justice Ginsburg urged, the majority offered an unduly "cramped interpretation" of Title VII's prohibition of gender discrimination.[21] Congress responded to Justice Ginsburg's eloquent argument, rapidly enacting the Lilly Ledbetter Fair Pay Act to overturn the Court's decision.[22]

Notably, Justice Ginsburg's pursuit of gender equality benefited people of all gender identities. She made her first constitutional claim for gender equality on behalf of Charles Moritz, a man who had been denied a caretaker's tax exemption available to women.[23] Moritz, as Justice Ginsburg often told audiences, "took good care of his mother,

---

[18.] United States v. Virginia, 518 U.S. at 550.

[19.] 550 U.S. 618 (2007).

[20.] *Id.* at 645 (Ginsburg, J., dissenting).

[21.] *Id.* at 661.

[22.] Pub. L. No. 111-2, 123 Stat. 5 (2009) (codified as amended in scattered sections of 29 U.S.C.A. and 42 U.S.C.A.).

[23.] Moritz v. Comm'r, 469 F.2d 466 (10th Cir. 1972).

though she was ninety-three."[24] The elderly Mrs. Moritz did not want to enter a nursing home, so Charles Moritz cared for her in his home. To cover his mother's needs while he was at work, Moritz engaged a caretaking assistant. A daughter in his situation would have been able to deduct that caretaking expense, but the Internal Revenue Code denied the deduction to bachelors like Moritz. Then Professor Ginsburg, arguing the case with her husband (and tax expert) Martin Ginsburg, persuaded the Court of Appeals for the Tenth Circuit that the statutory distinction was an "invidious discrimination" that "made a special discrimination premised on sex alone, which cannot stand."[25]

Several of Justice Ginsburg's arguments before the Supreme Court similarly featured male plaintiffs who had been hurt by gender stereotypes.[26] One of her favorite plaintiffs was Stephen Wiesenfeld, a new father whose wife Paula Polatschek tragically died in childbirth.[27] At that time, the Social Security Act paid survivors' benefits to widows, but not widowers. So, although Paula had contributed to Social Security for many years, Stephen could not afford to stay home to care for their newborn child. Then Professor Ginsburg argued his case to the Supreme Court and secured a unanimous victory. Even Justice Rehnquist agreed that the statute was unconstitutional although, as Justice Ginsburg sometimes wryly noted, he

---

[24.] *Ohio State Transcript, supra* note 2, at 809. Justice Ginsburg's description plays upon the language of A. A. Milne's poem *Disobedience*, which begins:
James James
Morrison Morrison
Weatherby George Dupree
Took great
Care of his Mother,
Though he was only three.
All Poetry, https://allpoetry.com/disobedience (last visited Mar. 2, 2022).
[25.] Moritz, 469 F.2d at 470. The Ginsburgs' work on the *Moritz* case was memorialized in the 2018 movie *On the Basis of Sex*.
[26.] In addition to the *Wiesenfeld* case described in this paragraph, Justice Ginsburg represented male plaintiffs in *Duren v. Missouri*, 439 U.S. 357 (1979) (male defendant challenged state's automatic exemption for female jurors); *Califano v. Goldfarb*, 430 U.S. 199 (1977) (widower challenged social security provision that awarded benefits to widows but not widowers); and *Kahn v. Shevin*, 416 U.S. 351 (1974) (widower challenged state property tax exemption provided to widows but not widowers).
[27.] Weinberger v. Wiesenfeld, 420 U.S. 636 (1975).

focused on the discrimination against the baby rather than against the female wage earner.[28]

Once on the Court, Justice Ginsburg continued to challenge stereotypes that harmed both men and women. She contended, for example, that railroad workers (a group largely composed of men) should be able to recover liberally for emotional distress suffered on the job.[29] And she argued forcefully for the right of fathers, as well as mothers, to confer United States citizenship on a child born out of wedlock.[30] She failed to carry the Court in these cases, but her words stand as an eloquent call for gender equality. As she wrote in her dissent to the citizenship decision, "when the Government controls gates to opportunity, it may not exclude qualified individuals based on fixed notions concerning the roles and abilities of males and females."[31] Instead, men and women must have equal access to those opportunities.

Although Justice Ginsburg is best known for her pursuit of gender equality, her advocacy and jurisprudence embraced fairness and equity on many fronts. During the same years that she established gender equality as a constitutional principle, she coauthored the American Civil Liberties Union's (ACLU's) amicus brief in *Regents of the University of California v. Bakke*.[32] In that case, a White applicant to a public medical school challenged the school's race-based affirmative action program. Then Professor Ginsburg advised the Court: "The United States cannot remedy the egregious wrongs that blight the nation's history by leaving the victims of racism where *Brown v. Board of Education* found them."[33] Instead, she urged, affirmative

---

28. *Id.* at 1236, 1237 (Rehnquist, J., concurring in the result) ("it is irrational to distinguish between mothers and fathers when the sole question is whether a child of a deceased contributing worker should have the opportunity to receive the full-time attention of the only parent remaining to it"). *See also Ohio State Transcript, supra* note 2, at 815 ("Most of the Justices thought the law discriminated against the woman as wage earner. A minority thought the law discriminated against the male as parent. And one, the Justice who later became my Chief, thought it discriminated irrationally against the baby.") (footnotes omitted).

29. Consol. Rail Corp. v. Gottshall, 512 U.S. 532, 559 (1994) (Ginsburg, J., dissenting).

30. Miller v. Albright, 523 U.S. 420, 460 (1998) (Ginsburg, J., dissenting).

31. *Id.* at 469 (internal quotation marks omitted).

32. Regents of the University of California v. Bakke, No. 76-811, Brief for Amicus ACLU et al. (U.S. 1977), *available at* 1977 WL 187972.

33. *Id.* at 4.

action programs play an essential part in addressing "the elimination, root and branch, of all vestiges of racism" in the United States.[34] The Supreme Court agreed, holding that institutions of higher education could consider race as one of many factors in admissions.

When the Court revisited affirmative action programs a quarter century later, Justice Ginsburg was on the Bench. She joined four colleagues in upholding one of the challenged programs, declaring, "It is well documented that conscious and unconscious race bias, even rank discrimination based on race, remain alive in our land, impeding realization of our highest values and ideals."[35] She then chided her colleagues for striking the affirmative action program in a companion case, stressing the importance of "measures taken to hasten the day when entrenched discrimination and its aftereffects have been extirpated."[36]

Justice Ginsburg's most compelling discussion of racial equality came in *Shelby County, Alabama v. Holder.*[37] In that case, five Justices struck down a key section of the Voting Rights Act. In dissent, Justice Ginsburg powerfully defended Congress's constitutional authority to enact the contested provision. She also detailed the many ways in which racial discrimination continues to hamper voting and politics. "The grand aim of the Act," she reminded her colleagues, "is to secure to all in our polity equal citizenship stature, a voice in our democracy undiluted by race."[38] That essential work, she warned, is far from complete and is likely to founder without the Voting Rights Act as a foundation.

Justice Ginsburg also sought to assure equal stature for individuals with disabilities. In *Olmstead v. L.C. ex rel. Zimring,*[39] she authored an opinion for the Court holding that "unjustified institutional isolation of persons with disabilities is a form of discrimination" violating the Americans with Disabilities Act.[40] Citing cases condemning gender and racial stereotypes, Justice Ginsburg observed that the "institutional placement of persons who can handle and

---

[34.] *Id.* at 2.
[35.] Grutter v. Bollinger, 539 U.S. 306, 345 (2003) (Ginsburg, J., concurring).
[36.] Gratz v. Bollinger, 539 U.S. 244, 301 (2003) (Ginsburg, J., dissenting).
[37.] 570 U.S. 529 (2013).
[38.] *Id.* At 592 (Ginsburg, J., dissenting).
[39.] 527 U.S. 581 (1999).
[40.] *Id.* at 600.

benefit from community settings perpetuates unwarranted assumptions that persons so isolated are incapable or unworthy of participating in community life."[41] Prejudices based on disabilities, she concluded, are as harmful as those founded on race or gender.

Justice Ginsburg did not author an opinion in *Obergefell v. Hodges*, the landmark decision recognizing a constitutional right for same-sex couples to marry.[42] She preferred, instead, to allow Justice Kennedy to speak for a unified five-Justice majority. In the years after *Obergefell*, Justice Ginsburg took particular delight in performing wedding ceremonies for same-sex couples. She also authored a key decision that recognized the rights of LGBTQ+ students, holding that a law school could refuse formal recognition to a student group that excluded LGBTQ+ members.[43]

Justice Ginsburg, finally, frequently sought to overcome inequality rooted in economic disadvantage. In *M.L.B. v. S.L.J.*, she persuaded a majority of the Court that the Constitution protects an indigent parent's right to appeal a decree terminating parental rights.[44] The state thus could not charge an indigent parent for a transcript needed on appeal. And she worried that any overruling of *Roe v. Wade*[45] would primarily affect poor women rather than wealthy ones. "For any woman who has the money to buy a plane ticket or bus ticket," she reflected, "it's not a problem. She'll be taken care of. It's the women who don't have the wherewithal to avoid their State's restrictions by going elsewhere who will suffer."[46]

* * *

Justice Ginsburg thought of herself as a "path marker" rather than a "path breaker." She repeatedly broke through stereotypes and discrimination, but she was quick to recognize the writers and advocates who laid the foundation for her work. When she submitted her brief in *Reed v. Reed*, the first case described above, then Professor Ginsburg listed Pauli Murray and Dorothy Kenyon as coauthors

---

[41.] *Id.*

[42.] 576 U.S. 644 (2015).

[43.] Christian Legal Soc. Chapter of the Univ. of California, Hastings College of the Law v. Martinez, 561 U.S. 661 (2010).

[44.] 519 U.S. 102 (1996).

[45.] 410 U.S. 113 (1973).

[46.] Ginsburg & Stein, *supra* note 2, at 24.

of the brief.[47] Although those two did not contribute directly to the brief, which laid out the first constitutional argument for gender equality, both were lawyers who had argued for decades to advance racial, gender, and economic justice.[48] Murray, while still a student at Howard University Law School, had also developed the argument that Thurgood Marshall and others relied upon in *Brown v. Board of Education.*[49] Advocate Ginsburg paid tribute to these contributions by recognizing Murray and Kenyon as coauthors of her historic brief.

Justice Ginsburg also used the phrase "path marker" to signal that the pursuit of equality is not done: She helped mark the way, but the path is long. To populate the path ahead, Justice Ginsburg mentored more than two generations of students, law clerks, lawyers, and judges who continue her work. Beyond that circle, her example and words inspired many others—people she never met personally—to pursue a "richer system of justice" for all.

How do we, those who follow Justice Ginsburg, continue her work? And how do we preserve her legacy? Justice Ginsburg's writings point us to two essential tools. The first is our Constitution. Although written in the eighteenth century and amended only sparingly, Justice Ginsburg believed that the majestic words of that document have "growth potential, so that [the Constitution] can keep pace with society as it changes from generation to generation."[50]

The authors of the Fourteenth Amendment, she noted, certainly did not "think that the Equal Protection Clause meant women had the right to own property in their own names, contract in their own names, [or] sue and be sued in their own names."[51] But those same

---

[47.] *Reed v. Reed*, No. 70-4, Brief for Appellant (U.S. 1971), *available at* 1971 WL 133598.
[48.] For additional information about Murray and Kenyon, see, *e.g.*, Samantha Barbas, *Dorothy Kenyon and the Making of Modern Legal Feminism*, 5 STAN. J. CIV. RTS. & CIV. LIBERTIES 423 (2009); Serena Mayeri, *After Suffrage: The Unfinished Business of Feminist Legal Advocacy*, 129 YALE L. J. FORUM 512, 523 (2020). Interest in Justice Ginsburg has reawakened interest in her feminist forebears. Julie Cohen and Betsy West, for example, created a documentary about Pauli Murray (*My Name is Pauli Murray*, 2021) after completing their documentary of Justice Ginsburg (*RBG*, 2018).
[49.] Florence Wagman Roisman, *Lessons for Advocacy from the Life and Legacy of the Reverend Doctor Pauli Murray*, 20 U. MD. L. J. RACE, RELIGION, GENDER & CLASS 1, 12 (2020).
[50.] *Colorado Conversation, supra* note 3, at 923.
[51.] *Id.*

authors would have recognized the fertility of their language and the promises it held for the future. "So I think," Justice Ginsburg told one audience, "the people who wrote the Equal Protection Clause would probably say, 'Yes, in the twenty-first century, it certainly includes—we meant it to include, people who were once left out.'"[52]

A majority of Americans agree with Justice Ginsburg's theory of the Constitution,[53] and many Supreme Court decisions reflect that wisdom. Landmark cases like *Brown v. Board of Education*[54] and *Gideon v. Wainwright*[55] rest on the assumption that the people who wrote and ratified the Constitution simply marked the beginning of a pathway. They did not complete our nation's journey toward democratic rule, liberty, and equality. Similarly, the drafters and ratifiers of the Fourteenth Amendment continued that journey; they did not mean to cement nineteenth-century sensibilities into the Constitution. To protect Justice Ginsburg's legacy and continue her work, it is essential to press her constitutional theory—shared by so many other lawyers and citizens—at every opportunity.

Our second resource is ourselves and the people around us. Justice Ginsburg frequently observed that the plaintiffs she represented as an advocate were "everyday people" who "had suffered an injustice and believed that the system of justice in the United States was capable of righting that wrong."[56] The ACLU did not seek these plaintiffs for test cases; the future plaintiffs stepped forward to claim justice on their own. As long as everyday people retain "faith in our system of justice and . . . the bravery to test that faith," Justice Ginsburg believed, our laws will continue their progress towards serving "*all* the people."

Today, many people are discouraged by our system of justice. Racial bias infects every stage of the criminal justice process, from surveillance to incarceration. Partisan strife impedes progress in legislative

---

[52.] *Id.* at 924.

[53.] Kristen Bialik, *Growing Share of Americans Say Supreme Court Should Base Its Rulings on What Constitution Means Today*, Pew Research Center, *available at* https://www.pewresearch.org/fact-tank/2018/05/11/growing-share-of-americans-say-supreme-court-should-base-its-rulings-on-what-constitution-means-today/ (May 11, 2018).

[54.] 347 U.S. 483 (1954) (striking down racial segregation in public schools).

[55.] 372 U.S. 335 (1963) (requiring states to provide counsel to indigent felony defendants).

[56.] Ginsburg & Greenhouse, *supra* note 17, at 288.

bodies. Social divisions, cash-heavy campaigns, and the isolation of a long pandemic make us despair of achieving any type of consensus. It is easy to give up in the face of these obstacles.

Seemingly intractable hurdles, however, have always stood in the way of progress. Justice Ginsburg and the other jurists included in this volume fought to secure their victories. They struggled to gain a foothold in the workplace, to balance jobs and family, and to persuade colleagues of their worth. They battled equally hard to advance the law and achieve a more inclusive system of justice. They didn't always win: Some of Justice Ginsburg's most forceful words appear in dissenting opinions. But they persevered, always believing that our Constitution and democratic processes could move us ever closer to justice.

Now it is our turn. When we look at the long road ahead of us, we need to draw strength from how far we have already traveled. In 1960, Ruth Bader Ginsburg was denied a Supreme Court clerkship because she was a woman—but she persevered to become a Supreme Court Justice in 1993. If she could travel that far in thirty-three years, how much farther can we advance in the next thirty-three?

Justice Ginsburg would not want us to throw up our hands in despair, pointing to the conservative majority on the current Court, backlashes against progress, disinformation campaigns, and a physical attack on the Capitol. Democracy prevailed on January 6, and it gives us the tools to continue her fight. The path is uneven, and sometimes doubles back on itself, but Justice Ginsburg firmly believed that courageous people could always move us closer to justice and equality.

BIO

Deborah Jones Merritt

Deborah Jones Merritt is a Distinguished University Professor and the John Deaver Drinko/Baker & Hostetler Chair in Law Emerita at The Ohio State University's Moritz College of Law. Professor Merritt was fortunate to learn Constitutional Law from then Professor Ruth Bader Ginsburg at Columbia Law School during the 1970s. After earning her JD, Merritt clerked for then Judge Ginsburg during her first term on the Court of Appeals for the District of Columbia Circuit. Merritt also clerked for Justice Sandra Day O'Connor during her first term on the Supreme Court of the United States.

As a professor, Merritt has won university-wide awards for teaching, scholarship, service, and diversity enhancement. She has taught a wide range of courses at Moritz, including Torts, Evidence, Law & Psychology, Legal Writing, and the Criminal Justice Clinics. With Professor Ric Simmons, she coauthored the leading text on evidence law, *Learning Evidence: From the Federal Rules to the Courtroom.* The text, now in its fifth edition, adopts an innovative approach that became the cornerstone for a series of new law school textbooks.

As a scholar, Professor Merritt has published widely on issues related to constitutional law, legal education, the legal profession, diversity, and equality. Several of her articles address the status of women in legal education and the legal profession. She has also written frequently about Justice Ginsburg and her jurisprudence. Due to the interdisciplinary nature of her work, Professor Merritt holds courtesy appointments in the John Glenn College of Public Affairs, as well as the Departments of Sociology and Women's, Gender and Sexuality Studies at Ohio State.

In 2020, Professor Merritt published (with Logan Cornett of the Institute for the Advancement of the American Legal System) *Building a Better Bar: The Twelve Building Blocks of Minimum Competence.* That report, based on a nation-wide study of lawyers, provides an evidence-based foundation for structuring legal education and the licensing process. Task forces in several states have used the report to consider changes in their licensing systems.

In retirement, Professor Merritt continues to work toward making legal education and the profession more diverse, inclusive, accessible, and focused on excellent client service.

Acknowledgments

Book writing is generally a solitary endeavor where support is more about helping a writer find the extra time in a day (well, usually night) to get the job done. Editing an anthology is a vastly different experience. And editing an anthology where the contributions come from people who have spent decades of their career writing as distinguished lawyers and judges in a court of law borders on daunting.

Questions and worries never end, even as this is the last section I author in this book. First, there are the administrative worries. The task was complex—the focus was on submissions from women judges whose shared characteristic was that they have been honored by the American Bar Association's Commission on Women in the Profession with the prestigious Margaret Brent Women Lawyers of Achievement Award, a recognition given annually since 1991. How will we find everyone? How to best keep track of the responses—affirmative, negative, and equivocal? What is the best way to follow up? How many emails are too many? How much time do the authors need? How can we ever get to the end point with the frequent requests for more time from people who are extraordinarily busy, yet agreed to participate? How best to track the edits, bios, headshots, questions, answers, phone calls, and revisions?

Then there are the substantive concerns. How do you edit the submissions of people who, by their profession, have spent much of their careers as the ultimate arbiter of the work of other highly skilled individuals such as their clerks, assistants, and the lawyers who come before them? And after offering edits, how do you then ask for more information, more nuance, more description about difficult times in their lives? How do you best ensure that their stories show the relevance to the struggles of today?

Notwithstanding all these worries (many of which continue), part of the answer was found in the fact that the participants were more than worthy of their extraordinary reputations. They were open to the process and responded with grace and kindness. My first acknowledgment is, therefore, to every judge who shared aspects of the challenges they have faced on their path to—and while serving on—the bench. The stories they share and the lessons they provide are lasting gifts to readers of this book. The same is true for the highly distinguished lawyers and judge who gave of their time to write for icons in the judiciary who are no longer able to speak for themselves.

The process of locating contact information for those judges who have been out of the workforce for a long time, as well as selecting and finding authors for some of the judges who have passed away or could not otherwise participate, was not easy. It was, however, proof of the strength of a sisterhood who grasped what I was trying to accomplish and helped either reach out directly or find the friend of a friend who might have an email address. In this group there are far too many to thank individually, but my gratitude runs deep.

This book is a stronger collection because of two people. One is Drucilla Ramey, a California powerhouse and long-time ABA colleague whose relationship I treasure as an example of why bar association engagement can produce some of the most meaningful—and helpful—bonds one can experience. Because I knew the size of Dru's network was significant (including from her years as the Executive Director of the National Association of Women Judges), I called her often in the beginning for help in figuring out how to contact many of the judges. In one of those conversations, I mentioned my idea for what the book would include. Many days later, out of the blue, she called to tell me why my original vision was too narrow, and what I needed to do to fix it. She was 100 percent right. I will always appreciate her caring enough to make that call and setting me on a much stronger path. And, of course, she did not get away without an assignment—her chapter on Judge Joan Dempsey Klein is a wonderful addition to this book.

The second person who made this book stronger is Marcia Greenberger, the founder and co-president of the National Women's

Law Center, whose many accomplishments have been recognized by the National Women's Hall of Fame. I still have not had the honor of meeting Marcia in person, but was put in touch with her through the aid of Ginny Sloan, another example of the strength of bar association relationships. Marcia helped with my initial request, and then never stopped helping. Among the many ways she supported this project was to connect me to Marci Hamilton and Deborah Merritt, respectively, former law clerks to Supreme Court Justices Sandra Day O'Connor and Ruth Bader Ginsburg, who happily said yes to our request to write about these icons—doing so in the most meaningful ways. And, like Dru, Marcia ended up as an author on this project, writing a beautiful piece about Judge Patricia Wald. That Marcia enlisted as a coauthor Judge Wald's accomplished daughter, Sarah, made the piece that much more eloquent.

This book is being published by the American Bar Association, a bar where I have had the opportunity to serve in many leadership roles, including as chair of the Section of Civil Rights & Social Justice, an important ABA home for lawyers working to make our society more just. This is my third book published by the ABA, and, with each book, I become more grateful to and an admirer of Bryan Kay, Publishing Director, Editorial and Licensing, whose title does not reflect his admirable qualities of kindness, infinite patience, and helpful suggestions. I also thank Jeffrey Salyards, Executive Editor, Book Publishing, for guiding this book through the process and always being available to graciously answer my many questions.

The idea for this book came out of the ABA Judicial Division, whose nascent Editorial Board was thinking about interesting ideas to inaugurate their portfolio. I am grateful to the Editorial Board—and particularly Linda Strite Murnane (also an author here)—for both the idea and for thinking to ask me to shepherd this project. I am also appreciative of the early support from Judge Bernice Donald and Judge M. Margaret McKeown, whose initial letter to the authors requesting their participation was invaluable.

Thanks, as well, to the Editorial Board's chair, Judge Herbert Dixon (yet another ABA colleague), and to my liaison to the Editorial Board, Keith Roberts, for his sensitively handled and helpful edits.

A special thank-you also is owed to the Judicial Division Director, Tori Wible, who, like all ABA staff, plays a key role in facilitating the good work that gets done by ABA volunteer leaders.

When I was first contacted about this book idea in July of 2020, the world had just begun to grapple with a new virus. My hopes and expectations were that within a year, the book would be done, and Covid-19 would be a distant memory.

Also during that summer of 2020, I was asked to join the leadership team of a relatively new organization called Lawyers Defending American Democracy (LDAD)—a group dedicated to galvanizing the legal profession to address the rule-of-law abuses and threats to democracy that the country was facing. I agreed to become involved, assuming that these major challenges also would likely soon recede.

Clearly, the summer of 2020 was not a good time for predictions. I became increasingly involved with LDAD and am now serving as its interim executive director as well as board member, and the threats to our democracy have grown. This book, more than two years later, is finally completed.

These two roles have been in perfect counterpoint. Thinking about and working on ways to address what is happening to this country's democratic institutions can be draining; but then spending time reading and editing essays about these caring and inspiring judges restores the faith needed to keep focusing on what is ahead. My virtual friends and fellow leaders of LDAD have inspired me in this work, and I know they will be inspired by the stories that are told in these pages.

We all stand on the shoulders of giants who sacrificed and struggled to make this country better. And we all owe these giants our best efforts to continue to seek that more perfect union.

As with all things in life, I am grateful to my husband, Sander Rikleen, for his extraordinary help, support, and seemingly endless reservoir of patience. He enjoyed reading these stories that were so rich in history and detail, and always had sage advice. For a brilliant litigator, he's also pretty handy around the computer, providing crucial tech support in all manner of ways.

And, of course, I am thankful for the wonderful book-writing diversions of my amazing adult children, Alex and Ilyse, and their loving and lovable spouses, Leslie and Sam, and the pure joy of grandparenting the next generation in their miraculous early years.

Our family is fortunate for the legacy of love and support that has been passed down from my parents, Elaine and Joe Stiller, and Sander's parents, Rebecca and Alexander Rikleen. It is a testament to each of them to see that legacy continue through the generations.

It is much easier to write books when there is a loving, extended family that also includes siblings, cousins, nieces, nephews, and more who provide every reason to be grateful for loving diversions from a complicated world. I love you all.